P9-DHF-285

The EatingWell HEALTHY IN A HURRY COOKBOOK

Library of Congress Cataloging-in-Publication Data has been applied for.

ISBN 0-88150-687-7

Editor-in-Chief: James M. Lawrence
Editor: Jim Romanoff
Contributing Writers & Editors: Bruce Weinstein & Mark Scarbrough

Production Director: Alice Z. Lawrence **Managing Editor:** Wendy S. Ruopp
Test Kitchen: Stacy Fraser (Test Kitchen Manager), Jessica Price (Assistant Food Editor), Katie Webster (Recipe Developer), Carolyn Malcoun, Carolyn Casner
Associate Nutrition Editor: Sylvia Geiger, M.S., R.D.
Nutrition Intern: Alyssa Nathanson
Research Editor: Anne C. Treadwell **Proofreader:** David Grist

Art Director: Susan McClellan **Photographer:** Ken Burris

Front cover photograph: Wok-Seared Chicken Tenders with Asparagus & Pistachios *(page 111)*

Published by
The Countryman Press, P.O. Box 748, Woodstock, Vermont 05091
Distributed by
W.W. Norton & Company, Inc., 500 Fifth Avenue, New York, New York 10110
Printed in China by R.R. Donnelley

10 9 8 7 6 5 4 3 2 1

The EatingWell HEALTHY IN A HURRY COOKBOOK

150 delicious recipes for simple, everyday suppers in 45 minutes or less

JIM ROMANOFF
and the editors of

The Countryman Press
Woodstock, Vermont

Acknowledgments

Healthy in a Hurry is dedicated to my parents, Marge and Al, who are the source of my love for food, and also to my wife, Sue, and daughter, Nina, who make my passion for getting a delicious dinner on the table worth the effort. Special thanks to: Katie Webster for her hard work as lead recipe developer, Jessie Price and Stacy Fraser for their thorough (and good-humored) work helping to edit this volume, and Carolyn Malcoun for her diligent editorial support. Thanks to art director Susan McClellan and photographer Ken Burris, whose talents made this book as inviting to use as it is handsome. Also I thank James Lawrence for his friendship and for pushing me to make this book even better than I knew it could be. Most important, thanks to Wendy Ruopp who has been the true driving force behind this project and has made the creation of this book a pleasure. *—J.R.*

Recipe Guidelines & Nutrient Analyses

Defining "Active minutes" and "Total":
Testers in the EatingWell Test Kitchen keep track of the time needed for each recipe. ACTIVE MINUTES includes prep time (the time it takes to chop, dice, puree, mix, combine, etc. before cooking begins), but it also includes the time spent tending something on the stovetop, in the oven or on the grill—and getting it to the table. If you can't walk away from it, we consider it active minutes. TOTAL includes both active and inactive minutes and indicates the entire amount of time required for each recipe, start to finish. TO MAKE AHEAD gives storage instructions to help you plan. If special EQUIPMENT is needed, we tell you that at the top of the recipe too.

Analysis notes:
Each recipe is analyzed for calories, total fat, saturated (SAT) and monounsaturated (MONO) fat, cholesterol, carbohydrate, protein, fiber and sodium. (Less than 0.5 gram is rounded down to 0; 0.5-0.9 gram is rounded up to 1.) We use Food Processor software (ESHA Research), version 8.5.

When a recipe states a measure of salt "or to taste," we analyze the measured quantity. (Readers on sodium-restricted diets can reduce or eliminate the salt.) Recipes are tested with iodized table salt unless otherwise indicated. Kosher or sea salt is called for when the recipe will benefit from the unique texture or flavor. We assume that rinsing reduces the sodium in canned beans by 35%.

Butter is analyzed as unsalted. We do not include trimmings or marinade that is not absorbed. When alternative ingredients are listed, we analyze the first one suggested. Optional ingredients and garnishes are not analyzed. Portion sizes are consistent with healthy-eating guidelines.

Nutrition icons:
Our nutritionists have highlighted recipes likely to be of interest to those following various dietary plans. Recipes that meet specific guidelines are marked with these icons:

Healthy Weight
An entree has reduced calories, carbohydrate, fats and saturated fats, as follows:

CALORIES ≤ 350, CARBS ≤ 33g, TOTAL FAT ≤ 20g, SAT FAT ≤ 10g

Lower Carbs
Recipe has 22 grams or less of carbohydrate per serving.

High Fiber
Recipe provides 5 grams or more of fiber per serving.

Nutrition bonuses:
Nutrition bonuses are indicated for recipes that provide 15% or more of the daily value (dv) of specific nutrients. The daily values are the average daily recommended nutrient intakes for most adults that you see listed on food labels. In addition to the nutrients listed on food labels (vitamins A and C, calcium, iron and fiber), we have included bonus information for other nutrients, such as folate, magnesium, potassium, selenium, niacin and zinc, when a recipe is particularly high in one of these. We have chosen to highlight these nutrients because of their importance to good health and the fact that many Americans may have inadequate intakes of them.

Contents

Delicious Alchemy

"Wow! Can I get this recipe? I'd make it for supper tonight." This sort of response during a staff tasting session is the holy grail of compliments in the EatingWell Test Kitchen. After all, even though our day's work is all about helping our readers get a delicious, healthy meal on their dinner table, we know we've got big problems if we don't want that same meal to end up on ours.

This collection of our favorite faster recipes had its genesis in EatingWell Magazine's single-most-popular regular feature—"Healthy in a Hurry"—where we put our skills to work creating everyday meals that can be made with minimal fuss and with notably short prep and cooking times. *Healthy in a Hurry* represents the very best of these recipes and includes many new ones developed specifically for this volume.

This cookbook is built around recipes that have passed the scrutiny of many and varied eaters. Every recipe has survived multiple tastings by EatingWell editors, staff members and our families. Not only outstanding in flavor, texture and visual appeal, each recipe must also pass muster in nutritional analysis for calorie content, fats, carbohydrates, sodium and various other vital dietary measures.

Meals that fall within our definition of healthy in a hurry are made possible by an alchemy of sorts—taking a foolproof recipe with great nutrition credentials, adding fresh, wholesome ingredients and mixing in a helping of good solid kitchen smarts (*see "Getting Started, Getting Organized," page 8*). What emerges from the cauldron should be something you know is nutritionist-approved, something you will be proud to serve—and something virtually guaranteed to draw raves from those who try it.

How do we manage to combine speed, nutrition and delicious taste? Katie Webster, one of our lead recipe developers, who has a degree from the New England Culinary Institute, points to a few key concepts of professional cooking that benefit the *Healthy in a Hurry* cook.

"To get a meal made quickly and keep your sanity, you need to be organized from the start and not be afraid to turn the heat up. High heat sears food and delivers big flavor fast."

Jessie Price, our assistant food editor, speaks for our home cooks when she says, "At the dinnertime rush hour, there isn't time to allow flavor to develop using long cooking methods. Pick produce and cuts of meat, poultry and fish that cook quickly and start out tender. Use ingredients with bold tastes and add seasonings and fresh herbs for excitement."

Our test kitchen manager, Stacy Fraser, runs our recipe testing and development facility with the same skills she used to manage the kitchen of Penny Cluse Café, one of the busiest restaurants in our hometown of Burlington, Vermont. At home, she plans her meals a week at a time, creating a detailed shopping list and making one grand shopping trip, thus avoiding the daily conundrum of what's for dinner.

Quick home suppers that I cook can range from a great tuna melt to an exotic duck curry, but all start with flavorful ingredients. My philosophy: start with fresh, high-quality and in-season ingredients, cook them quickly with creativity, and success is assured. With my five-year-old daughter, Nina, at my feet, I don't have time for complicated cooking.

At EatingWell, we strive to cook with foods available in most larger supermarkets. Prepared convenience products are used judiciously, only after being thoroughly checked out in our Test Kitchen. Frozen vegetables, prewashed salad mixes and canned broths can, without a doubt, shave prep time without sacrificing quality, but many preseasoned convenience products are loaded with salt and hydrogenated fat, along with objectionable or downright nasty tastes.

The EatingWell Test Kitchen crew during the final testing days for *Healthy in a Hurry*: Stacy Fraser, Jim Romanoff, Jessie Price, Katie Webster, Carolyn Malcoun.

Finally, we take great pride in our ability to put ourselves in your shoes. You're health-conscious and you love good food, but you don't have the time or desire to spend a major portion of every day shopping and cooking to get a good meal on the table. With *Healthy in a Hurry*, you now have the recipes, the shopping tips, and the cooking secrets to give your family hundreds of different nutritious meals—all deemed delicious by demanding people like you who value both good health and great food.

—Jim Romanoff
EatingWell *Food Editor*
Charlotte, Vermont

Getting Started, Getting Organized

All too often, the frantic pace of modern life seems to be the perfect recipe for just one thing: last-minute take-out dinners. Luckily, for those of us who still prefer to sit down to a delicious, healthy dinner, good meals ready in 30 to 40 minutes are—more than ever—easily within our reach.

But why bother? Take-out, packaged and fast restaurant foods are everywhere, always available and seemingly cheap. However, they are increasingly being linked to the worrisome state of nutrition in modern society. To sell well, many prepared foods are intentionally overloaded with calories, fats, added sweeteners and sodium. Plus, they frequently deliver more of the cheap, less desirable carbohydrates (white flour, white rice, white sugar, white potatoes) than any of us really need. Home cooking can be our best defense against the nutritional pitfalls that work against keeping our good health and vitality.

Equally important, food we make ourselves provides rich flavors and satisfaction that take-out and processed foods cannot hope to deliver. We can use the best, freshest, most delicious ingredients—and know we are doing the right thing for ourselves and our family members.

Getting a healthy meal on the table in a hurry depends on a few approaches that any cook can master. We need to be mindful of what we are doing, we need to shop with time shortcuts in mind, we need an organized, properly equipped kitchen—and we need the right recipes.

The advice and recipes that follow are all you need to start turning the notion of *Healthy in a Hurry* into an everyday reality in your own kitchen.

Plan ahead.

Commonsensical advice, for sure, but it's hard to underestimate it. If you don't plan ahead, it's like setting out on a car trip without a map. Sure, you might get where you're going, but exactly when you'll get there is another matter entirely.

1. **Each week, take a few moments** over the weekend or one night after dinner to plan out your meals for the coming days. Don't wait until you get home from work on Tuesday night to figure out what's for dinner. That's just an invitation to order in pizza or Chinese.

2. **Make a detailed shopping list,** grouping what you need based on the layout of your favorite market and how you like to work your way through it. If you can avoid having to backtrack from the dairy section to the produce department for the forgotten onions, you can save much time and stress.

3. **Work ahead on your more leisurely days.** Consider planning to cook twice on a weekend or a low-pressure evening and then reheating a dish on a busier day. Some foods can easily be cooked in larger volumes and kept refrigerated or frozen in anticipation of days when time is really short. It's a good idea to blanch lots of fresh vegetables, such as green beans and broccoli, at the beginning of the week and store them in resealable bags. Quickly rewarmed or sautéed and then seasoned, these make for almost-instant side dishes.

Shop smart.

Going to any large supermarket can seem like a trip to some culinary fantasy land these days: all that produce, all those convenience products, all seductively displayed. Frankly, it's hard to keep your wits about you. But remember this: in the end, it's all about getting dinner on the table. All the recipes in this book are developed with expediency in mind but never at the expense of excellent flavor. You will find they tend to call for quick-cooking cuts of meat and poultry whenever possible. Save the pot roast for the weekend when you have more time to do some slow cooking. During the week, cutlets, chops and fillets will keep your cooking times to a minimum, leaving more time for the rest of life. Precut vegetables and fruits can be a godsend when saving time is important. On the other hand, it pays to choose your convenience products judiciously. While broths and other prepared products, such as canned tomatoes and beans, are lifesavers at times, they can be loaded with salt and sometimes short on good flavor. Experiment to find out which brands appeal to you the most and always read the labels to avoid ending up with a lot of unwanted ingredients.

With list in hand, you're ready for the market. Stick to your plan and follow our top four secrets for getting on with the raw materials for a meal.

1. **Be a picky shopper.** Ripe fruits and vegetables cook faster and add much more flavor than their immature counterparts. But how do you tell what's ripe? Many people shake, rattle and roll their way

The Well-Stocked Pantry
Oils, Vinegars & Condiments

- Extra-virgin olive oil for cooking and salad dressings
- Canola oil for cooking and baking
- Flavorful nut and seed oils for salad dressings and stir-fry seasonings: toasted sesame oil, walnut oil
- Butter, preferably unsalted. Store in the freezer if you use infrequently.
- Reduced-fat mayonnaise
- Vinegars: balsamic, red-wine, white-wine, rice (or rice-wine), apple cider
- Asian condiments and flavorings: reduced-sodium soy sauce, fish sauce, hoisin sauce, mirin, oyster sauce, chile-garlic sauce, curry paste
- Kalamata olives, green olives
- Dijon mustard
- Capers
- Ketchup
- Barbecue sauce
- Worcestershire sauce

through the produce aisle and clearly some occasional squeezing is required (with an avocado there's no other way). However, there's one cardinal rule for almost all fruits and vegetables: if it doesn't smell like anything, it won't taste like anything. Forgo the smell-less (and thus, tasteless) and go for what's ripe, fresh and ready to cook.

The same goes for meat and fish. Ask the fishmonger or butcher if you can smell before you buy. Fish and shellfish should smell like blue ocean at high tide on a spring morning, never like the tidal flats on an August afternoon. Meat should smell clean and bright, not like copper, soured yogurt or very runny cheese.

You may get a reputation for being a kook, but you'll win accolades at home when dinner is reliably full of the true flavors of good food. After all, underripe or spoiled ingredients only mean a lackluster dinner—or even a delay while you pull the car out of the garage and head back to the supermarket.

2. **When time is of the essence, more is sometimes less.** While it's cost-saving to buy fresh produce or meat in bulk, it can be time-killing too. You buy that whole bag of peppers or those 12 jumbo mangoes at the big-box warehouse store, and then you have to do something with them before they go bad. It naturally leads to cooking vats of food, racks of casseroles—or outright waste, something all good cooks try to avoid. It also leads to a depressing sameness in your menu. That eight-pound side of salmon looks like a deal, but by the third night, it's a catalyst for culinary ennui—and outright rebellion from your patrons.

If you need one celery stalk or a handful of diced peppers, consider shopping at the salad bar in your market and buying exactly what you can use, and no more. In the end, quick cooking is often about measuring the gap between cost and convenience. The price per pound of a single celery stalk may be higher than that for a big bag with multiple heads, but you'll have exactly what you need at the ready.

3. **Precut vegetables and fruits are lifesavers—but watch the bulk.** While buying fresh produce and meat in bulk may end up as more work than bargained for, using bags of frozen vegetables and precut fresh vegetables can trim time and effort from any cooking endeavor. Look for good-quality vegetables in your market's freezer case or produce section—not those doped with salt solutions or chemical preservatives. Prewashed bags of salad mixes might cost more than whole heads, but you often end up with less waste and more variety.

Of course, you needn't buy produce prechopped. The next time you're chopping an onion, consider doing two and putting the second in a ziplock bag for tomorrow's dinner. Or slice up a second head of broccoli or cauliflower and keep the florets in the freezer. You wouldn't use frozen vegetables in a recipe that showcases fresh ones, but you can take them right from the freezer to your skillet for any cooked dish.

New convenience items are appearing with great regularity these days. We've lately taken a shine to containers of peeled garlic cloves and refrigerated jars of chopped ginger, both usually available in the produce section. Frozen and pan-ready mushrooms, onions, peppers and other ingredients can make speedy cooking a weeknight breeze.

4. **Shop with your pantry in mind (*see suggestions on pages 10-14*).** A well-stocked kitchen helps you avoid the there's-nothing-to-eat-so-let's-go-out moment. Of course, you needn't run out and buy this list before you start; it's just a handy guide to things that will keep for months on end. But always plan on restocking essential pantry items when they run low. It's so irritating to have to stop cooking when you suddenly find there's no olive oil in the house.

Use the right tools for the job.

The bevy of remodeling shows on TV goads us all into thinking of our kitchens as blank canvases for today's hippest designers. Don't get us wrong: the kitchen should be a pleasant place to work—nice colors, family mementos. But there's no cause for unwarranted fussiness. After all, the tiles on your stove's backsplash, while compelling, don't put dinner on the table. In the end, you just need to make sure your pots and implements are all handy, your sink is cleared out and work surfaces are clean.

Like any good workspace, your kitchen needs good tools. We recommend:

1. **One full set of measuring spoons, two full sets of measuring cups.** We recommend one set of larger measuring containers for liquids, containers complete with handles and pour spouts, and one graduated set (1/4 cup, 1/3 cup, 1/2 cup, etc.) for dry ingredients that can be scooped up and/or leveled off.

2. **At least two cutting boards.** Ideally, there should be one that you use for produce and one for protein to avoid cross-contamination. Some cooks even use a full range of colored cutting

The Well-Stocked Pantry
Flavorings

- Kosher salt, coarse sea salt, fine salt
- Black peppercorns
- Onions
- Fresh garlic
- Fresh ginger
- Anchovies or anchovy paste for flavoring pasta sauces and salad dressings
- Dried herbs: bay leaves, dill, crumbled dried sage, dried thyme leaves, oregano, tarragon, Italian seasoning blend
- Spices: allspice (whole berries or ground), caraway seeds, chili powder, cinnamon sticks, ground cinnamon, coriander seeds, cumin seeds, ground cumin, curry powder, ground ginger, dry mustard, nutmeg, paprika, cayenne pepper, crushed red pepper, turmeric
- Lemons, limes, oranges. The zest is as valuable as the juice. Organic fruit is recommended when you use a lot of zest.
- Granulated sugar
- Brown sugar
- Honey
- Pure maple syrup
- Unsweetened cocoa powder, natural and/or Dutch-processed
- Bittersweet chocolate, semisweet chocolate chips

The Well-Stocked Pantry

Canned Goods & Bottled Items

- Canned tomatoes, tomato paste
- Reduced-sodium chicken broth, beef broth and/or vegetable broth
- Clam juice
- "Lite" coconut milk for Asian curries and soups
- Canned beans: cannellini beans, great northern beans, chickpeas, black beans, red kidney beans
- Canned lentils
- Chunk light tuna and salmon

Grains & Legumes

- Whole-wheat flour and whole-wheat pastry flour (Store opened packages in the refrigerator or freezer.)
- All-purpose flour
- Assorted whole-wheat pastas
- Brown rice and instant brown rice
- Pearl barley, quick-cooking barley
- Rolled oats
- Whole-wheat couscous
- Bulgur
- Dried lentils
- Yellow cornmeal
- Plain dry breadcrumbs

boards—the yellow one always for onions and garlic (which can leave a lingering flavor that wouldn't go well with fruit), the red always for chicken and beef, the blue for....

3. **A 2- or 3-inch paring knife, an 8-inch chef's knife.** The most important thing we can tell you is to buy a knife in a store, not over the Internet or from TV. You need to feel it in your hand. It should be a natural extension of your arm, its heft and weight commensurate with your own. Buy the best heavy-duty knives you can afford. Cheap, lightweight models make for harder work, slower prep times and even less safety for the cook. We recommend carbon-steel alloy blades, which do not require sharpening as often as nonalloy blades.

4. **Two flat-bottom 12-inch skillets with slightly angled sides, one nonstick and one stainless steel, preferably with one lid that fits both. A preseasoned cast-iron skillet is also a must-have for its natural nonstick surface and great searing ability.** Nonstick cookware is a modern marvel and essential when cooking with little or no fat. There are a few things to keep in mind about the surface. It can be nicked or scratched by metal utensils, rendering it unusable, and it should never be exposed to high heat without ingredients in the pan. Your stainless-steel or cast-iron skillet will simply be more durable; use the nonstick only when a recipe requires it.

5. **Two-quart and 4-quart saucepans, as well as a Dutch oven or covered casserole, preferably 8-quart or larger, all with lids.** We prefer multi-ply, stainless-steel, copper-core pots. While they'll set your budget back a notch or two, no amount of fancy cooking techniques can overcome poor-quality cookware.

6. **A set of three stainless-steel mixing bowls (small, medium and large).** Glass mixing bowls, while beautiful, chip and break. Stainless-steel bowls are relatively indestructible and have a natural nonstick and nonreactive finish. Lately, stainless-steel bowls with rubber outer coatings have come on the market—they do not slip across a counter, a boon to cooks everywhere.

7. **A kitchen scale.** Healthy cooking is calibrated cooking—you want exactly what the recipe calls for. Buy a kitchen scale with a

"tare function"—in other words, it can "zero out." You can set a small plate on it or a large measuring cup, reset the machine to zero, and then measure what you add without subtracting the weight of the container.

8. **An instant-read thermometer.** Accurately checking temperature is the only way to tell for sure if a piece of meat or poultry is cooked to the proper doneness. A thermometer with a simple dial gauge, available at supermarkets, will work as well as a fancy digital one.

9. **Two or three wooden spoons for stirring; a plastic or metal slotted spoon for draining**

10. **A sturdy colander** that fits in your sink, stands up well to heat and is easy to clean.

Think like a chef.

You need never have been a short-order cook to do meals in a hurry, but we can all gain a bit of culinary wisdom from those who have had to prepare hundreds of meals in a single day.

1. **Before you start cooking,** put on some music and pour yourself a glass of wine, fruit juice or iced tea. A relaxed, composed cook is a more efficient one.

2. **Read the recipe through** ahead of time so you know everything that's going to happen. Give yourself a minute to imagine doing the steps.

3. **Lay out your ingredients.** Ever wonder how your favorite cooking celebrities can pull a dish together so quickly? Ever noticed how they've got all the ingredients in little bowls right in front of them? Having everything at your fingertips means the dish will come together faster. Cutting an onion before you start to cook is actually a time-saver; cutting it when the cooking's already started is a time-waster—you have to take the skillet off the heat, then heat it back up when you're done chopping. That being said, remember that quick cooking is about getting maximal results in a minimal amount of time. So, for instance, if a recipe calls for cooking an ingredient first, make use of that cooking time to get some of your other prep work done.

The Well-Stocked Pantry

Nuts, Seeds & Fruits

- Walnuts
- Pecans
- Almonds
- Hazelnuts
- Dry-roasted unsalted peanuts
- Pine nuts
- Sesame seeds

(*Store opened packages of nuts and seeds in the refrigerator or freezer.*)

- Natural peanut butter
- Tahini
- Assorted dried fruits, such as apricots, prunes, cherries, cranberries, dates, figs, raisins

Refrigerator Basics

- Low-fat milk or soymilk
- Low-fat or nonfat plain yogurt and/or vanilla yogurt
- Reduced-fat sour cream
- Good-quality Parmesan cheese and/or Romano cheese
- Sharp Cheddar cheese
- Eggs (large). Keep them on hand for fast omelets and frittatas.
- Orange juice
- Dry white wine. If you wish, substitute nonalcoholic wine.
- Water-packed tofu

The Well-Stocked Pantry
Freezer Basics

- Fruit-juice concentrates (orange, apple, pineapple)
- Frozen vegetables: edamame soy beans, peas, spinach, broccoli, bell pepper and onion mix, corn, chopped onions, small whole onions, uncooked hash browns
- Frozen berries
- Italian turkey sausage and sliced prosciutto to flavor fast pasta sauces
- Low-fat vanilla ice cream or frozen yogurt for impromptu desserts

4. **Room-temperature vegetables cook faster than cold ones.** While we don't advocate letting meat, poultry, fish or dairy sit out, we do know that room-temperature vegetables sear quickly, cook evenly and blend more readily with other ingredients.

5. **Substitute carefully.** Although some substitutions seem obvious, they can be tricky business (*see page 246*). A ruined dish is a waste of time.

6. **Measure accurately.** Nothing wrecks a quick-cooking sauté like a double portion of flour or an overdose of salt.

7. **Work in a bigger bowl than you think you need.** Ever seen someone try to make tuna salad for four in a cereal bowl? Get out the big bowls—you'll avoid a mess on the counter, and you won't have to transfer things to bigger bowls once they become unwieldy.

8. **Do messy work in the sink, if at all possible.** Stir batters, coatings and spice mixtures in bowls set in the sink. Spills are simply washed down the drain.

9. **Turn up the heat.** While you shouldn't sauté onions in butter over high heat (the butter solids will burn and the onions will then

Basics of Food Safety

When to shop: If possible, go grocery shopping as your last errand before you head home. If you must run other errands, put a cooler in your car and buy a bag of ice to keep the perishables chilled until you get back home. In fact, in hotter climates, you need a cooler in the car even if shopping is your last errand of the day. Forty-five minutes in summertime traffic can render meat rancid, milk spoiled and butter liquid.

While you're shopping: Put meats or fish in plastic bags before you stick them in your cart so they don't drip on the vegetables or pantry items.

When you get home: Get the perishables in your refrigerator or freezer ASAP. Never store eggs, milk and the like on the door of your refrigerator. This is the place with the greatest temperature swings—where food freshness is most quickly compromised. We recommend you set your refrigerator for 40°F, but save the door for ketchup and convenience products.

Freezing: It's recommended that your freezer be kept at 2°F for safe frozen-food storage.

Defrosting: Defrost foods in the refrigerator or the microwave, not on the counter, to deter bacterial growth.

stick and scorch), you also shouldn't do so over low (the onions will just wilt and turn greasy). Don't be afraid of higher temperatures—within reason. If you're minding the skillet, the ingredients will not burn.

10. **Always have towels and oven mitts at the ready.** And make sure they're dry. Wet mitts conduct heat right to your hands. Have plenty of dish towels for every emergency.

11. **Clean up your area as you cook.** True, you don't have to become a Kitchen Retentive, a whisk in one hand and a sponge in the other. But consider putting things in the dishwasher while you're waiting for the onions to soften, or try washing the cutting boards and mixing bowls while you're waiting for the tomato sauce to come to a simmer. Always put each tool back in the same place—so you will know exactly where to find it the next time it's needed. Aim to start and finish with a clean kitchen. (Don't be afraid to recruit help from the ranks of those who will be eating what you cook.)

12. **A watched pot always boils.** Pay attention to the dish as it cooks; don't just set a timer and leave it. All timing guidelines are just that: guidelines. They're not laws from Sinai. Pay more attention to the visual and olfactory cues.

Before you start cooking: Wash your hands with soap under warm water for at least 20 seconds (about as long as it takes to sing the chorus of "Jingle Bells"). Then rinse off fruits and vegetables under cool running water.

Poultry, meat, fish: Do not rinse off poultry, meat or fish. The bacterial contaminants can only be killed at temperatures above 160°F, far hotter than the hot water in our homes. Rinsing only allows for random splashes—and thus cross-contamination on counters and cabinets.

Unwrap meats and fish in the sink and leave them in their container or paper until you're ready to use them. Immediately throw out the container or paper; never reuse it.

Avoid cross-contamination by having at least two cutting boards, one for the meat or fish and another for fresh produce.

When you're cleaning up: Wash plastic cutting boards in the dishwasher; wash your knives in hot, soapy water. And wash your counters with hot, soapy water. An occasional thorough once-over with a kitchen disinfectant spray is a good idea.

Basics of Cooking Techniques

With a Knife

Mince. This is the finest chop of all, less than 1/8 inch, achieved by first cutting, then rocking the knife back and forth across the ingredients, all the while rotating the blade around on the cutting board.

Dice. While the most common definition is to create cubes between 1/4 and 1/2 inch in size, dicing is actually not an aesthetic decision. Recipes call for a dice when vegetables are to be cooked quickly but evenly together—thus all the pieces should be the same size.

Cube. Like "dice," this is a chopping technique all about cooking time, not aesthetics; it's usually accompanied by a measurement to indicate the preferred size for even cooking (such as "cut into 1-inch cubes").

Chop. This is a slightly looser measurement, usually between 1/2- and 1-inch pieces. Here, the decision is less about cooking time and more about texture.

Roughly Chop. This is the loosest measurement of all: 1- to 2-inch uneven pieces.

Over the Heat

For the best flavor, heat the oil in a skillet or saucepan before you add the food. Never overcrowd the pan; if necessary, work in batches so you can cook in one layer. Watch the pan carefully, shaking the ingredients and turning them to keep them from sticking.

Simmering involves steady if fairly low heat (thus the constant reminder to "reduce heat" before simmering) and often a covered or partially covered pan. It's a slow cooking process that renders the melange of ingredients succulent and flavorful. One reminder: a covered pot will boil more quickly than an uncovered one, so watch the temperature carefully to keep the simmer low and steady.

"Braising" is the culinary term for "stewing," in some ways a subset of simmering. You add more liquid to the dish and let it go for a longer time over an even lower heat. Braising has traditionally been used for tough cuts of meat.

Stir-frying is a high-heat method of searing meats and vegetables, usually associated with Asian cooking. You must use oil for stir-frying, otherwise, the high temperature will cause the natural sugars to burn and foods will stick to the pan, even a nonstick one. While a wok is preferred, a high-sided skillet or sauté pan will also get the job done.

When you **steam** over moist, high heat, you preserve much of an ingredient's otherwise water-soluble nutrients. To steam effectively, you need a pot large enough to hold both the steamer basket and 1 or 2 inches of water with plenty of air flow all around the basket. The food must never sit in the water. Check the water level from time to time to make sure the pan isn't dry, and shake the pan gently once or twice to rearrange the food, ensuring even cooking.

Whether at a high or low heat, **roasting** involves a steady, even, dry heat that cooks from the outside in (the opposite, then, of microwaving, which cooks from the inside out). Air (and thus heat) should circulate freely around whatever's being roasted; the oven rack should be placed in the center of the oven unless otherwise stated in the recipe. If roasting vegetables, add a small amount of fat to the pan to sear them while they cook; if roasting meats, use a small rack to lift them off the bottom of the roaster, allowing the heat to circulate evenly underneath them (and thereby lifting them out of the fat). A good roasting pan is a heavy, metal pan with a shiny interior surface that holds heat and reflects it back onto the food.

Broiling, an indoor cousin of grilling, sears food with high, direct heat. A broiler should always be preheated for at least 5 minutes; food should be placed so that it (not the broiler pan) is 4 to 6 inches from the heat source. Foods blotted dry broil with less mess. Pour off rendered fat occasionally to avoid nasty fires.

There are actually two methods of cooking on a **grill**. Grilling involves placing ingredients directly over the heat source. Barbecuing, by contrast, involves putting the food on one side of the grill, the coals or heat source on the other, thereby cooking the food over indirect heat. Experienced grillers test their grills by "feel." Place your open palm 5 inches above the grill grate; the fire is...

> **high** if you have to move your hand in 2 seconds,
> **medium** if you have to move your hand in 5 seconds
> and **low** if you have to move your hand in 10 seconds.

Pattern for Health

What does a healthy eating pattern look like? One simple visualization winning praise across the board is the "Divide Your Plate" strategy.

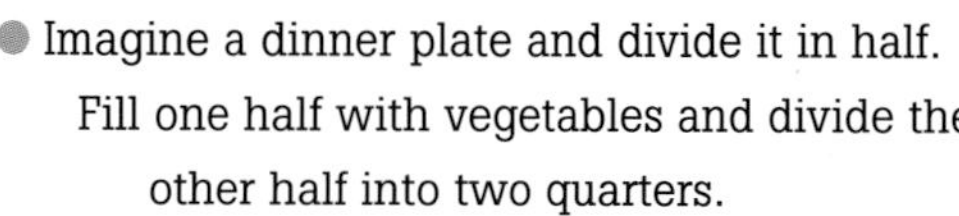

- Imagine a dinner plate and divide it in half. Fill one half with vegetables and divide the other half into two quarters.
- Fill one quarter with lean protein, such as fish, skinless poultry, lean beef, beans or tofu.
- Fill the other quarter with a grain-based or starchy side dish, preferably a whole grain like brown rice, whole-wheat pasta or a slice of whole-grain bread.

What this method lacks in precision, it more than makes up for in good sense. If you focus on making most of your meals look this way, you'll automatically be following sound nutrition guidelines and choosing appropriate portions—without having to pull out a nutrition guide or a measuring cup every time.

Remember that eating well means:

- selecting a variety of foods in sensible portions
- considering no food either a magic bullet or a forbidden fruit
- choosing whole foods over processed ones as often as possible
- embracing plant foods like vegetables, fruits, beans and whole grains
- including low-fat dairy products, fish and shellfish, lean meats and poultry
- relying on seasoning and cooking dishes with olive oil and the other "good fats" that make food tastier and more satisfying, while keeping a watchful eye on saturated fat and trans fat.

But most of all, eating well means eating with pleasure—in a relaxed and friendly environment. Enjoy every bite!

Menu Suggestions

Winter

Roasted Cod with Warm Tomato-Olive-Caper Tapenade (*page 153*)

Dressed-Up Rice (*page 229*) with currants, pine nuts & fresh parsley
Cinnamon Oranges (*page 239*)

Beef Stroganoff with Portobello Mushrooms (*page 192*)

Whole-wheat egg noodles
Roasted broccoli (*page 233*)

Spring

Sichuan-Style Shrimp (*page 177*)

Brown basmati rice (*page 238*)
Watercress Salad (*page 229*)

Herbed Lamb Chops with Greek Couscous Salad (*page 224*)

Roasted asparagus (*page 232*)
Strawberries with Minted Yogurt (*page 241*)

Summer

Grilled Steak with Fresh Corn Salad (*page 194*)

Grilled summer squash *or* zucchini (*page 236*)
Summer Blackberries (*page 241*)

Jerk Chicken Breasts (*page 121*)

Fresh Fruit Salsa with pineapple (*page 229*)
Carrot-Cumin Salad (*page 228*)

Fall

Rigatoni with Turkey Sausage, Cheese & Pepper (*page 144*)

TriColor Salad (*page 229*)
Crusty whole-wheat bread
Coffee-Cognac Coupe (*page 240*)

Chicken Tortilla Soup (*page 57*)

Quesadillas (*page 230*)

Entertaining

Miso-Glazed Scallops with Soba Noodles (*page 171*)

Cucumber Salad (*page 228*)
Pineapple with Mango Coulis (*page 240*)

Chicken Stuffed with Golden Onions & Fontina (*page 114*)

Asparagus with Fresh Tomato Garnish (*page 231*)
Brown Rice & Greens (*page 229*)
Gingered Peach Gratin (*page 240*)

Family Meals

Loaded Twice-Baked Potatoes (*page 198*)

Steamed green beans (*page 235*)
Strawberries Dipped in Chocolate (*page 241*)

Almond-Crusted Chicken Fingers (*page 123*)

Zucchini Noodles (*page 231*)
Steamed corn (*page 234*)

Vegetarian

Sweet & Sour Tofu (*page 98*)

Instant brown rice
Sesame Green Beans (*page 231*)

Zucchini-Potato Latkes with Tzatziki (*page 107*)

Chopped Tomato Salad (*page 228*)
Wilted Spinach with Garlic (*page 231*)
Aromatic Rice Pudding (*page 239*)

Chapter 1: Dinner Salads

Chicken

Lobster, Seafood, Tuna, Salmon & Shrimp

Pork, Beef & Lamb

Vegetarian

Vietnamese Chicken & Noodle Salad

Fish sauce is the soy sauce of Southeast Asia—more pungent at first blush but very aromatic and malleable when combined with other flavors, like the chicken, vegetables and peanuts in this light, refreshing salad.

1 pound boneless, skinless chicken breasts, trimmed of fat
4 ounces wide rice noodles
1/2 cup rice-wine vinegar
1 tablespoon fish sauce (*see Ingredient Note, page 243*)
2 teaspoons sugar, or to taste
3 cups shredded napa cabbage
1 English cucumber, halved, seeded and thinly sliced
1 cup shredded carrot
1 cup slivered fresh basil
1/2 cup finely chopped unsalted roasted peanuts

1. Place chicken in a skillet or saucepan and add enough water to cover; bring to a boil. Cover, reduce heat and gently simmer until the chicken is cooked through and no longer pink in the middle, 10 to 12 minutes. Transfer to a cutting board. When cool enough to handle, shred into bite-size strips.

2. Meanwhile, bring a large pot of water to a boil. Stir in rice noodles and cook until just tender, 6 to 8 minutes, or according to package directions. Drain and rinse under cold water.

3. Whisk vinegar, fish sauce and sugar to taste in a large bowl until the sugar is dissolved. Add the chicken, noodles, cabbage, cucumber, carrot, basil and peanuts; toss to combine. Serve immediately.

Makes 4 servings, 2 1/2 cups each.

Active Minutes: 40

Total: 40 minutes

To Make Ahead: Prepare salad up to 8 hours in advance. Toss with peanuts just before serving.

Per Serving: 402 calories; 12 g fat (2 g sat, 5 g mono); 63 mg cholesterol; 44 g carbohydrate; 31 g protein; 5 g fiber; 667 mg sodium.

Nutrition Bonus: Vitamin A (100% daily value), Vitamin K (60% dv), Vitamin C (40% dv), Selenium (37% dv).

High ↑ Fiber

Roasted Chicken Salad with Garlic Toasts

Rotisserie chickens have become all the rage in our local supermarkets—and why not? They can be the base of a quick, almost-homemade dinner in no time. Here, roasted chicken turns into an easy salad with some crusty garlic bread on the side.

2 cloves garlic, peeled
3 tablespoons cider vinegar *or* white-wine vinegar
3 tablespoons extra-virgin olive oil
1/4 cup Kalamata olives, pitted and chopped
8 cups mixed salad greens
4 1/2-inch slices whole-wheat country bread, toasted
1 2-pound roasted chicken (hot or cold), skin discarded, sliced into large pieces

1. Mince one garlic clove and whisk with vinegar, oil and olives in a medium bowl. Toss greens in the dressing to coat well.

2. Rub each bread slice with the remaining garlic clove. (Discard garlic.) Divide the salad among 4 plates, place chicken on top and serve with the bread.

Makes 4 servings.

Active Minutes: 20

Total: 20 minutes

Per Serving: 394 calories; 20 g fat (4 g sat, 12 g mono); 77 mg cholesterol; 22 g carbohydrate; 29 g protein; 2 g fiber; 435 mg sodium.

Nutrition Bonus: Selenium (28% daily value), Vitamin A (15% dv).

Lower Carbs

ingredient note:

- **Store-bought rotisserie chicken is convenient and practical—but much higher in sodium than a home-roasted bird. Even the unseasoned varieties have been marinated or seasoned with salty flavorings. People with hypertension should think twice before choosing store-bought.**
- **4 ounces home-roasted chicken: ≤100 mg sodium**
- **4 ounces rotisserie chicken: 350-450 mg sodium**

Five-Spice Chicken & Orange Salad

Five-spice powder has been a Chinese shortcut for years, a way to combine all the aromatics in one convenient package. Tossed with orange juice and chicken, it makes a terrific, flavorful salad with a complex, layered taste that belies the simple recipe.

- **6 teaspoons extra-virgin olive oil, divided**
- **1 teaspoon five-spice powder**
- **1 teaspoon kosher salt, divided**
- **1/2 teaspoon freshly ground pepper, plus more to taste**
- **1 pound boneless, skinless chicken breasts, trimmed of fat**
- **3 oranges**
- **12 cups mixed Asian *or* salad greens**
- **1 red bell pepper, cut into thin strips**
- **1/2 cup slivered red onion**
- **3 tablespoons cider vinegar**
- **1 tablespoon Dijon mustard**

1. Preheat oven to 450°F. Combine 1 teaspoon oil, five-spice powder, 1/2 teaspoon salt and 1/2 teaspoon pepper in a small bowl. Rub the mixture into both sides of the chicken breasts.

2. Heat 1 teaspoon oil in a large ovenproof nonstick skillet over medium-high heat. Add chicken; cook until browned on one side, 3 to 5 minutes. Turn it over and transfer the pan to the oven. Roast until the chicken is just cooked through (an instant-read thermometer inserted into the center should read 165°F), 6 to 8 minutes. Transfer the chicken to a cutting board; let rest for 5 minutes (it will finish cooking as it rests).

3. Meanwhile, peel and segment two of the oranges (*see Tip*). Collect segments and any juice in a large bowl. (Discard membranes, pith and skin.) Add the greens, bell pepper and onion to the bowl. Zest and juice the remaining orange. Place the zest and juice in a small bowl; whisk in vinegar, mustard, the remaining 4 teaspoons oil, remaining 1/2 teaspoon salt and freshly ground pepper to taste. Pour the dressing over the salad; toss to combine. Slice the chicken and serve on the salad.

Makes 4 servings.

Active Minutes: 35

Total: 35 minutes

To Make Ahead: Prepare through Step 2. Cover the cooked chicken and refrigerate for up to 2 days. Slice before serving chilled.

Per Serving: 278 calories; 10 g fat (2 g sat, 6 g mono); 63 mg cholesterol; 23 g carbohydrate; 26 g protein; 7 g fiber; 681 mg sodium.

Nutrition Bonus: Vitamin C (170% daily value), Vitamin A (140% dv), Selenium (30% dv), Iron (15% dv).

Healthy Weight

High Fiber

to segment a citrus fruit:

Using a sharp knife, cut off the peel and white pith from the fruit. To make attractive segments, hold the fruit over a bowl (to catch the juice) and slice between each segment and its surrounding membranes.

Grilled Lobster Tails with Nectarine-Avocado Salad

Sophisticated and yet very quick, this easy composed salad can be a meal on its own—or a wonderful starter to a weekend dinner party. All it needs is a glass of champagne. Shrimp or other sweet and meaty fish can stand in for the lobster.

3 nectarines, diced
1 avocado, diced
1 scallion, sliced
1 tablespoon lime juice, plus lime wedges for garnish
1 teaspoon kosher salt, divided
Freshly ground pepper to taste
3 lobster tails, fresh *or* frozen, thawed (8 ounces each)
2 teaspoons extra-virgin olive oil

1. Preheat grill to medium-high.

2. Toss nectarines, avocado, scallion, lime juice, 1/2 teaspoon salt and pepper in a medium bowl.

3. Lay lobster tails on a cutting board with the soft side of the shell facing up. Cut the tails in half lengthwise starting from the fan. Run your fingertips along the inside of the shell to loosen meat from shell. Brush the meat with oil and sprinkle with the remaining 1/2 teaspoon salt.

4. Lay the tails on the grill, cut-side down, and cook until the meat is lightly charred and the shell is beginning to turn red, 5 to 6 minutes. Turn and continue grilling until the meat is opaque and cooked through and the shell is completely red, 2 to 4 minutes more. Remove the lobster meat from the shells and serve with the nectarine salad.

Makes 4 servings.

Active Minutes: 40

Total: 40 minutes

Per Serving: 179 calories; 8 g fat (1 g sat, 5 g mono); 32 mg cholesterol; 18 g carbohydrate; 11 g protein; 4 g fiber; 642 mg sodium.

Nutrition Bonus: Vitamin K (30% daily value), Selenium (27% dv), Vitamin C (25% dv), Potassium (18% dv).

Healthy Weight

Lower Carbs

Seafood Salad with Citrus Vinaigrette

Active Minutes: 25

Total: 25 minutes

Per Serving: 441 calories; 28 g fat (5 g sat, 11 g mono); 74 mg cholesterol; 22 g carbohydrate; 30 g protein; 11 g fiber; 569 mg sodium.

Nutrition Bonus: Vitamin A (130% daily value), Vitamin C (120% dv), Folate (35% dv), Potassium (30% dv).

Lower ↓ Carbs

High ↑ Fiber

shopping for 2:

- **What if you want just six cherry tomatoes, not a whole container full? Shop the salad bar at your local supermarket. The produce may cost a little more, but you're guaranteed not to waste any of it since you'll buy just what you need.**

Crab and scallops combine with creamy avocados and a spiky orange dressing for a salad that's light, summery and very fast. The recipe can be easily doubled or tripled.

4 medium dry sea scallops (*see Ingredient Note, page 246*), quartered (about 3 ounces), tough muscle removed
1 small grapefruit, preferably ruby-red
1 small shallot, minced
3 tablespoons white-wine vinegar
1 teaspoon Dijon mustard
Salt to taste
1/4 teaspoon freshly ground pepper
2 tablespoons extra-virgin olive oil
6 ounces lump crabmeat
1 small head romaine lettuce, shredded (about 3 cups)
6 cherry tomatoes, halved (*see Tip*)
1 small avocado, peeled, pitted and diced

1. Bring a small saucepan of water to a boil. Add scallops and cook until firm, opaque and just cooked through, about 1 minute. Drain and rinse under cold water until cool.

2. Slice 1/4 inch off the bottom and top of the grapefruit; stand it on a cutting board. Using a sharp paring knife, remove the peel and pith. Hold the fruit over a medium bowl and cut between the membranes to release individual grapefruit sections into the bowl, collecting any juice as well. Discard membranes, pith, peel and any seeds. Transfer just the grapefruit sections to a serving bowl.

3. Whisk shallot, vinegar, mustard, salt and pepper into the bowl with the grapefruit juice. Whisk in oil in a slow, steady stream. Add the scallops and crab to the dressing; toss well to coat.

4. Add lettuce, tomatoes and avocado to the bowl with the grapefruit; toss to combine. Add the seafood and dressing; toss gently.

Makes 2 servings, 3 cups each.

Tuscan-Style Tuna Salad

Active Minutes: 10

Total: 10 minutes

To Make Ahead: Cover and refrigerate for up to 2 days.

Per Serving: 253 calories; 8 g fat (1 g sat, 5 g mono); 53 mg cholesterol; 20 g carbohydrate; 31 g protein; 6 g fiber; 453 mg sodium.

Nutrition Bonus: Fiber (25% daily value), Vitamin C (20% dv).

Healthy Weight

Lower Carbs

High Fiber

ingredient note:

- **When you use canned beans in a recipe, be sure to rinse them first in a colander under cold running water, as their canning liquid often contains a fair amount of sodium.**

This streamlined version of a northern Italian idea is perfect for a summer evening: no-fuss, no-cook and big taste. You can even make it ahead and store it, covered, in the refrigerator for several days. If you do, use it as a wrap filling for the next day's lunch.

2 6-ounce cans chunk light tuna, drained
1 15-ounce can small white beans, such as cannellini *or* great northern, rinsed (*see Note*)
10 cherry tomatoes, quartered
4 scallions, trimmed and sliced
2 tablespoons extra-virgin olive oil
2 tablespoons lemon juice
1/4 teaspoon salt
Freshly ground pepper to taste

1. Combine tuna, beans, tomatoes, scallions, oil, lemon juice, salt and pepper in a medium bowl. Stir gently. Refrigerate until ready to serve.

Makes 4 servings, 1 cup each.

Chopped Salad al Tonno

Why have the same mayonnaise-laden tuna when you can make a light, fresh salad that won't hold you back while you chase the kids around the yard?

1/4 cup lemon juice
3 tablespoons extra-virgin olive oil
1/2 teaspoon garlic salt
Freshly ground pepper to taste
8 cups chopped hearts of romaine
2 medium tomatoes, diced
1/2 cup sliced pimiento-stuffed green olives
2 6-ounce cans chunk light tuna, drained

1. Whisk lemon juice, oil, garlic salt and pepper in a large bowl. Add romaine, tomatoes and olives; toss to coat. Add tuna and toss again.

Makes 4 servings, generous 2 cups each.

Active Minutes: 15

Total: 15 minutes

Per Serving: 258 calories; 13 g fat (2 g sat, 9 g mono); 53 mg cholesterol; 8 g carbohydrate; 26 g protein; 3 g fiber; 428 mg sodium.

Nutrition Bonus: Vitamin A (110% daily value), Vitamin C (60% dv), Folate (32% dv).

Healthy Weight

Lower Carbs

ingredient note:

- Canned white tuna **comes from the large albacore and can be high in mercury content.** Chunk light**, on the other hand, which comes from smaller fish, skipjack or yellowfin, is best for health-conscious eaters. According to a recent study, canned white tuna samples averaged about 315 percent more mercury than chunk light tuna samples.**

Nouveau Niçoise

This quick, easy remake of the Provençal standard turns a couple of cans of tuna into a main-course salad that's just waiting for a glass of crisp Chardonnay.

8 cups water
8 ounces green beans, trimmed and halved
8 small red potatoes
2 eggs
1/4 cup minced shallots
1/4 cup red-wine vinegar
2 tablespoons Dijon mustard
1/4 teaspoon salt
1/4 teaspoon freshly ground pepper
3 tablespoons extra-virgin olive oil
6 cups mixed salad greens
2 6-ounce cans chunk light tuna, drained
12 Niçoise *or* Kalamata olives

1. Bring water to a boil in a 3- to 4-quart saucepan. Add green beans and cook until just tender and bright green, 1 to 2 minutes. Using a slotted spoon, transfer the beans to a colander, rinse under cold water and set aside in a large bowl. Carefully place potatoes and eggs into the boiling water. Cook the eggs until hard, 12 minutes. Using a slotted spoon, transfer the eggs to the colander, rinse under cold water until cool and set aside. Continue cooking the potatoes until fork-tender, 3 minutes more. Drain the potatoes; rinse under cold water until cool enough to handle.

2. Meanwhile, combine shallots, vinegar, mustard, salt and pepper in a small bowl. Slowly whisk in oil.

3. Cut the potatoes into quarters or eighths, depending on their size. Add to the bowl with the beans. Add greens, tuna and the dressing. Toss well. Peel the eggs and cut into wedges. Divide the salad among 4 plates. Top with egg wedges and olives. Serve immediately.

Makes 4 servings, generous 2 cups each.

Active Minutes: 30

Total: 40 minutes

To Make Ahead: Cook green beans, potatoes and eggs; dry, cover and refrigerate for up to 1 day.

Per Serving: 436 calories; 16 g fat (3 g sat, 11 g mono); 159 mg cholesterol; 38 g carbohydrate; 33 g protein; 6 g fiber; 547 mg sodium.

Nutrition Bonus: Vitamin C (90% daily value), Potassium (33% dv), Vitamin A (30% dv), Folate (26% dv), Iron (15% dv).

High ↑ Fiber

Warm Salmon Salad with Crispy Potatoes

Active Minutes: 25

Total: 25 minutes

Per Serving: 260 calories; 11 g fat (1 g sat, 5 g mono); 71 mg cholesterol; 15 g carbohydrate; 28 g protein; 2 g fiber; 708 mg sodium.

Nutrition Bonus: Vitamin C (32% daily value), Vitamin A (9% dv).

Healthy Weight

Lower Carbs

In a kind of updated homage to Swiss rösti, this light salad combines things we love: a bed of crispy potatoes, some delicious fish, flavorful greens and a perk-you-up dressing.

2 tablespoons extra-virgin olive oil, divided
2 small yellow-fleshed potatoes, such as Yukon Gold, scrubbed and cut into 1/8-inch slices
1/2 teaspoon salt, divided
1 medium shallot, thinly sliced
2 teaspoons rice vinegar
1/4 cup buttermilk
2 7-ounce cans boneless, skinless salmon, drained
4 cups arugula

1. Heat 1 tablespoon oil in a large nonstick skillet over medium-high heat. Add potatoes and cook, turning once, until brown and crispy, 5 to 6 minutes per side. Transfer to a plate and season with 1/4 teaspoon salt; cover with foil to keep warm.

2. Combine the remaining 1 tablespoon oil, 1/4 teaspoon salt, shallot and vinegar in a small saucepan. Bring to a boil over medium heat. Remove from the heat and whisk in buttermilk. Place salmon in a medium bowl and toss with the warm dressing. Divide arugula among 4 plates and top with the potatoes and salmon.

Makes 4 servings.

Lemony Lentil Salad with Salmon

Active Minutes: 30

Total: 30 minutes

To Make Ahead: Cover and refrigerate for up to 8 hours.

Per Serving: 354 calories; 18 g fat (3 g sat, 12 g mono); 31 mg cholesterol; 25 g carbohydrate; 24 g protein; 9 g fiber; 194 mg sodium.

Nutrition Bonus: Vitamin C (80% daily value), Folate (49% dv), Selenium (40% dv), Iron (25% dv), Potassium (21% dv), Calcium (20% dv).

High Fiber

to cook lentils:

- **Place in a saucepan, cover with water and bring to a boil. Reduce heat to a simmer and cook until just tender, about 20 minutes for green lentils and 30 minutes for brown. Drain and rinse under cold water.**

Salmon and lentils are a familiar combo in French bistro cooking. For the best presentation, flake the salmon with a fork, then stir gently into the salad to keep it in chunks, not tiny bits.

1/3 cup lemon juice
1/3 cup chopped fresh dill
2 teaspoons Dijon mustard
1/4 teaspoon salt, or to taste
Freshly ground pepper to taste
1/3 cup extra-virgin olive oil
1 medium red bell pepper, seeded and diced
1 cup diced seedless cucumber
1/2 cup finely chopped red onion
2 15-ounce cans lentils, rinsed, *or* 3 cups cooked brown *or* green lentils (*see Tip*)
2 7-ounce cans salmon, drained and flaked, *or* 1 1/2 cups flaked cooked salmon

1. Whisk lemon juice, dill, mustard, salt and pepper in a large bowl. Gradually whisk in oil. Add bell pepper, cucumber, onion, lentils and salmon; toss to coat.

Makes 6 servings, 1 cup each.

Warm Shrimp & Arugula Salad

Bursting with vibrant flavors, this summery salad makes a terrific supper, light but still satisfying. Fresh, raw corn kernels lend a sweet, candylike crunch to the dish—and work well against the salty shrimp and peppery arugula.

Active Minutes: 25

Total: 25 minutes

Per Serving: 343 calories; 21 g fat (5 g sat, 11 g mono); 181 mg cholesterol; 16 g carbohydrate; 25 g protein; 4 g fiber; 637 mg sodium.

Nutrition Bonus: Selenium (50% daily value), Vitamin A (50% dv), Vitamin C (50% dv), Calcium (25% dv), Iron (25% dv), Potassium (19% dv), Folate (18% dv).

Lower Carbs

- **12 cups loosely packed arugula leaves**
- **2 cups loosely packed fresh basil leaves, torn if large**
- **1 1/2 cups fresh corn kernels (from about 2 ears)**
- **1 1/2 cups cherry tomatoes *or* grape tomatoes, halved**
- **4 tablespoons extra-virgin olive oil, divided**
- **1 1/2 tablespoons lemon juice**
- **1 1/2 tablespoons balsamic vinegar**
- **2 teaspoons grainy mustard**
- **1/2 teaspoon coarse sea salt *or* kosher salt, divided**
- **1 pound raw shrimp (21-25 per pound), peeled and deveined, tails removed if desired**
- **2 cups herb-garlic croutons, preferably whole-grain (optional)**
- **Freshly ground pepper to taste**
- **1/2 cup grated Asiago *or* Parmesan cheese**

1. Combine arugula, basil, corn and tomatoes in a large bowl. Whisk 3 tablespoons oil, lemon juice, vinegar, mustard and 1/4 teaspoon salt in a small bowl.

2. Sprinkle shrimp with the remaining 1/4 teaspoon salt. Heat the remaining 1 tablespoon oil in a large nonstick skillet over high heat. Add the shrimp and cook, turning from time to time, just until they turn pink and are opaque in the center, 2 to 3 minutes. Add to the arugula mixture along with croutons, if using.

3. Whisk the dressing again and drizzle over the salad; toss to coat. Divide the salad among 4 plates. Grind pepper over the salads and sprinkle with cheese.

Makes 4 servings, about 3 cups each.

Shrimp Caesar

While most Caesars drown the greens in a heavy dressing, this lemony version lets the taste of the shrimp shine through. Don't worry about the anchovies—they'll mellow in the dressing, giving it a rich taste that can't be duplicated.

- **3 tablespoons lemon juice, plus 4 lemon wedges for garnish**
- **2 teaspoons Dijon mustard**
- **3 anchovies, coarsely chopped, *or* 1 teaspoon anchovy paste, or to taste**
- **1 small clove garlic, coarsely chopped**
- **2 tablespoons extra-virgin olive oil**
- **1/2 cup grated Asiago cheese, divided**
- **1/2 teaspoon freshly ground pepper**
- **8 cups chopped hearts of romaine (about 2 hearts)**
- **1 pound peeled cooked shrimp (21-25 per pound; thawed if frozen)**
- **1 cup croutons, preferably whole-grain (*see Tip*)**

1. Place lemon juice, mustard, anchovies (or anchovy paste) and garlic in a food processor; process until smooth. With the motor running, gradually add oil; process until creamy. Add 1/4 cup Asiago cheese and pepper; pulse until combined.

2. Combine romaine, shrimp and croutons in a large bowl. Add the dressing and toss to coat. Divide among 4 plates, top with the remaining 1/4 cup Asiago cheese and garnish with a lemon wedge.

Makes 4 servings, about 2 1/2 cups each.

Active Minutes: 20

Total: 20 minutes

To Make Ahead: The dressing (Step 1) will keep, in a jar in the refrigerator, for up to 3 days. Shake vigorously just before tossing with the salad.

Per Serving: 312 calories; 16 g fat (4 g sat, 8 g mono); 235 mg cholesterol; 13 g carbohydrate; 31 g protein; 2 g fiber; 669 mg sodium.

Nutrition Bonus: Vitamin A (50% daily value), Vitamin C (45% dv), Iron (30% dv), Calcium (20% dv).

Healthy Weight

Lower Carbs

homemade croutons:

- **Toss 1 cup whole-grain bread cubes with 1 tablespoon extra-virgin olive oil, a pinch each of salt, pepper and garlic powder. Spread out on a baking sheet and toast at 350°F until crispy, turning occasionally, 15 to 20 minutes.**

Shrimp Salad-Stuffed Tomatoes

Active Minutes: 35

Total: 35 minutes

To Make Ahead: Prepare the salad (Step 1). Cover and refrigerate for up to 1 day.

Per Serving: 192 calories; 5 g fat (1 g sat, 2 g mono); 223 mg cholesterol; 12 g carbohydrate; 26 g protein; 2 g fiber; 504 mg sodium.

Nutrition Bonus: Vitamin C (80% daily value), Iron (25% dv), Vitamin A (25% dv).

Healthy Weight

Lower Carbs

kitchen tip:

- **Save the scooped-out tomato insides to use in fresh tomato soup or pasta sauce. Store in the refrigerator for up to 3 days or in the freezer for up to 6 months.**

Hollowed-out tomatoes were the secret to elegant lunches in the '50s—and they deserve a comeback today. Look for bright red, aromatic tomatoes without any mushy spots or discolorations. You can also stuff these tomatoes with the barley salad on page 41 or the curried tofu salad on page 50.

- **1 pound peeled cooked shrimp (21-25 per pound; thawed if frozen), tails removed, chopped**
- **1 stalk celery, finely diced**
- **1/4 cup minced fresh basil**
- **10 Kalamata olives, pitted and finely chopped**
- **1 medium shallot, minced**
- **2 tablespoons reduced-fat mayonnaise**
- **1 tablespoon white-wine vinegar**
- **Pinch of freshly ground pepper**
- **4 large ripe tomatoes, cored**

1. Combine shrimp, celery, basil, olives, shallot, mayonnaise, vinegar and pepper in a medium bowl. Stir to combine.

2. Carefully hollow out the inside of each tomato using a melon baller or small spoon; reserve the scooped tomato for another use (*see Tip*). To serve, fill each tomato with a generous 1/2 cup of the shrimp salad.

Makes 4 servings.

Bacony Barley Salad with Marinated Shrimp

Here's a great example of how to cook a healthy dish in minutes—simply cook the bacon in the same pan as the barley to enrich the flavor, add some purchased cooked shrimp, a few aromatic vegetables, and you've got dinner (or a hearty potluck dish) in no time flat.

3 strips bacon, chopped
1 1/3 cups water
1/2 teaspoon salt
2/3 cup quick-cooking barley
1 pound peeled cooked shrimp (21-25 per pound; thawed if frozen), tails removed, coarsely chopped
1/3 cup lime juice
2 cups cherry tomatoes, halved
1/2 cup finely diced red onion
1/2 cup chopped fresh cilantro
2 tablespoons extra-virgin olive oil
Freshly ground pepper to taste
1 avocado, peeled and diced

1. Cook bacon in a small saucepan over medium heat, stirring often, until crispy, about 4 minutes. Drain on paper towel; discard fat.

2. Add water and salt to the pan and bring to a boil. Add barley and return to a simmer. Reduce heat to low, cover and simmer until all the liquid is absorbed, 10 to 12 minutes.

3. Combine shrimp and lime juice in a large bowl. Add the cooked barley; toss to coat. Let stand for 10 minutes, stirring occasionally, to allow the barley to absorb some of the lime juice. Add tomatoes, onion, cilantro and the bacon; toss to coat. Add oil and pepper and toss again. Stir in avocado and serve.

Makes 4 servings, 1 3/4 cups each.

Active Minutes: 40

Total: 40 minutes

To Make Ahead: Prepare without avocado, cover and refrigerate for up to 2 days. Stir in the avocado just before serving.

Per Serving: 393 calories; 18 g fat (3 g sat, 11 g mono); 228 mg cholesterol; 30 g carbohydrate; 31 g protein; 7 g fiber; 671 mg sodium.

Nutrition Bonus: Vitamin C (50% daily value), Fiber (29% dv), Iron (25% dv), Folate (15% dv).

High ↑ Fiber

Light Salade aux Lardons

Active Minutes: 20

Total: 25 minutes

Per Serving: 263 calories; 18 g fat (4 g sat, 11 g mono); 232 mg cholesterol; 8 g carbohydrate; 17 g protein; 3 g fiber; 902 mg sodium.

Nutrition Bonus: Vitamin A (50% daily value), Folate (43% dv), Selenium (36% dv), Potassium (17% dv), Iron (15% dv), Vitamin C (15% dv).

Healthy Weight

Lower Carbs

This French bistro salad is usually made with fatty bacon from the pig's belly. With Canadian bacon, it's lighter, leaner and just as tasty. You can cut down on the salt by parboiling the bacon for 1 minute before dicing. A poached egg nestled into the greens completes the dish—and turns it into a substantial brunch or supper.

- **3 tablespoons olive oil, divided**
- **8 ounces Canadian bacon, cut into 1/2-inch dice (1 3/4 cups)**
- **2 medium heads frisée *or* curly-leaf endive lettuce, torn (8 cups)**
- **1 large shallot, minced**
- **3 tablespoons white-wine vinegar**
- **1 teaspoon Dijon mustard**
- **1/4 teaspoon salt**
- **1/4 teaspoon freshly ground pepper, plus more to taste**
- **4 eggs**

1. Heat 1 tablespoon oil in a skillet over medium-high heat. Add bacon; cook, stirring, until brown and crisp, about 8 minutes.

2. Use a slotted spoon to transfer the bacon to a large bowl. Add lettuce to the bowl. Add shallot to the skillet and cook over medium heat, stirring, until softened, about 2 minutes. Remove from the heat and stir in the remaining 2 tablespoons oil, vinegar, mustard, salt and pepper. Pour this mixture onto the lettuce; toss to coat.

3. Meanwhile, bring about 1 inch of water to a boil in a medium skillet. Crack each egg into a small bowl and slip them one at a time into the boiling water, taking care not to break the yolks. Reduce heat to low. Cover the pan and poach the eggs until the yolks are just set, 4 to 5 minutes.

4. Divide salad among 4 plates. Top each serving with a poached egg. Grind pepper over the top and serve immediately.

Makes 4 servings, about 2 cups each.

Steak Salad-Stuffed Pockets

Here's a healthy dinner on the go, an easy sandwich you can pack up and take in the car when you're rushing the kids off to soccer or band. It's also a quick favorite when the adults just want to hang out on the deck on Saturday night with a pitcher of sangria on the side.

Active Minutes: 20

Total: 30 minutes

Per Serving: 410 calories; 15 g fat (3 g sat, 8 g mono); 65 mg cholesterol; 37 g carbohydrate; 33 g protein; 6 g fiber; 529 mg sodium.

Nutrition Bonus: Vitamin A (70% daily value), Selenium (66% dv), Vitamin C (45% dv), Folate (29% dv), Iron (25% dv), Magnesium (20% dv).

High ↑ Fiber

- **1/4 cup lemon juice**
- **3 tablespoons extra-virgin olive oil**
- **2 teaspoons Dijon mustard**
- **1/4 teaspoon salt, or to taste**
- **Freshly ground pepper to taste**
- **1 pound top round steak, 1 1/2 inches thick, trimmed**
- **4 cups romaine lettuce, chopped**
- **1 medium cucumber, diced**
- **1 large tomato, diced**
- **8 4-inch whole-wheat pitas *or* four 8-inch pitas, split open (*see Tip*)**

1. Position rack in upper third of oven; preheat broiler.

2. Whisk lemon juice, oil, mustard, salt and pepper in a large bowl. Place steak in a shallow dish and pour half the dressing over it. Let marinate at room temperature, turning once, for 10 minutes.

3. Meanwhile, prepare the salad by adding lettuce, cucumber and tomato to the remaining dressing in the bowl; toss to coat.

4. Transfer the meat to a broiling pan. Broil for 5 minutes on each side for medium-rare, or until it reaches desired doneness. Transfer to a cutting board, let rest for 3 minutes, then slice thinly against the grain. Mix the meat with the salad and fill each pita. Serve immediately.

Makes 4 servings.

tip:

- **Warm pitas on the bottom rack of the oven while the steak is broiling.**

Bistro Beef Salad

Shallot vinaigrette unifies a simple salad of leftover beef, potatoes and cherry tomatoes; serve with a loaf of crusty whole-wheat bread and a glass of Cabernet.

Active Minutes: 15

Total: 25 minutes

Per Serving: 357 calories; 15 g fat (5 g sat, 8 g mono); 69 mg cholesterol; 26 g carbohydrate; 28 g protein; 3 g fiber; 286 mg sodium.

Nutrition Bonus: Vitamin A (100% daily value), Vitamin C (70% dv), Zinc (44% dv), Selenium (29% dv), Iron (25% dv).

4 red potatoes, scrubbed and cut into quarters (1 pound)
Salt to taste
2 tablespoons chopped shallots
2 tablespoons white-wine vinegar
1 tablespoon Dijon mustard
1 tablespoon chopped fresh parsley
1 tablespoon chopped fresh tarragon *or* 1 teaspoon dried
2 tablespoons cold water
1 tablespoon extra-virgin olive oil
Freshly ground black pepper to taste
1 large head red leaf lettuce, torn (8 cups)
2 cups red *or* yellow cherry tomatoes, cut in half
12 ounces cooked roast beef *or* steak, thinly sliced

1. Place potatoes in a medium saucepan and cover with lightly salted water by 1 inch. Bring to a boil over medium heat and cook until tender, about 15 minutes.

2. Meanwhile, whisk shallots, vinegar, mustard, parsley, tarragon and water in a small bowl. Slowly whisk in oil. Season with salt and pepper.

3. Drain the potatoes and rinse with cold water. Divide lettuce among 4 plates; arrange the potatoes, tomatoes and beef on top. Drizzle with the dressing and serve.

Makes 4 servings.

Mediterranean Lamb Salad

Here's an example of everyday simplicity taken to elegant heights—a lovely chickpea and vegetable salad, topped with warm strips of lamb. Hearty yet light for a warm night, this supper could be followed up with Iced Lychees (*page 240*).

1 pound boneless leg of lamb steaks, 1-1 1/2 inches thick (*see Note*)
1 1/2 teaspoons kosher salt, divided
Freshly ground pepper to taste
2 medium cucumbers, peeled, halved, seeded and diced
2 large tomatoes, diced
1 15-ounce can chickpeas, rinsed
1/2 cup minced red onion
1/4 cup crumbled feta cheese
1/4 cup sliced fresh mint leaves
1/4 cup lemon juice
1 teaspoon extra-virgin olive oil

1. Preheat grill to high. Sprinkle lamb with 1/2 teaspoon salt and pepper. Grill the lamb for 2 to 4 minutes per side for medium, depending on the thickness of the steaks. Transfer to a cutting board and let rest for at least 5 minutes before thinly slicing across the grain.

2. Meanwhile, place cucumbers, tomatoes, chickpeas, onion, feta cheese and mint in a large bowl. Add lemon juice, oil, the remaining 1 teaspoon salt and more pepper to taste; stir to combine. Serve topped with the sliced lamb.

Makes 6 servings.

Active Minutes: 30

Total: 30 minutes

Per Serving: 256 calories; 9 g fat (3 g sat, 4 g mono); 54 mg cholesterol; 23 g carbohydrate; 21 g protein; 5 g fiber; 713 mg sodium.

Nutrition Bonus: Vitamin C (35% daily value), Selenium (29% dv), Zinc (27% dv), Folate (23% dv), Potassium (19% dv), Iron (15% dv), Vitamin A (15% dv).

Healthy Weight

High Fiber

ingredient note:

Leg of lamb is lean, flavorful and cooks quickly when cut into steaks. Steaks will vary in thickness, depending on the butcher. If leg of lamb steaks are unavailable in your supermarket, trimmed, deboned lamb shoulder chops are a good substitute.

Asian Tofu Salad

Active Minutes: 25

Total: 25 minutes

To Make Ahead: The dressing (Step 1) will keep, covered, in the refrigerator for up to 2 days. Whisk just before using.

Per Serving: 237 calories; 16 g fat (2 g sat, 8 g mono); 0 mg cholesterol; 16 g carbohydrate; 11 g protein; 5 g fiber; 454 mg sodium.

Nutrition Bonus: Vitamin A (180% daily value), Folate (41% dv), Vitamin C (38% dv), Calcium (29% dv).

Healthy Weight

Lower Carbs

High Fiber

The best thing about tofu—besides its nutritional value—is the way it carries other flavors, such as the tanginess of this sesame dressing. Serve this warm salad with crunchy breadsticks and a tall glass of iced jasmine tea.

3 tablespoons canola oil
2 tablespoons rice vinegar
1 tablespoon honey
2 teaspoons reduced-sodium soy sauce
1 teaspoon toasted sesame oil
1 teaspoon minced fresh ginger
1/2 teaspoon salt
1 14-ounce package extra-firm, water-packed tofu, rinsed, patted dry and cut into 1-inch cubes
8 cups mixed salad greens
2 medium carrots, peeled, halved lengthwise and sliced
1 large cucumber, chopped

1. Whisk canola oil, vinegar, honey, soy sauce, sesame oil, ginger and salt in a bowl.

2. Place tofu and 2 tablespoons of the dressing in a large nonstick skillet. Cook over medium-high heat, turning every 2 to 3 minutes, until golden brown, 12 to 15 minutes total. Remove from the heat, add 1 tablespoon of the dressing to the pan and stir to coat.

3. Toss greens, carrots and cucumber with the remaining dressing. Serve immediately, topped with the warm tofu.

Makes 4 servings.

Curried Tofu Salad

Call this one the EatingWell philosophy in a single dish: heart-healthy tofu and walnuts, ripe grapes, a few aromatics and a light version of curried mayo dressing. All together, it makes a brilliant, quick lunch or dinner, full of flavor and ready in minutes.

Active Minutes: 20

Total: 20 minutes

To Make Ahead: Cover and refrigerate for up to 2 days.

Per Serving: 140 calories; 8 g fat (1 g sat, 2 g mono); 2 mg cholesterol; 13 g carbohydrate; 7 g protein; 2 g fiber; 241 mg sodium.

Nutrition Bonus: Calcium (15% daily value).

Healthy Weight

Lower Carbs

3 tablespoons low-fat plain yogurt
2 tablespoons reduced-fat mayonnaise
2 tablespoons prepared mango chutney
2 teaspoons curry powder, preferably hot Madras
1/4 teaspoon salt
Freshly ground pepper to taste
1 14-ounce package extra-firm water-packed tofu, drained, rinsed and finely crumbled
2 stalks celery, diced
1 cup red grapes, sliced in half
1/2 cup sliced scallions
1/4 cup chopped walnuts

1. Whisk yogurt, mayonnaise, chutney, curry powder, salt and pepper in a large bowl. Add tofu, celery, grapes, scallions and walnuts; stir to combine.

Makes 6 servings, 2/3 cup each.

ingredient note:

- **We prefer water-packed tofu from the refrigerated section of the supermarket. Crumbling it into uneven pieces creates more surface area, improving the texture and avoiding the blocky look that turns many people away.**

Greek Diner Salad

The secret to this New York diner-style salad is to dice the vegetables to the same size, so that the flavors can meld in one bite. The tangy dressing really perks up the vegetables and makes this dish a stand-alone entree or a zippy accompaniment to barbecued or roasted meats.

3 tablespoons nonfat plain yogurt
3 tablespoons reduced-fat mayonnaise
2 tablespoons lemon juice
2 tablespoons chopped fresh mint
1 clove garlic, minced
1 teaspoon honey
1/2 teaspoon salt
1 medium zucchini, finely diced
1 large red bell pepper, finely diced
1 bunch radishes, finely diced
1 15-ounce can chickpeas, rinsed
4 large Boston lettuce leaves, for serving

1. Whisk yogurt, mayonnaise, lemon juice, mint, garlic, honey and salt in a small bowl until creamy.

2. Toss zucchini, bell pepper, radishes and chickpeas in a large bowl. Pour the dressing over the vegetables; toss gently. To serve, spoon into lettuce leaves, using them as cups.

Makes 4 servings, 1 1/3 cups each.

Active Minutes: 35

Total: 35 minutes

To Make Ahead: Store the chopped salad and dressing separately, tightly covered, in the refrigerator for up to 1 day.

Per Serving: 202 calories; 4 g fat (1 g sat, 1 g mono); 3 mg cholesterol; 35 g carbohydrate; 7 g protein; 7 g fiber; 585 mg sodium.

Nutrition Bonus: Vitamin C (180% daily value), Vitamin A (70% dv), Folate (29% dv), Iron (15% dv), Potassium (15% dv).

High ↑ Fiber

Southwestern Corn & Black Bean Salad

Active Minutes: 25

Total: 25 minutes

To Make Ahead: Cover and refrigerate for up to 1 day.

Per Serving: 410 calories; 16 g fat (2 g sat, 8 g mono); 0 mg cholesterol; 57 g carbohydrate; 16 g protein; 13 g fiber; 482 mg sodium.

Nutrition Bonus: Vitamin C (80% daily value), Iron (25% dv), Vitamin A (20% dv), Potassium (15% dv).

High Fiber

tip:

Convenient preshredded cabbage can be purchased, in bags, in the produce section of most supermarkets.

Here's a great make-ahead lunch—or take the leftovers to work in a resealable plastic container. If you make it ahead, don't add the salt and pepper until just before serving. That way, the salt won't render the vegetables soggy and the pepper won't lose its bite.

- **3 large ears of corn, husked**
- **1/3 cup pine nuts**
- **1/4 cup lime juice**
- **2 tablespoons extra-virgin olive oil**
- **1/4 cup chopped fresh cilantro**
- **1/2 teaspoon salt**
- **Freshly ground pepper to taste**
- **2 15-ounce cans black beans, rinsed**
- **2 cups shredded red cabbage (*see Tip*)**
- **1 large tomato, diced**
- **1/2 cup minced red onion**

1. Bring 1 inch of water to a boil in a Dutch oven. Add corn, cover and cook until just tender, about 3 minutes. When cool enough to handle, cut the kernels from the cobs using a sharp knife.

2. Meanwhile, place pine nuts in a small dry skillet over medium-low heat and cook, stirring, until fragrant and lightly browned, 2 to 4 minutes.

3. Whisk lime juice, oil, cilantro, salt and pepper in a large bowl. Add the corn, pine nuts, beans, cabbage, tomato and onion; stir to coat. Refrigerate until ready to serve.

Makes 4 servings, 2 cups each.

Warm Quinoa Salad with Edamame & Tarragon

Quinoa, a super food from South America, is packed with protein and fiber. Toasting it gives it a slightly nutty taste, a complement to the walnuts and a foil to the lemony tarragon dressing. Try this salad over greens of any sort: fresh arugula, Boston lettuce leaves or wilted spinach.

Active Minutes: 25

Total: 25 minutes

To Make Ahead: Prepare through Step 3. Cover and refrigerate for up to 2 days.

Per Serving: 404 calories; 17 g fat (1 g sat, 6 g mono); 0 mg cholesterol; 47 g carbohydrate; 16 g protein; 8 g fiber; 528 mg sodium.

Nutrition Bonus: Fiber (31% daily value), Iron (25% dv), Vitamin A (20% dv), Vitamin C (20% dv).

High Fiber

- **1 cup quinoa (*see Note*)**
- **2 cups vegetable broth**
- **2 cups frozen shelled edamame, thawed (10 ounces)**
- **1 tablespoon freshly grated lemon zest**
- **2 tablespoons lemon juice**
- **2 tablespoons extra-virgin olive oil**
- **2 tablespoons chopped fresh tarragon *or* 2 teaspoons dried**
- **1/2 teaspoon salt**
- **1/2 cup drained and diced jarred roasted red peppers (3 ounces)**
- **1/4 cup chopped walnuts, preferably toasted (*see Cooking Tip, page 242*)**

1. Toast quinoa in a dry skillet over medium heat, stirring often, until it becomes aromatic and begins to crackle, about 5 minutes. Transfer to a fine sieve and rinse thoroughly.

2. Meanwhile, bring broth to a boil in a medium saucepan over high heat. Add the quinoa and return to a boil. Cover, reduce heat to a simmer and cook gently for 8 minutes. Remove the lid and, without disturbing the quinoa, add edamame. Cover and continue to cook until the edamame and quinoa are tender, 7 to 8 minutes longer. Drain any remaining water, if necessary.

3. Whisk lemon zest and juice, oil, tarragon and salt in a large bowl. Add peppers and the quinoa mixture. Toss to combine. Divide among 4 plates and top with walnuts.

Makes 4 servings, 1 1/2 cups each.

ingredient note:

Quinoa is a delicately flavored grain that was a staple in the ancient Incas' diet. It is available in most natural-foods stores and the natural-foods sections of many supermarkets. Toasting the grain before cooking enhances its flavor and rinsing removes any residue of saponin, quinoa's natural, bitter protective covering.

Quinoa Salad with Dried Apricots & Baby Spinach

Active Minutes: 30

Total: 45 minutes

To Make Ahead: Prepare through Step 3. Cover and refrigerate the quinoa and dressing separately for up to 2 days.

Per Serving: 325 calories; 10 g fat (1 g sat, 5 g mono); 0 mg cholesterol; 51 g carbohydrate; 11 g protein; 7 g fiber; 214 mg sodium.

Nutrition Bonus: Vitamin A (120% daily value), Vitamin C (50% dv), Folate (32% dv), Iron (30% dv), Potassium (25% dv).

High Fiber

This spicy salad with little jewels of dried apricot in the mix would be welcome at lunch or a simple weekday dinner. You can prepare the salad and dressing ahead of time.

- **1 cup quinoa (*see Ingredient Note, page 53*)**
- **2 teaspoons extra-virgin olive oil**
- **2 cloves garlic, minced**
- **1/2 cup dried apricots, coarsely chopped**
- **2 cups water**
- **1/4 teaspoon salt**
- **2/3 cup Moroccan-Spiced Lemon Dressing (*page 227*), divided**
- **1 cup cherry tomatoes *or* grape tomatoes, halved**
- **1 small red onion, chopped**
- **8 cups baby spinach**
- **1/4 cup sliced almonds, toasted (*see Cooking Tip, page 242*)**

1. Toast quinoa in a dry skillet over medium heat, stirring often, until it becomes aromatic and begins to crackle, about 5 minutes. Transfer to a fine sieve and rinse thoroughly.

2. Heat oil in a medium saucepan over medium heat. Add garlic and cook, stirring constantly, until golden, about 1 minute. Add apricots and the quinoa; continue cooking, stirring often, until the quinoa has dried out and turned light golden, 3 to 4 minutes. Add water and salt; bring to a boil. Reduce heat to medium-low and simmer, uncovered, until the quinoa is tender and the liquid is absorbed, 15 to 18 minutes.

3. Meanwhile, make Moroccan-Spiced Lemon Dressing. Transfer the quinoa to a medium bowl and toss with 1/3 cup of the dressing. Let cool for 10 minutes.

4. Just before serving, add tomatoes and onion to the quinoa; toss to coat. Toss spinach with the remaining 1/3 cup dressing in a large bowl. Divide the spinach among 4 plates. Mound the quinoa salad on the spinach and sprinkle with almonds.

Makes 4 servings.

Chapter 2:
Soups & Stews

Chicken

Clams & Shrimp

Beef & Pork

Vegetarian

Chicken Tortilla Soup

Making soups may have once been an all-day affair, but here's a great example of how a few choice convenience products can renovate an old favorite for our modern, hectic lives. Some frozen vegetables, a few canned tomatoes and canned broth—and voilà! a Tex-Mex favorite in minutes.

4 soft corn tortillas, cut into 1-by-2-inch strips
1 tablespoon extra-virgin olive oil
1 pound boneless, skinless chicken breast, trimmed of fat and diced
3 cups frozen bell pepper and onion mix (about 10 ounces)
1 tablespoon ground cumin
2 14-ounce cans reduced-sodium chicken broth
1 15-ounce can diced tomatoes, preferably with green chiles
1/4 teaspoon freshly ground pepper
2 tablespoons lime juice
1/2 cup chopped fresh cilantro
3/4 cup shredded reduced-fat Cheddar *or* Monterey Jack cheese

1. Preheat oven to 350°F. Spread tortillas in a single layer on a baking sheet. Bake until lightly browned and crisp, 10 to 12 minutes.

2. Meanwhile, heat oil in a Dutch oven over medium-high heat. Add chicken and cook, stirring occasionally, until beginning to brown, 3 to 4 minutes. Transfer to a plate using a slotted spoon. Add pepper-onion mix and cumin to the pot. Cook, stirring occasionally, until the onions are lightly browned, about 4 minutes. Add broth, tomatoes, pepper and lime juice; bring to a simmer and cook, stirring often, until the vegetables are tender, about 3 minutes more. Return the chicken and any accumulated juice to the pot and cook, stirring, until heated through, about 1 minute. Remove from the heat; stir in cilantro. Serve topped with the toasted tortilla strips and cheese.

Makes 4 servings, about 1 1/3 cups each.

Active Minutes: 35

Total: 35 minutes

To Make Ahead: Cover and refrigerate, without the tortilla strips, for up to 2 days. Top with toasted tortilla strips just before serving.

Per Serving: 357 calories; 12 g fat (5 g sat, 4 g mono); 87 mg cholesterol; 24 g carbohydrate; 37 g protein; 4 g fiber; 603 mg sodium.

Nutrition Bonus: Selenium (30% daily value), Calcium (20% dv), Vitamin C (15% dv), Zinc (15% dv).

Chicken & White Bean Soup

Once again, rotisserie chickens can really relieve the dinner-rush pressure—especially in this Italian-inspired soup that cries out for a piece of crusty bread and a glass of red wine.

- **2 teaspoons extra-virgin olive oil**
- **2 leeks, white and light green parts only, cut into 1/4-inch rounds**
- **1 tablespoon chopped fresh sage *or* 1/4 teaspoon dried**
- **2 14-ounce cans reduced-sodium chicken broth**
- **2 cups water**
- **1 15-ounce can cannellini beans, rinsed**
- **1 2-pound roasted chicken, skin discarded, meat removed from bones and shredded (4 cups)**

1. Heat oil in a Dutch oven over medium-high heat. Add leeks and cook, stirring often, until soft, about 3 minutes. Stir in sage and continue cooking until aromatic, about 30 seconds. Stir in broth and water, increase heat to high, cover and bring to a boil. Add beans and chicken and cook, uncovered, stirring occasionally, until heated through, about 3 minutes. Serve hot.

Makes 6 servings, 1 1/2 cups each.

Active Minutes: 25

Total: 25 minutes

To Make Ahead: Cover and refrigerate for up to 2 days.

Per Serving: 199 calories; 6 g fat (1 g sat, 3 g mono); 52 mg cholesterol; 16 g carbohydrate; 23 g protein; 4 g fiber; 530 mg sodium.

Nutrition Bonus: Selenium (19% daily value), Iron (15% dv).

Healthy Weight

Lower Carbs

Greek Lemon & Rice Soup

Citrus soups are a global favorite, from the Yucatán to (as here) the Greek Isles. Smooth silken tofu replaces the egg in our version. For a refreshing light meal, serve with Endive & Watercress Salad (*page 228*) and some crusty whole-grain rolls.

Active Minutes: 15

Total: 30 minutes

To Make Ahead: Cover and refrigerate for up to 2 days.

Per Serving: 178 calories; 7 g fat (1 g sat, 3 g mono); 5 mg cholesterol; 18 g carbohydrate; 11 g protein; 0 g fiber; 147 mg sodium.

Healthy Weight

Lower Carbs

- **4 cups reduced-sodium chicken broth**
- **1/3 cup white rice**
- **1 12-ounce package silken tofu (about 1 1/2 cups)**
- **1 tablespoon extra-virgin olive oil**
- **1/4 teaspoon turmeric**
- **1/4 cup lemon juice**
- **2 tablespoons chopped fresh dill**
- **1/4 teaspoon freshly ground pepper**

1. Bring broth and rice to a boil in a large saucepan. Reduce heat to a simmer and cook until the rice is very tender, about 15 minutes.

2. Carefully transfer 2 cups of the rice mixture to a blender. Add tofu, oil and turmeric; process until smooth. (Use caution when pureeing hot liquids.) Whisk the tofu mixture, lemon juice, dill and pepper into the soup remaining in the pan. Heat through.

Makes 4 servings, about 1 1/3 cups each.

Chicken-Sausage & Kale Stew

Active Minutes: 30

Total: 45 minutes

To Make Ahead: Cover and refrigerate for up to 2 days.

Per Serving: 214 calories; 7 g fat (1 g sat, 2 g mono); 40 mg cholesterol; 26 g carbohydrate; 14 g protein; 3 g fiber; 345 mg sodium.

Nutrition Bonus: Vitamin A (140% daily value), Vitamin C (120% dv), Potassium (20% dv).

Healthy Weight

ingredient note:

- **Convenient cooked and diced potatoes can be found in the refrigerated section of the produce and/or dairy department of the supermarket.**

A splash of vinegar is a long-standing chef's trick for soups. Added just before you serve the soup, vinegar brightens the taste considerably. Use your favorite style of chicken sausage to add variety to this dish.

1 tablespoon extra-virgin olive oil
1 large onion, diced
4 cups kale, torn into bite-size pieces and rinsed
2 14-ounce cans reduced-sodium chicken broth
4 plum tomatoes, chopped
2 cups diced cooked potatoes (*see Note*), preferably red-skinned
1 teaspoon chopped fresh rosemary
1/2 teaspoon freshly ground pepper
1 12-ounce package cooked chicken sausages, halved lengthwise and sliced
1 tablespoon cider vinegar

1. Heat oil in a Dutch oven over medium-high heat. Add onion and kale and cook, stirring often, until the onion starts to soften, 5 to 7 minutes.

2. Stir in broth, tomatoes, potatoes, rosemary and pepper. Cover, increase heat to high and bring to a boil, stirring occasionally. Reduce heat and simmer, covered, until the vegetables are just tender, about 15 minutes. Stir in sausage and vinegar and continue to cook, stirring often, until heated through, about 2 minutes more.

Makes 6 servings, about 1 1/2 cups each.

Manhattan Clam Chowder

There's long been a feud between Manhattan's tomato-based chowder and the cream-based New England varieties. The whole thing got so heated that in 1939, the Maine Assembly debated a bill that would have made it a crime to put tomatoes in chowder! No matter which you prefer, you can't deny that this easy chowder will put dinner on the table before you can debate your preferences.

Active Minutes: 30

Total: 40 minutes

Per Serving: 319 calories; 4 g fat (1 g sat, 2 g mono); 53 mg cholesterol; 38 g carbohydrate; 25 g protein; 5 g fiber; 604 mg sodium.

Nutrition Bonus: Iron (130% daily value), Vitamin C (90% dv), Selenium (71% dv), Potassium (32% dv), Vitamin A (20% dv), Zinc (17% dv).

High ↑ Fiber

- **1 tablespoon extra-virgin olive oil**
- **1 large onion, diced**
- **1 bulb fennel, cored and finely diced, plus 1/4 cup chopped feathery fronds**
- **4 cloves garlic, minced**
- **1 teaspoon dried thyme leaves**
- **3 1/2 cups diced cooked potatoes (*see Ingredient Note, page 62*), preferably red-skinned**
- **2 15-ounce cans diced tomatoes**
- **2 14-ounce cans reduced-sodium chicken broth**
- **3/4 cup white wine**
- **1/2 teaspoon freshly ground pepper**
- **1/4 teaspoon salt**
- **1 pound minced shucked clams (*see Note*)**

1. Heat oil in a Dutch oven over medium heat. Add onion, diced fennel, garlic and thyme. Cover and cook, stirring occasionally, until just soft and beginning to brown, 6 to 8 minutes. Stir in potatoes, tomatoes, broth, wine, pepper and salt. Bring to a simmer and cook, stirring occasionally, until the vegetables are tender, 8 to 10 minutes. Stir in clams, any clam juice and the fennel fronds; cook until just heated through, 1 to 2 minutes.

Makes 6 servings, 2 cups each.

ingredient note:

- **Fresh clams, shucked and minced, are available by the pound in the seafood department in large supermarkets. They are superior to canned varieties in both flavor and texture.**

Express Shrimp & Sausage Jambalaya

Active Minutes: 15

Total: 25 minutes

Per Serving: 412 calories; 10 g fat (3 g sat, 1 g mono); 142 mg cholesterol; 44 g carbohydrate; 31 g protein; 3 g fiber; 685 mg sodium.

Nutrition Bonus: Selenium (31% daily value), Vitamin C (25% dv).

ingredient note:

- **Andouille sausage is a smoky, mildly spicy pork sausage commonly used in Cajun cooking. Look for it near other smoked sausages in large supermarkets or specialty food stores.**

You don't have to sacrifice the traditional smoky punch of this Cajun favorite just because you're short on time. All you need is some purchased sausage and quick-cooking brown rice to create a rich, satisfying dinner on any weeknight. Have some sliced berries for dessert to cool off your palate!

- **1 teaspoon canola oil**
- **8 ounces andouille sausage (*see Note*) *or* low-fat kielbasa, cut into 1/4-inch-thick slices**
- **1 16-ounce bag frozen bell pepper and onion mix**
- **1 14-ounce can reduced-sodium chicken broth**
- **2 cups instant brown rice**
- **8 ounces raw shrimp (26-30 per pound), peeled and deveined**

1. Heat oil in a Dutch oven over medium-high heat. Add sausage and pepper-onion mix; cook, stirring occasionally, until the vegetables soften, 3 to 5 minutes.

2. Add broth to the pot and bring to a boil. Add rice, stir once, cover and cook for 5 minutes. Add shrimp and stir to incorporate. Remove from the heat and let stand, covered, until the shrimp are opaque and cooked through, 5 to 6 minutes. Fluff with a fork and serve.

Makes 4 servings, 1 1/2 cups each.

Vietnamese-Style Beef & Noodle Broth

Inspired by *pho*—a traditional Vietnamese soup—this one-pot meal is garnished with crunchy mung bean sprouts and chopped fresh basil. You could also serve it with lime wedges and a bottle of Asian chile sauce, such as sriracha, on the side.

2 teaspoons canola oil
1 pound beef flank steak, very thinly sliced against the grain (*see Tip*)
4 cups chopped bok choy (1 small head, about 1 pound)
4 cups reduced-sodium chicken broth
1 cup water
4 ounces wide rice noodles
2 teaspoons reduced-sodium soy sauce
1 1/2 cups mung bean sprouts
4 tablespoons chopped fresh basil, or to taste

1. Heat oil in a Dutch oven or soup pot over high heat. Add beef and cook, stirring often, until just cooked, about 2 minutes. Transfer to a plate using tongs, leaving the juices in the pot.

2. Add bok choy to the pot and cook, stirring, until wilted, about 2 minutes. Add broth and water, cover and bring to a boil. Add noodles and soy sauce; simmer until the noodles are soft, about 4 minutes. Return the beef to the pot and cook until heated through, 1 to 2 minutes more. Ladle into bowls and sprinkle with bean sprouts and basil. Serve hot.

Makes 6 servings, 1 1/3 cups each.

Active Minutes: 15

Total: 30 minutes

Per Serving: 235 calories; 8 g fat (3 g sat, 3 g mono); 33 mg cholesterol; 19 g carbohydrate; 22 g protein; 1 g fiber; 209 mg sodium.

Nutrition Bonus: Vitamin A (40% daily value), Zinc (27% dv), Vitamin C (25% dv).

Healthy Weight

Lower Carbs

kitchen tip:

If you have a little extra time before dinner, put the flank steak in the freezer for about 20 minutes to help make it easier to slice thinly.

Pork & Plantain Chili

Plantains and orange juice balance this thick, Latin American pork-and-bean stew with some sweetness and also a little acidity. Top with nonfat sour cream or yogurt, if you like.

Active Minutes: 35

Total: 45 minutes

To Make Ahead: Cover and refrigerate for up to 3 days or freeze for up to 2 months.

Per Serving: 305 calories; 7 g fat (1 g sat, 3 g mono); 42 mg cholesterol; 39 g carbohydrate; 23 g protein; 10 g fiber; 527 mg sodium.

Nutrition Bonus: Vitamin C (100% daily value), Selenium (38% dv), Iron (20% dv), Vitamin A (20% dv), Calcium (15% dv).

High ⬆ Fiber

3 teaspoons extra-virgin olive oil, divided
1 pound pork tenderloin, trimmed of fat, cut into 1-inch cubes
1 large onion, finely diced
1 very ripe plantain (*see Note*) *or* sweet potato, peeled and diced
1 red bell pepper, diced
1 tablespoon ground cumin
1/2 teaspoon freshly ground pepper
1/4 teaspoon salt
1/4 teaspoon cinnamon
1/2 cup orange juice
2 cups water
1 15-ounce can black beans, rinsed
2 4-ounce cans diced green chiles
1 15-ounce can refried beans, preferably black beans

1. Heat 1 teaspoon oil in a Dutch oven over medium-high heat. Add pork and cook, stirring occasionally, until just browned, 2 to 3 minutes. Transfer to a plate using a slotted spoon.

2. Reduce heat to medium and add the remaining 2 teaspoons oil to the pot. Add onion, plantain, bell pepper, cumin, pepper, salt and cinnamon and cook, stirring often, until the vegetables are beginning to soften, 3 to 5 minutes. Add orange juice, increase heat to high, and cook until most of the liquid has evaporated, about 1 minute.

3. Stir in water and black beans and bring to a boil. Reduce heat to a simmer and cook, stirring occasionally, until the onion and plantain are tender, 10 to 14 minutes. Stir in chiles, refried beans and the pork along with any accumulated juices. Increase heat to medium-high and cook, stirring constantly, until the mixture is thick and the pork is just cooked through, about 2 minutes.

Makes 6 servings, about 1 1/2 cups each.

ingredient note:

- **Plantains are a starchy, less-sweet relative of the banana. They are typically sold underripe, with yellow skin, but are best when the skin is almost completely black. Buy underripe plantains about one week in advance and ripen on the counter.**

Pork Posole

Traditionally a long-simmered stew, this Mexican-inspired stew is quick and easy, thanks to canned hominy. Searing the pork loin in the pot before making the stew gives you a great base of flavors so the stew seems as if it indeed simmered all afternoon. Garnish with chopped cilantro and serve with warm tortillas on the side.

- **1 tablespoon canola oil**
- **3/4 pound boneless pork loin chops, trimmed of fat and diced**
- **1 large onion, diced**
- **2 tablespoons plus 2 cups water, divided**
- **4 cloves garlic, minced**
- **2 teaspoons ground cumin**
- **2 teaspoons ground coriander**
- **1 14-ounce can reduced-sodium chicken broth**
- **1/4 cup cornmeal**
- **2 15-ounce cans hominy, rinsed (*see Note*)**
- **2 4-ounce cans diced green chiles**
- **1/2 teaspoon freshly ground pepper**
- **1/4 teaspoon salt**
- **1-2 tablespoons lime juice**

1. Heat oil in a Dutch oven over medium-high heat. Add pork and cook, stirring once, until just browned on one or two sides, 1 to 2 minutes. Transfer to a plate using a slotted spoon.

2. Reduce heat to medium-low; add onion and 2 tablespoons water. Cook, stirring occasionally, until the onion is soft and golden brown and any moisture has evaporated, 5 to 7 minutes. Stir in garlic, cumin and coriander and cook, stirring constantly, until fragrant, 30 seconds to 1 minute. Whisk in the remaining 2 cups water, broth and cornmeal. Bring to a simmer over high heat, stirring often. Add hominy, chiles, pepper and salt; return to a simmer. Reduce heat to medium-low and cook, stirring often, until the onion is very soft and the mixture is thickened, about 5 minutes. Stir in lime juice to taste.

3. Return the pork and any accumulated juices to the pot; cook, stirring occasionally, until the pork is just cooked through, 1 to 2 minutes.

Makes 6 servings, 1 1/3 cups each.

Active Minutes: 30

Total: 30 minutes

To Make Ahead: Cover and refrigerate for up to 3 days or freeze for up to 2 months.

Per Serving: 251 calories; 7 g fat (2 g sat, 3 g mono); 34 mg cholesterol; 29 g carbohydrate; 16 g protein; 5 g fiber; 510 mg sodium.

Nutrition Bonus: Selenium (33% daily value), Vitamin C (25% dv).

Healthy Weight

High Fiber

ingredient note:

Hominy is white or yellow corn that has been treated with lime to remove the tough hull and germ. Dried, ground hominy is the main ingredient in grits. Canned, cooked hominy can be found in the Mexican section of large supermarkets—near the beans.

Asparagus Soup

This creamless but still creamy soup is a great lunch or summer-night dinner on its own—but you can also spoon it over lump crabmeat, cooked shrimp or cubed tofu for a heftier meal.

Active Minutes: 20

Total: 30 minutes

To Make Ahead: Prepare the soup (Steps 1 & 3), cover and refrigerate for up to 2 days. Top with prosciutto just before serving.

Per Serving: 174 calories; 3 g fat (1 g sat, 0 g mono); 22 mg cholesterol; 24 g carbohydrate; 14 g protein; 5 g fiber; 658 mg sodium.

Nutrition Bonus: Vitamin C (50% daily value), Iron (30% dv), Vitamin A (25% dv), Folate (22% dv).

Healthy Weight

High Fiber

kitchen tip:

- **Hot liquids can splatter out of a blender when it's turned on. To avoid this, remove the center piece of the lid. Loosely cover the hole with a folded kitchen towel and turn the blender on. Better airflow will keep the contents from spewing all over the kitchen.**

1 14-ounce can reduced-sodium chicken broth
1/4 cup water
1 yellow-fleshed potato, such as Yukon Gold (6 ounces), peeled and cut into 1/2-inch cubes
1 medium shallot, thinly sliced
1 clove garlic, thinly sliced
1/2 teaspoon dried thyme
1/2 teaspoon dried savory *or* marjoram leaves
1/8 teaspoon salt
12 ounces asparagus, woody ends removed, sliced into 1-inch pieces
1 1/2 ounces thinly sliced prosciutto, chopped
Freshly ground pepper to taste

1. Place broth, water, potato, shallot, garlic, thyme, savory (or marjoram) and salt in a large saucepan. Bring to a boil over high heat. Reduce heat to medium-low, cover, and simmer until the potato is tender, about 8 minutes. Add asparagus, return to a simmer, and cook, covered, until the asparagus is tender, about 5 minutes more.

2. Meanwhile, cook prosciutto in a small skillet over medium heat, stirring, until crisp, about 5 minutes.

3. Pour the soup into a large blender or food processor (*see Tip*); puree until smooth, scraping down the sides if necessary. Season with pepper. Serve topped with the crisped prosciutto.

Makes 2 servings, 1 1/2 cups each.

Creamy Tomato Bisque with Mozzarella Crostini

Active Minutes: 20

Total: 35 minutes

To Make Ahead: Prepare the soup (Steps 1 & 3), cover and refrigerate for up to 2 days. Preheat oven, make crostini (Steps 2 & 4) and reheat the soup when ready to serve.

Per Serving: 219 calories; 8 g fat (1 g sat, 4 g mono); 3 mg cholesterol; 32 g carbohydrate; 8 g protein; 4 g fiber; 354 mg sodium.

Nutrition Bonus: Vitamin C (25% daily value), Vitamin A (20% dv), Iron (15% dv).

Healthy Weight

You don't have to lard a soup with cream just to have a creamy soup. Here, a little rice cooked into the broth and silken tofu thicken this French-inspired soup. And once you forgo the cream, you can certainly splurge on a cheesy crostini!

- **2 tablespoons extra-virgin olive oil**
- **1 large onion, chopped**
- **4 cloves garlic, crushed and peeled**
- **1 14-ounce can reduced-sodium chicken broth**
- **2 cups water**
- **1/4 cup white rice**
- **1 28-ounce can crushed tomatoes**
- **1/2 cup silken tofu**
- **1 tablespoon rice vinegar**
- **6 3/4-inch-thick slices baguette**
- **3 tablespoons shredded part-skim mozzarella cheese**

1. Heat oil in a Dutch oven over medium heat. Add onion and garlic and cook, stirring occasionally, until beginning to soften, about 3 minutes. Stir in broth, water and rice; bring to a boil. Reduce heat to a simmer and cook, stirring occasionally, until the rice is very tender, about 15 minutes.

2. Preheat oven to 450°F.

3. Stir tomatoes, tofu and vinegar into the soup. Remove from the heat and puree, in batches, in a blender. (Use caution when pureeing hot liquids.) Return the soup to the pot and reheat over medium-high heat, stirring often.

4. Meanwhile, top slices of baguette with mozzarella and place on a baking sheet. Bake until the cheese is melted and bubbly, about 5 minutes. Ladle soup into bowls and top with a cheesy crostini.

Makes 6 servings, about 1 1/2 cups each.

Tortellini & Zucchini Soup

Everyone knows purchased tortellini makes a quick weeknight pasta dinner—but in an easy vegetable soup, they can also provide the added kick that'll bring everyone to the table. One caveat: Read the label carefully; avoid pasta products made with hydrogenated oils or unnecessary preservatives.

2 tablespoons extra-virgin olive oil
2 large carrots, finely chopped
1 large onion, diced
2 tablespoons minced garlic
1 teaspoon chopped fresh rosemary
2 14-ounce cans vegetable broth
2 medium zucchini, diced
9 ounces (about 2 cups) fresh *or* frozen tortellini, preferably spinach-and-cheese
4 plum tomatoes, diced
2 tablespoons red-wine vinegar

1. Heat oil in a Dutch oven over medium heat. Add carrots and onion; stir, cover and cook, stirring occasionally, until the onion is soft and just beginning to brown, 6 to 7 minutes. Stir in garlic and rosemary and cook, stirring often, until fragrant, about 1 minute.

2. Stir in broth and zucchini; bring to a boil. Reduce heat to a simmer and cook, stirring occasionally, until the zucchini is beginning to soften, about 3 minutes. Add tortellini and tomatoes and simmer until the tortellini is plump and the tomatoes are beginning to break down, 6 to 10 minutes. Stir vinegar into the hot soup just before serving.

Makes 6 servings, about 1 1/2 cups each.

Active Minutes: 25

Total: 40 minutes

Per Serving: 204 calories; 8 g fat (2 g sat, 4 g mono); 10 mg cholesterol; 28 g carbohydrate; 7 g protein; 4 g fiber; 386 mg sodium.

Nutrition Bonus: Vitamin A (80% daily value), Vitamin C (35% dv).

Healthy Weight

Escarole & White Bean Soup

Active Minutes: 40

Total: 40 minutes

To Make Ahead: Cover and refrigerate for up to 2 days.

Per Serving: 281 calories; 13 g fat (3 g sat, 8 g mono); 5 mg cholesterol; 38 g carbohydrate; 14 g protein; 12 g fiber; 759 mg sodium.

Nutrition Bonus: Vitamin A (80% daily value), Folate (36% dv), Potassium (25% dv), Calcium (25% dv), Vitamin C (25% dv), Iron (15% dv).

High ↑ Fiber

This Italian soup is made with escarole, a bitter green that looks like frilly romaine and cooks down to a surprisingly buttery smoothness. Rinse escarole carefully because grime often lurks in the leaves. If you can't find escarole, substitute a 10-ounce bag of spinach leaves with the large, woody stems removed.

- **1/4 cup extra-virgin olive oil**
- **1 large onion, chopped**
- **1 cup halved cherry tomatoes**
- **1/2 cup finely chopped celery**
- **1/2 cup finely chopped carrot**
- **1/4 cup chopped garlic**
- **2 teaspoons Italian seasoning**
- **1/2 teaspoon freshly ground pepper**
- **2 14-ounce cans vegetable broth *or* reduced-sodium chicken broth**
- **2 15-ounce cans cannellini beans, rinsed**
- **1 head escarole, chopped and rinsed**
- **1/2 cup freshly shredded hard Italian cheese, such as Parmesan, Romano *or* Asiago**

1. Heat oil in a Dutch oven over medium heat. Add onion, tomatoes, celery, carrot, garlic, Italian seasoning and pepper and cook, stirring often, until the vegetables are beginning to soften and the onion is translucent, about 10 minutes. Add broth, bring to a simmer, and cook, stirring often, until the vegetables are tender. Stir in beans and escarole and cook, stirring often, until the escarole is just tender, about 5 minutes. Serve with a sprinkle of cheese.

Makes 6 servings, 1 1/2 cups each.

Spicy Vegetable Soup

Fresh basil adds a bright spark to this vinegary, vegetable-stuffed soup, full of the traditional flavors of the Mediterranean. Alternatively, pesto adds a nutty richness to the soup. Use store-bought or try our Basic Basil Pesto recipe on page 226.

Active Minutes: 30

Total: 40 minutes

To Make Ahead: Cover and refrigerate for up to 2 days.

Per Serving: 253 calories; 8 g fat (1 g sat, 5 g mono); 0 mg cholesterol; 40 g carbohydrate; 9 g protein; 10 g fiber; 485 mg sodium.

Nutrition Bonus: Vitamin A (270% daily value), Vitamin C (60% dv), Folate (44% dv), Potassium (30% dv), Calcium (20% dv), Iron (20% dv).

High ↑ Fiber

- **2 tablespoons extra-virgin olive oil**
- **1 large onion, diced**
- **1-3 teaspoons hot paprika, or to taste**
- **2 14-ounce cans vegetable broth**
- **4 medium plum tomatoes, diced**
- **1 medium yellow summer squash, diced**
- **2 cups diced cooked potatoes (*see Ingredient Note, page 62*)**
- **1 1/2 cups green beans, cut into 2-inch pieces**
- **2 cups frozen spinach (5 ounces)**
- **2 tablespoons sherry vinegar *or* red-wine vinegar**
- **1/4 cup chopped fresh basil *or* prepared pesto**

1. Heat oil in a Dutch oven over medium heat. Add onion, cover and cook, stirring occasionally, until beginning to brown, about 6 minutes. Add paprika and cook, stirring, for 30 seconds. Add broth, tomatoes, squash, potatoes and beans; bring to a boil. Reduce heat to a simmer and cook, stirring occasionally, until the vegetables are just tender, about 12 minutes. Stir in spinach and vinegar; continue cooking until heated through, 2 to 4 minutes more. Ladle soup into bowls and top with fresh basil or a dollop of pesto.

Makes 4 servings, about 2 1/4 cups each.

Multi-Bean Chili

Even confirmed carnivores will love this meatless chili because it's rib-sticking thick. If you like, add a dollop of low-fat sour cream or nonfat plain yogurt to each serving. Or try it with minced scallions and a little shredded Cheddar. In any case, have bottled hot red pepper sauce on hand to pass alongside.

1 tablespoon canola oil
1 large onion, diced
4 cloves garlic, minced
3 tablespoons chili powder
1 tablespoon ground cumin
1/4–1/2 teaspoon ground chipotle chile *or* cayenne pepper, or to taste
1 28-ounce can crushed tomatoes
3 medium tomatoes, chopped
1 15-ounce can dark red kidney beans, rinsed
1 15-ounce can small white beans, such as navy beans, rinsed
1 15-ounce can black beans, rinsed
3 cups water
1/2 teaspoon freshly ground pepper

1. Heat oil in a Dutch oven over medium heat. Add onion and cook, stirring, until beginning to soften, 2 to 3 minutes. Reduce heat to medium-low and cook, stirring often, until very soft and just beginning to brown, 3 to 4 minutes. Add garlic, chili powder, cumin and chipotle (or cayenne) to taste and cook, stirring constantly, until fragrant, 30 seconds to 1 minute. Stir in canned and fresh tomatoes, kidney, white and black beans, water and pepper. Increase heat to high and bring to a boil, stirring often. Reduce heat to a simmer and cook, stirring occasionally, until the chili has reduced slightly, 10 to 15 minutes.

Makes 6 servings, scant 2 cups each.

Active Minutes: 20

Total: 35 minutes

To Make Ahead: Cover and refrigerate for up to 3 days or freeze for up to 2 months.

Per Serving: 294 calories; 4 g fat (0 g sat, 2 g mono); 0 mg cholesterol; 55 g carbohydrate; 16 g protein; 16 g fiber; 806 mg sodium.

Nutrition Bonus: Vitamin C (60% daily value), Vitamin A (45% dv), Iron (30% dv), Potassium (22% dv), Calcium (15% dv).

High ↑ Fiber

Chapter 3:
Vegetarian

Florentine Ravioli

The flavors of Italy are best expressed in simplicity: a dash of spices, a little oil, and dinner's on the table in minutes—especially if you use frozen spinach and frozen ravioli or tortellini for this fast supper.

- **1 20-ounce package frozen cheese ravioli *or* tortellini (4 cups) (*see Note*)**
- **6 teaspoons extra-virgin olive oil, divided**
- **4 cloves garlic, minced**
- **1/4 teaspoon salt**
- **1/8-1/4 teaspoon crushed red pepper**
- **1 16-ounce bag frozen chopped *or* whole-leaf spinach**
- **1/2 cup water**
- **1/4 cup freshly grated Parmesan cheese**

1. Bring a large pot of water to a boil; cook ravioli (or tortellini) according to package directions.

2. Meanwhile, heat 2 teaspoons oil in a large nonstick skillet over medium heat. Add garlic and cook, stirring, until fragrant, about 30 seconds. Add salt, crushed red pepper to taste, spinach and water. Cook, stirring frequently, until the spinach has thawed, wilted and heated through, 5 to 7 minutes. Divide among 4 bowls, top with the pasta and drizzle 1 teaspoon of the remaining oil over each portion. Serve immediately with a sprinkle of Parmesan.

Makes 4 servings, about 1 1/2 cups each.

Active Minutes: 20

Total: 20 minutes

Per Serving: 277 calories; 13 g fat (4 g sat, 7 g mono); 25 mg cholesterol; 28 g carbohydrate; 14 g protein; 6 g fiber; 654 mg sodium.

Nutrition Bonus: Vitamin A (270% daily value), Vitamin C (50% dv), Folate (44% dv), Calcium (35% dv), Potassium (20% dv).

Healthy Weight

High Fiber

shopping tip:

When buying frozen ravioli or tortellini, be sure to read the label—the fat content per serving can vary widely according to brand.

Fettuccine & Bells

Although fresh bell peppers give this dish a gorgeous, colorful splash, you can make a quicker supper by substituting a 1-pound package of frozen bell pepper and onion mix. Make sure you cook the frozen vegetables until they caramelize and most of the liquid has evaporated, about 12 to 14 minutes.

Active Minutes: 30

Total: 30 minutes

Per Serving: 314 calories; 8 g fat (2 g sat, 5 g mono); 4 mg cholesterol; 53 g carbohydrate; 11 g protein; 9 g fiber; 366 mg sodium.

Nutrition Bonus: Vitamin C (100% daily value), Selenium (61% dv), Iron (15% dv).

High ↑ Fiber

- **1 tablespoon extra-virgin olive oil**
- **3 medium bell peppers (red, yellow *and/or* orange), cut into 1 1/2-inch-long julienne strips**
- **1 1/2 cups thinly sliced onions**
- **3 cloves garlic, minced**
- **1/8 teaspoon crushed red pepper**
- **1/2 cup brine-cured black olives, pitted and halved**
- **1/4 cup dry white wine**
- **1/4 cup balsamic vinegar**
- **1/4 teaspoon salt, or to taste**
- **Freshly ground pepper to taste**
- **12 ounces whole-wheat fettuccine**
- **1/3 cup freshly grated Parmesan cheese**
- **1/2 cup slivered basil leaves, divided**

1. Put a large pot of water on to boil for cooking pasta.

2. Heat oil in a large skillet over medium-high heat. Add bell peppers and onions; cook, stirring, until tender, 8 to 12 minutes. Add garlic and crushed red pepper; cook, stirring, for 30 seconds. Stir in olives, wine and vinegar; cook, stirring, for 2 to 3 minutes. Season with salt and pepper.

3. Meanwhile, cook pasta until just tender, 9 to 11 minutes, or according to package directions. Reserving 1/4 cup of the cooking liquid, drain the pasta and place in a large bowl. Add the vegetable mixture, Parmesan cheese, 1/4 cup basil and the reserved cooking liquid; toss well. Serve immediately, sprinkled with the remaining 1/4 cup basil.

Makes 6 servings, about 1 1/2 cups each.

Penne with Braised Squash & Greens

Active Minutes: 40

Total: 40 minutes

Per Serving: 386 calories; 7 g fat (2 g sat, 3 g mono); 9 mg cholesterol; 66 g carbohydrate; 17 g protein; 10 g fiber; 715 mg sodium.

Nutrition Bonus: Vitamin A (340% daily value), Vitamin C (80% dv), Calcium (25% dv), Potassium (22% dv).

High ↑ Fiber

This chunky sauce is laced with chard and accented with smoked tofu. Convenient packages of peeled and diced butternut squash are available in most supermarkets in the fall and winter.

- **2 teaspoons extra-virgin olive oil**
- **4 ounces cubed smoked tofu**
- **1 medium onion, chopped**
- **3 cloves garlic, minced**
- **Pinch of crushed red pepper**
- **1 1/2 cups vegetable broth**
- **1 pound butternut squash, peeled and cut into 3/4-inch cubes (3 cups)**
- **1 small bunch Swiss chard, stems removed, leaves cut into 1-inch pieces**
- **8 ounces whole-wheat penne, rigatoni *or* fusilli**
- **1/2 cup freshly grated Parmesan cheese**
- **1/4 teaspoon salt, or to taste**
- **Freshly ground pepper to taste**

1. Put a large pot of water on to boil for cooking pasta.

2. Heat oil in a large nonstick skillet over medium heat. Add tofu and cook, stirring, until lightly browned, 3 to 5 minutes. Transfer to a plate. Add onion to the pan; cook, stirring often, until softened and golden, 2 to 3 minutes. Add garlic and crushed red pepper; cook, stirring, for 30 seconds. Return the tofu to the pan and add broth and squash; bring to a simmer. Cover and cook for 10 minutes. Add chard and stir to immerse. Cover and cook until the squash and chard are tender, about 5 minutes.

3. Meanwhile, cook pasta until just tender, 8 to 10 minutes or according to package directions. Drain and return to the pot. Add the squash mixture, Parmesan, salt and pepper; toss to coat.

Makes 4 servings, 1 3/4 cups each.

Pasta & Beans

A healthful combination of beans and greens makes this pasta dish evocative of the Italian countryside. By dropping the greens in the boiling water with the pasta, you've eliminated an extra step—and an extra pot to wash.

Active Minutes: 35

Total: 35 minutes

Per Serving: 443 calories; 14 g fat (3 g sat, 9 g mono); 5 mg cholesterol; 67 g carbohydrate; 20 g protein; 8 g fiber; 667 mg sodium.

Nutrition Bonus: Vitamin C (190% daily value), Vitamin A (160% dv), Folate (31% dv), Iron (30% dv).

High ↑ Fiber

- **3 tablespoons extra-virgin olive oil**
- **2 cloves garlic, minced**
- **4-5 medium plum tomatoes, chopped**
- **1/2 teaspoon dried oregano**
- **Pinch of crushed red pepper**
- **1 15-ounce can cannellini beans, rinsed**
- **1/2 teaspoon salt, or to taste**
- **Freshly ground pepper to taste**
- **8 ounces orecchiette, radiatore *or* other short pasta**
- **1 pound broccoli rabe, stem ends trimmed, rinsed and cut into 1 1/2-inch pieces**
- **1/4 cup freshly grated Parmesan *or* Pecorino Romano cheese**

1. Put a large pot of water on to boil for cooking pasta.

2. Heat oil in a large skillet over low heat. Add garlic and cook, stirring, until fragrant but not colored, about 1 minute. Add tomatoes, oregano and crushed red pepper; cover and increase heat to medium. Cook, stirring occasionally, until the tomatoes start to break down and release their juices, 5 to 10 minutes. Add beans, reduce heat to low and simmer, covered, until heated through. Season with salt and pepper.

3. Meanwhile, cook pasta in the boiling water for 4 minutes. Add broccoli rabe and cook until the pasta is just tender and the broccoli rabe is tender, 4 to 5 minutes more. Reserving 1/2 cup of the cooking liquid, drain the pasta and broccoli rabe and place in a large bowl. Add the tomato mixture and the reserved cooking liquid; toss to coat. The dish should be slightly soupy. Sprinkle each serving with cheese.

Makes 4 servings, about 2 cups each.

White Beans, Spinach & Tomatoes over Parmesan Toasts

Three words describe this dish to a T: comforting, simple and fast. You can even make the spinach-and-bean mixture in advance; store it covered in the refrigerator for up to 2 days, then reheat it in the microwave while you make the cheesy toasts.

Active Minutes: 25

Total: 25 minutes

Per Serving: 270 calories; 10 g fat (2 g sat, 6 g mono); 4 mg cholesterol; 44 g carbohydrate; 13 g protein; 15 g fiber; 729 mg sodium.

Nutrition Bonus: Vitamin A (70% daily value), Vitamin C (35% dv), Calcium (30% dv), Iron (25% dv).

High Fiber

- **4 thick slices country-style whole-wheat bread**
- **1/4 cup freshly grated Parmesan cheese**
- **2 tablespoons extra-virgin olive oil**
- **4 cloves garlic, chopped**
- **4 medium plum tomatoes, chopped**
- **1 15-ounce can white beans, rinsed**
- **1 10-ounce bag baby spinach**
- **1/2 teaspoon freshly ground pepper**
- **1/4 teaspoon salt**
- **1/2 cup vegetable broth**
- **1/4 cup sliced fresh basil *or* 2 tablespoons prepared pesto**

1. Preheat oven to 450°F.

2. Top bread with Parmesan, place on a baking sheet and bake until the bread is crispy and the cheese is melted, 5 to 7 minutes.

3. Heat oil in a large nonstick skillet over medium-high heat. Add garlic and cook, stirring constantly, until fragrant, 30 seconds to 1 minute. Stir in tomatoes and beans and cook, stirring often, until the tomatoes are beginning to soften and the beans are heated through, 2 to 4 minutes. Stir in spinach, pepper, salt and broth and cook, stirring constantly, until the spinach is just wilted, 2 to 3 minutes. Remove from the heat and stir in basil (or pesto). Spoon the bean-and-spinach mixture over the Parmesan toasts and serve hot.

Makes 4 servings.

Chickpea Burgers & Tahini Sauce

Active Minutes: 25

Total: 25 minutes

To Make Ahead: Cover and refrigerate the uncooked burger mixture and tahini sauce for up to 2 days.

Per Serving: 399 calories; 16 g fat (3 g sat, 8 g mono); 55 mg cholesterol; 53 g carbohydrate; 15 g protein; 9 g fiber; 742 mg sodium.

Nutrition Bonus: Fiber (37% daily value), Folate (32% dv), Vitamin C (30% dv), Iron (20% dv).

High ↑ Fiber

ingredient note:

- **Tahini is a smooth, thick paste made from ground sesame seeds and commonly used in Middle Eastern foods. Look for it in the Middle Eastern section or near other nut butters in large supermarkets.**

Rather than a heavy, fried falafel, here's an updated version of this pocket sandwich: a light chickpea patty served in a whole-wheat pita with a flavorful but light tahini sauce.

Chickpea Burgers

- **1 19-ounce can chickpeas, rinsed**
- **4 scallions, trimmed and sliced**
- **1 egg**
- **2 tablespoons all-purpose flour**
- **1 tablespoon chopped fresh oregano**
- **1/2 teaspoon ground cumin**
- **1/4 teaspoon salt**
- **2 tablespoons extra-virgin olive oil**
- **2 6 1/2-inch whole-wheat pitas, halved and warmed, if desired**

Tahini Sauce

- **1/2 cup low-fat plain yogurt**
- **2 tablespoons tahini (*see Note*)**
- **1 tablespoon lemon juice**
- **1/3 cup chopped flat-leaf parsley**
- **1/4 teaspoon salt**

1. **To prepare burgers:** Place chickpeas, scallions, egg, flour, oregano, cumin and 1/4 teaspoon salt in a food processor. Pulse, stopping once or twice to scrape down the sides, until a coarse mixture forms that holds together when pressed. (The mixture will be moist.) Form into 4 patties.

2. Heat oil in a large nonstick skillet over medium-high heat. Add patties and cook until golden and beginning to crisp, 4 to 5 minutes. Carefully flip and cook until golden brown, 2 to 4 minutes more.

3. **To prepare sauce & serve:** Meanwhile, combine yogurt, tahini, lemon juice, parsley and 1/4 teaspoon salt in a medium bowl. Divide the patties among the pitas and serve with the sauce.

Makes 4 servings.

Mock Risotto

Risotto is hardly quick fare, what with all that stirring over a hot stove. But instant brown rice and creamy Neufchâtel cheese can make a nutty, rich, stand-in version that's sure to be a family favorite. Substitute any vegetables you wish for the asparagus and bell pepper.

Active Minutes: 40

Total: 40 minutes

Per Serving: 378 calories; 14 g fat (6 g sat, 5 g mono); 29 mg cholesterol; 54 g carbohydrate; 13 g protein; 7 g fiber; 663 mg sodium.

Nutrition Bonus: Vitamin C (120% daily value), Vitamin A (70% dv), Folate (32% dv).

High ↑ Fiber

- **1 tablespoon extra-virgin olive oil**
- **1 medium onion, diced**
- **1/4 teaspoon salt**
- **2 cups instant brown rice**
- **4 cloves garlic, chopped**
- **2 1/2 cups vegetable *or* reduced-sodium chicken broth**
- **1 pound asparagus, trimmed and cut into 1/4-inch pieces**
- **1 red bell pepper, finely diced**
- **1 cup frozen peas, thawed**
- **4 ounces reduced-fat cream cheese (Neufchâtel)**
- **1/2 cup grated Asiago *or* Parmesan cheese, plus more for passing**
- **1/4 cup minced chives *or* scallions**

1. Heat oil in a large nonstick skillet over medium-low heat. Add onion and salt and cook, stirring often, until soft and just beginning to brown, 4 to 6 minutes. Add rice and garlic and cook until the garlic is fragrant, 30 seconds to 1 minute. Add broth, cover, reduce heat to a simmer and cook for 5 minutes.

2. Spread asparagus and bell pepper on top of the simmering rice—do not stir into the rice mixture. Cover and continue simmering, adjusting the heat if necessary, until the liquid is almost absorbed and the asparagus is bright green but still very crisp, about 5 minutes.

3. Add peas and cream cheese; stir until the mixture is creamy and the cream cheese is incorporated. Return to a simmer and continue cooking until the liquid has evaporated and the asparagus is tender, about 5 minutes more. Stir in 1/2 cup Asiago (or Parmesan). Serve hot topped with chives (or scallions) and additional grated cheese.

Makes 4 servings, 1 1/2 cups each.

Crispy Potatoes with Green Beans & Eggs

This is a one-skillet meal, reminiscent of diner fare at roadside restaurants across the U.S. It can be made with either leftover or raw potatoes. Even while making dinner in a hurry, don't rush this dish: you want to cook the potato cubes until they are crispy outside but still creamy inside.

1 cup fresh *or* cooked green beans, cut into 1-inch pieces
2 tablespoons extra-virgin olive oil
2 pounds boiling potatoes, peeled and cut into 1/2-inch dice, *or* 5 cups diced cooked potatoes
2 cloves garlic, minced
1/8 teaspoon crushed red pepper
1/2 teaspoon salt, or to taste
Freshly ground pepper to taste
4 large eggs
Pinch of paprika (optional)

1. If using fresh green beans, cook in a large saucepan of boiling water until crisp-tender, about 3 minutes. Drain and refresh under cold running water.

2. Heat oil in a large nonstick or cast-iron skillet over medium heat until hot enough to sizzle a piece of potato. Spread potatoes in an even layer and cook, turning every few minutes with a wide spatula, until tender and browned, 15 to 20 minutes for raw potatoes, 10 to 12 minutes for cooked. Stir in the green beans, garlic, crushed red pepper, salt and pepper.

3. Crack each egg into a small bowl and slip them one at a time into the skillet on top of the vegetables, spacing evenly. Cover and cook over medium heat until the whites are set and the yolks are cooked to your taste, 3 to 5 minutes. Sprinkle the eggs with paprika, if desired, and serve immediately.

Makes 4 servings.

Active Minutes: 35

Total: 40 minutes

Per Serving: 315 calories; 12 g fat (3 g sat, 7 g mono); 212 mg cholesterol; 42 g carbohydrate; 10 g protein; 5 g fiber; 371 mg sodium.

Nutrition Bonus: Vitamin C (30% daily value), Selenium (24% dv), Potassium (22% dv).

High ↑ Fiber

Golden Polenta & Egg with Mustard Sauce

Active Minutes: 25

Total: 30 minutes

Per Serving 278 calories; 13 g fat (3 g sat, 5 g mono); 219 mg cholesterol; 27 g carbohydrate; 12 g protein; 4 g fiber; 528 mg sodium.

Nutrition Bonus: Vitamin A (20% daily value), Vitamin C (20% dv), Calcium (15% dv).

Healthy Weight

Here's a streamlined version of Eggs Benedict: purchased polenta, boiled eggs and an easy, no-cook homage to hollandaise. It's a quick dinner any night of the week—or a great weekend brunch.

- **1/2 cup low-fat plain yogurt**
- **1/3 cup reduced-fat mayonnaise**
- **1 tablespoon Dijon mustard**
- **1 tablespoon lemon juice**
- **1 tablespoon water**
- **1 pound green beans, trimmed**
- **4 eggs**
- **2 teaspoons extra-virgin olive oil**
- **12 ounces prepared polenta, sliced into eight 1/2-inch rounds**

1. Combine yogurt, mayonnaise, mustard, lemon juice and water in a small bowl. Set aside.

2. Bring 6 cups of lightly salted water to a boil in a medium saucepan. Add green beans and cook until just tender, 4 minutes. Remove the green beans with a slotted spoon and divide among 4 plates.

3. Return the water to a boil; place eggs, one by one, in the boiling water and set the timer: 5 minutes for a soft-boiled egg, 8 minutes for hard-boiled. When cool enough to handle, peel and slice the eggs in half.

4. Meanwhile, heat the oil in a large nonstick skillet over medium-high heat, add polenta rounds in a single layer and cook, turning once, until crispy and golden, about 4 minutes per side. Place 2 polenta rounds on each plate and keep warm. Add the reserved sauce to the pan and cook over medium-low heat, stirring constantly to avoid scorching, until heated through, about 3 minutes.

5. Divide the polenta rounds among the plates, top with egg halves and drizzle with the sauce. Serve immediately.

Makes 4 servings.

Red Pepper & Goat Cheese Frittata

Active Minutes: 40

Total: 40 minutes

To Make Ahead: Let cool, cover and refrigerate for up to 1 day; serve cold.

Per Serving: 179 calories; 13 g fat (4 g sat, 7 g mono); 286 mg cholesterol; 4 g carbohydrate; 11 g protein; 1 g fiber; 326 mg sodium.

Nutrition Bonus: Vitamin C (60% daily value), Selenium (31% dv), Vitamin A (25% dv).

Healthy Weight

Lower Carbs

A frittata is a baked omelet, far easier because it lacks that pesky step of flipping it. Frittatas appeared on the *Saturnia*, a fashionable Italian cruise ship in the post-WWII years. The dish was an elegant lunch on transatlantic crossings and became a U.S. craze when *The New York Times* ran the first English-language recipe in 1952.

- **8 eggs**
- **2 tablespoons finely chopped fresh oregano**
- **1/2 teaspoon salt**
- **1/4 teaspoon freshly ground pepper**
- **2 tablespoons extra-virgin olive oil**
- **1 cup sliced red bell pepper**
- **1 bunch scallions, trimmed and sliced**
- **1/2 cup crumbled goat cheese**

1. Position rack in upper third of oven; preheat broiler.

2. Whisk eggs, oregano, salt and pepper in a medium bowl. Heat oil in a large, ovenproof, nonstick skillet over medium heat. Add bell pepper and scallions and cook, stirring constantly, until the scallions are just wilted, 30 seconds to 1 minute.

3. Pour the egg mixture over the vegetables and cook, lifting the edges of the frittata to allow the uncooked egg to flow underneath, until the bottom is light golden, 2 to 3 minutes. Dot the top of the frittata with cheese, transfer the pan to the oven and broil until puffy and lightly golden on top, 2 to 3 minutes. Let rest for about 3 minutes before serving. Serve hot or cold.

Makes 6 servings.

Polenta & Vegetable Bake

This healthful casserole is perfect on a fall night with a glass of crisp Chardonnay—or any time of year when you want to remember those clear, brisk October evenings.

- 2 tablespoons extra-virgin olive oil
- 1 medium eggplant, diced
- 1 small zucchini, finely diced
- 1/2 teaspoon salt
- 1/2 teaspoon freshly ground pepper
- 1/2 cup water
- 1 10-ounce bag baby spinach
- 1 1/2 cups prepared marinara sauce, preferably lower-sodium
- 1/2 cup chopped fresh basil
- 1 14-ounce tube prepared polenta, sliced lengthwise into 6 thin slices
- 1 1/2 cups shredded part-skim mozzarella, divided

1. Preheat oven to 450°F. Coat a 9-by-13-inch baking dish with cooking spray.

2. Heat oil in a large nonstick skillet over medium-high heat. Add eggplant, zucchini, salt and pepper and cook, stirring occasionally, until the vegetables are tender and just beginning to brown, 4 to 6 minutes. Add water and spinach; cover and cook until wilted, stirring once, about 3 minutes. Stir marinara sauce into the vegetables and heat through, 1 to 2 minutes. Remove from the heat and stir in basil.

3. Place polenta slices in a single layer in the prepared baking dish, trimming to fit if necessary. Sprinkle with 3/4 cup cheese, top with the eggplant mixture and sprinkle with the remaining 3/4 cup cheese. Bake until bubbling and the cheese has just melted, 12 to 15 minutes. Let stand for about 5 minutes before serving.

Makes 8 servings.

Active Minutes: 35

Total: 40 minutes

Per Serving: 215 calories; 8 g fat (3 g sat, 4 g mono); 14 mg cholesterol; 27 g carbohydrate; 9 g protein; 6 g fiber; 670 mg sodium.

Nutrition Bonus: Vitamin A (35% daily value), Calcium (25% dv), Vitamin C (25% dv), Fiber (23% dv).

Healthy Weight

High Fiber

Pear, Walnut & Gorgonzola Pizzas

Active Minutes: 20

Total: 35 minutes

Per Serving: 361 calories; 14 g fat (4 g sat, 4 g mono); 13 mg cholesterol; 53 g carbohydrate; 12 g protein; 8 g fiber; 543 mg sodium.

Nutrition Bonus: Selenium (43% daily value), Fiber (33% dv), Iron (15% dv).

High ↑ Fiber

Pita rounds make quick pizza crusts. But topped with the classic combination of pears, walnuts and blue cheese, they're taken to elegant heights. These pizzas are great with a green salad for a quick supper; wedges can also be served up as cocktail-hour fare.

- **1 tablespoon extra-virgin olive oil**
- **1 large sweet onion, sliced**
- **1 medium ripe pear, sliced**
- **2 tablespoons balsamic vinegar**
- **1/2 teaspoon freshly ground pepper**
- **4 6 1/2-inch *or* eight 4-inch whole-wheat pita breads**
- **1/2 cup crumbled blue cheese, such as Gorgonzola**
- **1/4 cup chopped walnuts**

1. Preheat oven to 450°F.

2. Heat oil in a large nonstick skillet over medium-high heat. Add onion and cook, stirring often, until soft and golden, about 7 minutes. Stir in pear and cook, stirring often, until slightly soft and heated through, 1 to 2 minutes. Add vinegar and pepper and continue cooking, stirring often, until the liquid has evaporated and the onion is tender and coated with a dark glaze, about 2 minutes more.

3. Divide the onion-pear mixture among the pitas; sprinkle with cheese and walnuts. Transfer the pitas to a large baking sheet and bake until crispy and the cheese is melted, 10 to 15 minutes.

Makes 4 servings.

Tomato-&-Olive-Stuffed Portobello Caps

Portobello caps make excellent mini casseroles. Here, they hold a tomato, cheese and olive stuffing that grills up to a smoky perfection. Serve them with whole-wheat couscous and a mixed green salad for an easy meal.

- **2/3 cup chopped plum tomatoes**
- **1/2 cup shredded part-skim mozzarella cheese**
- **1/4 cup chopped Kalamata olives**
- **1 teaspoon minced garlic**
- **2 teaspoons extra-virgin olive oil, divided**
- **1/2 teaspoon finely chopped fresh rosemary *or* 1/8 teaspoon dried**
- **1/8 teaspoon freshly ground pepper**
- **4 portobello mushroom caps, 5 inches wide**
- **2 tablespoons lemon juice**
- **2 teaspoons reduced-sodium soy sauce**

1. Combine tomatoes, cheese, olives, garlic, 1 teaspoon oil, rosemary and pepper in a small bowl.

2. Preheat grill to medium.

3. Discard mushroom stems. Remove brown gills from the undersides of the caps using a spoon; discard gills. Mix the remaining 1 teaspoon oil, lemon juice and soy sauce in a small bowl. Brush the mixture over both sides of the caps.

4. Oil a grill rack (*see Tip, page 242*). Place the caps on the rack, stem sides down, cover and grill until soft, about 5 minutes per side. Remove from the grill and fill with the tomato mixture. Return to the grill, cover, and cook until the cheese is melted, about 3 minutes more.

Makes 4 servings.

Active Minutes: 35

Total: 40 minutes

Per Serving: 122 calories; 7 g fat (2 g sat, 4 g mono); 9 mg cholesterol; 9 g carbohydrate; 7 g protein; 3 g fiber; 339 mg sodium.

Nutrition Bonus: Vitamin C (25% daily value), Potassium (17% dv), Calcium (15% dv).

Healthy Weight

Lower Carbs

Tofu Cutlets Marsala

Slices of extra-firm tofu are dredged and sautéed to golden perfection, just as you would with any cutlet. Try this technique with your favorite pan sauce.

Active Minutes: 40

Total: 40 minutes

Per Serving: 334 calories; 18 g fat (3 g sat, 12 g mono); 0 mg cholesterol; 25 g carbohydrate; 11 g protein; 2 g fiber; 256 mg sodium.

Nutrition Bonus: Selenium (41% daily value), Calcium (25% dv), Potassium (16% dv), Iron (15% dv).

Healthy ⋊ Weight

ingredient note:

- **Marsala, a fortified wine, is a flavorful and wonderfully economical addition to many sauces. An opened bottle can be stored in a cool, dry place for months—unlike wine, which starts to decline within hours of being uncorked.**

1/4 cup plus 2 teaspoons cornstarch, divided
1/4 cup all-purpose flour
1/4 teaspoon salt
1/4 teaspoon freshly ground pepper
1 14-ounce block extra-firm tofu, drained, rinsed and cut crosswise into eight 1/2-inch-thick slices
4 tablespoons extra-virgin olive oil, divided
2 large shallots, minced
1 teaspoon dried thyme
6 cups sliced cremini *or* white mushrooms (about 1 pound)
1/2 cup dry Marsala wine (*see Note*)
1 cup vegetable broth *or* reduced-sodium chicken broth
1 tablespoon tomato paste

1. Whisk 1/4 cup cornstarch, flour, salt and pepper in a shallow dish. Pat tofu with paper towel to remove excess moisture. Heat 2 tablespoons oil in a large nonstick skillet over medium-high heat. Dredge 4 tofu slices in the flour mixture, add them to the pan and cook until crispy and golden, about 3 minutes per side. Place the tofu on a baking sheet and transfer to a 300°F oven to keep warm. Dredge the remaining tofu and cook with another tablespoon of oil, adjusting the heat if necessary to prevent scorching. Keep warm in the oven.

2. Add the remaining 1 tablespoon oil, shallots and thyme to the skillet. Cook over medium heat, stirring constantly, until the shallots are slightly soft and beginning to brown, 1 to 2 minutes. Add mushrooms and cook, stirring often, until tender and lightly browned, 3 to 5 minutes. Stir in Marsala and simmer until the mixture is slightly reduced, about 1 minute.

3. Whisk the remaining 2 teaspoons cornstarch with broth and tomato paste in a small bowl. Stir into the mushroom mixture, return to a simmer and cook, stirring constantly, until thick and glossy, about 4 minutes. To serve, spoon the hot sauce over the tofu.

Makes 4 servings.

Sweet & Sour Tofu

This easy stir-fry makes a great supper for the whole family, especially if you serve it over brown rice and alongside Asian Salad (*page 228*). If you want to spice it up, add a dash of crushed red pepper or chile-garlic sauce with the pineapple chunks.

Active Minutes: 35

Total: 40 minutes

To Make Ahead: The tofu can be marinated (Step 1) up to 30 minutes in advance.

Per Serving: 255 calories; 12 g fat (1 g sat, 5 g mono); 0 mg cholesterol; 32 g carbohydrate; 10 g protein; 4 g fiber; 368 mg sodium.

Nutrition Bonus: Vitamin C (230% daily value), Vitamin A (35% dv), Calcium (25% dv), Magnesium (17% dv), Iron (15% dv), Potassium (15% dv).

Healthy Weight

1 20-ounce can pineapple chunks *or* tidbits
3 tablespoons rice-wine vinegar
2 tablespoons ketchup
2 tablespoons reduced-sodium soy sauce
1 tablespoon brown sugar
1 14-ounce package water-packed extra-firm tofu, drained, rinsed and cut into 1/2-inch cubes
2 teaspoons cornstarch
2 tablespoons canola oil, divided
2 tablespoons minced garlic
1 tablespoon minced ginger
1 large red bell pepper, cut into 1/2-by-2-inch strips
1 large green bell pepper, cut into 1/2-by-2-inch strips

1. Drain pineapple and set aside, reserving 1/4 cup of the juice. Whisk the reserved juice, vinegar, ketchup, soy sauce and sugar in a medium bowl until smooth. Place tofu in a large bowl; toss with 3 tablespoons of the sauce. Let marinate for at least 5 minutes and up to 30 minutes. Add cornstarch to the remaining sauce and whisk until smooth.

2. Heat 1 tablespoon oil in a large nonstick skillet over medium-high heat. Transfer the tofu to the pan using a slotted spoon; whisk any remaining marinade into the bowl of reserved sauce. Cook the tofu, stirring every 1 to 2 minutes, until golden brown, 7 to 9 minutes total. Transfer to a plate.

3. Add the remaining oil to the pan and heat over medium heat. Add garlic and ginger and cook, stirring constantly, until fragrant, about 30 seconds. Add red and green peppers and cook, stirring often, until just tender, 2 to 3 minutes. Pour in the reserved sauce and cook, stirring, until thickened, about 30 seconds. Add the tofu and pineapple and cook, stirring gently, until heated through, about 2 minutes more.

Makes 4 servings, 1 1/2 cups each.

Asian-Style Grilled Tofu with Greens

Look for Asian greens (tatsoi, mizuna and/or pea shoots) packaged as a salad mix. They're slightly more bitter than many spring greens and will stand up well to this aromatic, vinegary dressing.

Dressing

- **1 small carrot, peeled and coarsely chopped**
- **1/2 cup prepared carrot juice**
- **2 tablespoons white *or* yellow miso (*see Ingredient Note, page 243*)**
- **2 tablespoons rice vinegar**
- **2 tablespoons canola oil**
- **1 tablespoon coarsely chopped fresh ginger**
- **1/2 teaspoon minced garlic**

Tofu & Greens

- **28 ounces water-packed firm tofu, drained and rinsed**
- **2 tablespoons honey**
- **2 tablespoons canola oil**
- **2 tablespoons reduced-sodium soy sauce**
- **1 tablespoon black bean-garlic sauce (*see Note*)**
- **2 teaspoons minced garlic**
- **10 ounces mixed Asian greens *or* baby spinach**

1. **To prepare dressing:** Puree carrot, carrot juice, miso, vinegar, oil, ginger and garlic in a blender or food processor until smooth.

2. **To prepare tofu:** Slice each tofu block crosswise into 5 slices; pat dry with paper towels. Combine honey, oil, soy sauce, black bean-garlic sauce and garlic in a small bowl. Spread half the marinade in a large baking dish and top with the tofu slices. Spread the remaining marinade over the tofu, covering completely.

3. Preheat grill to medium-high. Oil the grill rack (*see Cooking Tip, page 242*). Grill the tofu until heated through, 2 to 3 minutes per side. To serve, toss greens with the dressing. Divide among 6 plates and top with the tofu.

Makes 6 servings.

Active Minutes: 45

Total: 45 minutes

Per Serving: 240 calories; 16 g fat (2 g sat, 4 g mono); 0 mg cholesterol; 12 g carbohydrate; 17 g protein; 4 g fiber; 405 mg sodium.

Nutrition Bonus: Vitamin A (90% daily value), Iron (25% dv), Vitamin C (25% dv), Calcium (20% dv).

Healthy Weight

Lower Carbs

ingredient note:

Black bean-garlic sauce, a savory, salty sauce used in Chinese cooking, is made from fermented black beans, garlic and rice wine. It can be found in the Asian-food section of large supermarkets or at Asian markets. Use it in stir-fries and marinades for beef, chicken or tofu.

Sichuan-Style Tofu with Mushrooms

Because of the high moisture content of tofu, it can go from a stir-fry to a braise in seconds. We also recommend salting and drying the tofu in paper towels so oil doesn't splatter during frying.

14 ounces water-packed firm tofu, rinsed
1/2 teaspoon salt
2 tablespoons canola oil, divided
2 cloves garlic, smashed
2 scallions, trimmed and chopped
1 1/2 cups sliced white mushrooms (about 4 ounces)
Sichuan Sauce (*page 227*)

1. Place tofu on several paper towels and sprinkle with 1/4 teaspoon salt. Turn tofu over, sprinkle with the remaining 1/4 teaspoon salt, place more paper towels on top and weight the tofu down with a plate. Set aside for 5 minutes. Cut the tofu into roughly 1-inch cubes.

2. Heat a 14-inch flat-bottomed wok or large skillet over high heat until a bead of water vaporizes within 1 to 2 seconds of contact. Swirl in 1 tablespoon oil; add garlic and scallions and stir-fry until fragrant, 10 seconds. Add mushrooms and stir-fry until just beginning to soften, 1 minute. Transfer to a plate.

3. Swirl the remaining 1 tablespoon oil into the pan, reduce the heat to medium, add the tofu and pan-fry, turning midway through cooking, until it begins to brown, about 3 minutes. Swirl in Sichuan Sauce and the mushroom mixture; increase the heat to high and stir-fry until the tofu is just heated through and the sauce clings to it, 30 seconds to 1 minute. Discard the garlic. Serve immediately.

Makes 4 servings, about 3/4 cup each.

Active Minutes: 20

Total: 25 minutes

Per Serving: 233 calories; 16 g fat (2 g sat, 6 g mono); 0 mg cholesterol; 9 g carbohydrate; 17 g protein; 3 g fiber; 383 mg sodium.

Nutrition Bonus: Calcium (70% daily value), Magnesium (16% dv), Iron (15% dv).

Healthy Weight

Lower Carbs

TLT (Tofu, Lettuce & Tomato Sandwich)

With pickles, oven fries and a tall glass of minty iced tea, even the most devoted bacon fan won't remember what's missing in this smoky, spicy renovation of the sandwich favorite.

Active Minutes: 25

Total: 25 minutes

To Make Ahead: Prepare through Step 3. Wrap the baked tofu in plastic wrap and refrigerate for up to 3 days.

Per Serving: 363 calories; 9 g fat (1 g sat, 1 g mono); 4 mg cholesterol; 46 g carbohydrate; 17 g protein; 4 g fiber; 685 mg sodium.

Nutrition Bonus: Vitamin A (25% daily value), Vitamin C (20% dv), Fiber (17% dv).

1 tablespoon Dijon mustard
1 tablespoon reduced-sodium soy sauce
1 teaspoon adobo sauce from canned chipotle peppers (*see Note*), divided
14 ounces water-packed extra-firm tofu, drained and rinsed
4 tablespoons reduced-fat mayonnaise
8 slices crusty whole-wheat bread, toasted
4 pieces green-leaf lettuce
2 medium tomatoes, sliced

1. Preheat oven to 475°F. Coat a baking sheet with cooking spray.

2. Combine mustard, soy sauce and 1/2 teaspoon adobo sauce in a small bowl. Slice tofu crosswise into eight 1/2-inch-thick pieces. Pat dry with a paper towel and place on the prepared baking sheet. Using a spoon, spread half the mustard mixture on one side of the tofu. Turn the slices over and spread the remaining mixture on the other side.

3. Bake the tofu for 20 minutes.

4. Combine mayonnaise with the remaining 1/2 teaspoon adobo sauce in a small bowl. Spread the mixture on toasted bread. Divide the tofu, lettuce and tomato among 4 slices of toast and top with the remaining toast to make 4 sandwiches. Cut in half to serve.

Makes 4 servings.

ingredient note

- **Canned chipotle peppers (smoked jalapeños) add heat and smokiness to dishes; the adobo sauce alone adds a spicy zest without extra heat. Look for small cans with other Mexican foods in large supermarkets. Once opened, chipotles will keep for up to 2 weeks in the refrigerator or 6 months in the freezer.**

Grilled Eggplant Panini

Grilled eggplant is one of life's simpler pleasures: creamy and rich. Look for medium-size, purple eggplants with firm skins and no mushy spots. This end-of-summer treat will be even tastier if you can find the vegetables at a local farmstand—or in your own backyard!

Active Minutes: 35

Total: 35 minutes

Per Serving: 337 calories; 16 g fat (6 g sat, 6 g mono); 22 mg cholesterol; 36 g carbohydrate; 12 g protein; 7 g fiber; 659 mg sodium.

Nutrition Bonus: Folate (28% daily value), Calcium (25% dv), Selenium (23% dv), Iron (15% dv).

High ↑ Fiber

- **2 tablespoons reduced-fat mayonnaise**
- **2 tablespoons chopped fresh basil**
- **2 tablespoons extra-virgin olive oil, divided**
- **8 1/2-inch slices eggplant (about 1 small)**
- **1/2 teaspoon garlic salt**
- **8 slices whole-grain country bread**
- **8 thin slices fresh mozzarella cheese**
- **1/3 cup sliced jarred roasted red peppers**
- **4 thin slices red onion**

1. Preheat grill to medium-high.

2. Combine mayonnaise and basil in a small bowl. Using 1 tablespoon oil, lightly brush both sides of eggplant and sprinkle each slice with garlic salt. With the remaining 1 tablespoon oil, brush one side of each slice of bread.

3. Grill the eggplant for 6 minutes, turn with a spatula, top with cheese, and continue grilling until the cheese is melted and the eggplant is tender, about 4 minutes more. Toast the bread on the grill, 1 to 2 minutes per side.

4. **To assemble sandwiches:** Spread basil mayonnaise on four slices of bread. Top with the cheesy eggplant, red peppers, onion and the remaining slices of bread. Cut in half and serve warm.

Makes 4 sandwiches.

Portobello "Philly Cheese Steak" Sandwich

Active Minutes: 25

Total: 25 minutes

Per Serving: 268 calories; 10 g fat (4 g sat, 4 g mono); 15 mg cholesterol; 35 g carbohydrate; 13 g protein; 7 g fiber; 561 mg sodium.

Nutrition Bonus: Vitamin C (140% daily value), Selenium (49% dv), Calcium (25% dv), Potassium (20% dv), Magnesium (16% dv).

High ↑ Fiber

cooking tip:

- **The dark gills found on the underside of a portobello are edible, but if you like you can scrape them off with a spoon.**

Cheese steaks are a Philadelphia tradition: thin slices from a rich and very fatty slab of beef, fried up and topped with a heavy cheese sauce. We've cut down on the fat considerably—but not on the taste. All it needs is a cold beer on the side.

- **2 teaspoons extra-virgin olive oil**
- **1 medium onion, sliced**
- **4 large portobello mushrooms, stems and gills removed (*see Tip*), sliced**
- **1 large red bell pepper, thinly sliced**
- **2 tablespoons minced fresh oregano *or* 2 teaspoons dried**
- **1/2 teaspoon freshly ground pepper**
- **1 tablespoon all-purpose flour**
- **1/4 cup vegetable broth *or* reduced-sodium chicken broth**
- **1 tablespoon reduced-sodium soy sauce**
- **3 ounces thinly sliced reduced-fat provolone cheese**
- **4 whole-wheat buns, split and toasted**

1. Heat oil in a large nonstick skillet over medium-high heat. Add onion and cook, stirring often, until soft and beginning to brown, 2 to 3 minutes. Add mushrooms, bell pepper, oregano and pepper; cook, stirring often, until the vegetables are wilted and soft, about 7 minutes.

2. Reduce heat to low; sprinkle the vegetables with flour and stir to coat. Stir in broth and soy sauce; bring to a simmer. Remove from the heat, lay cheese slices on top of the vegetables, cover and let stand until melted, 1 to 2 minutes.

3. Divide the mixture into 4 portions with a spatula, leaving the melted cheese layer on top. Scoop a portion onto each toasted bun and serve immediately.

Makes 4 sandwiches.

Zucchini-Potato Latkes with Tzatziki

Call this an international version of potato pancakes: a vegetable patty that's served with a tangy Greek sauce. You can put the patties and sauce in pita pockets for a quick lunch on the go.

- **1 pound zucchini, shredded**
- **2 cups shredded cooked potato (*see Note*)**
- **2 medium shallots, minced, divided**
- **1 egg, beaten**
- **2 cups fresh whole-wheat breadcrumbs (*see Tip, page 242*)**
- **1/2 cup crumbled reduced-fat feta cheese**
- **2 tablespoons chopped fresh dill, divided**
- **1/2 teaspoon salt, divided**
- **1/2 teaspoon freshly ground pepper, divided**
- **2 tablespoons extra-virgin olive oil, divided**
- **1 cup low-fat plain yogurt**
- **1/2 medium cucumber, peeled, seeded and shredded**
- **1 tablespoon red-wine vinegar**

1. Preheat oven to 450°F. Coat a baking sheet with cooking spray.

2. Toss zucchini, potato, 3 tablespoons shallot and egg in a large bowl. Add breadcrumbs, feta, 1 tablespoon dill, 1/4 teaspoon salt and 1/4 teaspoon pepper; toss to combine. Form the mixture into 12 patties.

3. Heat 1 tablespoon oil in a large nonstick skillet over medium-high heat. Add 6 patties, cover and cook until crispy and browned on one side, 2 to 5 minutes. Carefully flip over onto the prepared sheet, browned-side down. Repeat with the remaining 1 tablespoon oil and patties. Transfer the latkes to the oven and bake until firm and hot all the way through, 10 to 12 minutes.

4. Meanwhile, combine yogurt, cucumber, vinegar, the remaining shallot, 1 tablespoon dill and 1/4 teaspoon each salt and pepper in a small bowl. Serve the latkes with the yogurt sauce on the side.

Makes 4 servings.

Active Minutes: 35

Total: 40 minutes

Per Serving: 325 calories; 12 g fat (3 g sat, 6 g mono); 62 mg cholesterol; 45 g carbohydrate; 14 g protein; 10 g fiber; 689 mg sodium.

Nutrition Bonus: Vitamin C (35% daily value), Calcium (30% dv), Folate (29% dv).

High ↑ Fiber

ingredient note:

Cooked and shredded potatoes for hash browns can be found in the refrigerated produce section and sometimes in the dairy section of most supermarkets. If you'd prefer to cook your own potatoes, boil them until you can just pierce them with a fork, but not until they are completely tender. Let cool slightly, then shred.

Chapter 4: Chicken, Duck & Turkey

Chicken Cacciatore

A cacciatore was a hunting-lodge dish, a way to slow-simmer tough game birds to tenderness. Flavorful chicken thighs need no special treatment but they do take so well to the traditional wine, tomato and mushroom sauce.

1/4 cup all-purpose flour
1 1/4 pounds boneless, skinless chicken thighs, trimmed of fat
1 tablespoon extra-virgin olive oil, divided
1 medium onion, sliced
10 ounces mushrooms, sliced
1 teaspoon chopped fresh rosemary
1 14-ounce can diced tomatoes
1 cup white wine
1/2 teaspoon salt
1/2 teaspoon freshly ground pepper
1 tablespoon chopped flat-leaf parsley

1. Place flour in a shallow dish. Lightly dredge each chicken thigh in the flour. Discard the remaining flour.

2. Heat 1 teaspoon oil in a large skillet over medium-high heat. Add the chicken and cook until golden, 2 to 4 minutes per side. Transfer to a plate, cover and keep warm.

3. Reduce heat to medium-low and add the remaining 2 teaspoons oil to the skillet. Add onion, mushrooms and rosemary and cook, stirring often, until the vegetables are lightly browned, about 5 minutes. Add tomatoes, white wine, salt and pepper and cook until the onion is very soft, about 5 minutes. Return the chicken to the pan, nestle into the sauce, reduce heat to a simmer and cook until the sauce is thickened and the chicken is cooked through and no longer pink in the middle, about 5 minutes. Sprinkle with parsley and serve.

Makes 4 servings.

Active Minutes: 40

Total: 40 minutes

Per Serving: 341 calories; 14 g fat (4 g sat, 7 g mono); 93 mg cholesterol; 12 g carbohydrate; 29 g protein; 2 g fiber; 620 mg sodium.

Nutrition Bonus: Selenium (53% daily value), Niacin (45% dv), Vitamin C (30% dv), Zinc (20% dv).

Healthy Weight

Lower Carbs

Wok-Seared Chicken Tenders with Asparagus & Pistachios

Here's an East-meets-West stir-fry that will soon become a family favorite. Serve it over rice or noodles, with a simple salad of arugula and orange sections dressed in a light vinaigrette.

- **1 tablespoon toasted sesame oil**
- **1 1/2 pounds fresh asparagus, tough ends trimmed, cut into 1-inch pieces**
- **1 pound chicken tenders (*see Note*), cut into bite-size pieces**
- **4 scallions, trimmed and cut into 1-inch pieces**
- **2 tablespoons minced fresh ginger**
- **1 tablespoon oyster-flavored sauce**
- **1 teaspoon chile-garlic sauce (*see Ingredient Note, page 243*)**
- **1/4 cup shelled salted pistachios, coarsely chopped**

1. Heat oil in a wok or large skillet over high heat. Add asparagus; cook, stirring, for 2 minutes. Add chicken; cook, stirring, for 4 minutes. Stir in scallions, ginger, oyster sauce and chile-garlic sauce; cook, stirring, until the chicken is juicy and just cooked through, 1 to 2 minutes more. Stir in pistachios and serve immediately.

Makes 4 servings, about 1 1/4 cups each.

Active Minutes: 25

Total: 25 minutes

Per Serving: 208 calories; 8 g fat (1 g sat, 3 g mono); 67 mg cholesterol; 7 g carbohydrate; 30 g protein; 3 g fiber; 175 mg sodium.

Nutrition Bonus: Folate (35% daily value), Vitamin A (20% dv), Vitamin C (15% dv).

Healthy Weight

Lower Carbs

ingredient note:

- **Chicken tenders, virtually fat-free, are a strip of rib meat typically found attached to the underside of the chicken breast, but they can also be purchased separately. Four 1-ounce tenders will yield a 3-ounce cooked portion. Tenders are perfect for quick stir-fries, chicken satay or kid-friendly breaded "chicken fingers."**

Roast Chicken Dal

A dal is traditionally a lentil side, often the accompaniment for curry. Here, combined with roast chicken (or rotisserie chicken), it moves from the side of the plate to its center for a quick lunch or an easy weeknight dinner.

Active Minutes: 25

Total: 25 minutes

Per Serving: 345 calories; 9 g fat (2 g sat, 4 g mono); 78 mg cholesterol; 30 g carbohydrate; 36 g protein; 10 g fiber; 361 mg sodium.

Nutrition Bonus: Folate (48% daily value), Iron (28% dv).

Healthy Weight

High Fiber

- **1 1/2 teaspoons canola oil**
- **1 small onion, minced**
- **2 teaspoons curry powder**
- **1 15-ounce can lentils, rinsed, *or* 2 cups cooked lentils (*see Tip, page 242*)**
- **1 14-ounce can diced tomatoes, preferably fire-roasted**
- **1 2-pound roasted chicken, skin discarded, meat removed from bones and diced (4 cups)**
- **1/4 teaspoon salt, or to taste**
- **1/4 cup low-fat plain yogurt**

1. Heat oil in a large heavy saucepan over medium-high heat. Add onion and cook, stirring, until softened but not browned, 3 to 4 minutes. Add curry powder and cook, stirring, until combined with the onion and intensely aromatic, 20 to 30 seconds. Stir in lentils, tomatoes, chicken and salt and cook, stirring often, until heated through. Remove from the heat and stir in yogurt. Serve immediately.

Makes 4 servings, about 1 1/2 cups each.

Penne with Roasted Chicken & Radicchio

Radicchio is a brawlingly bitter green that becomes impossibly meek and mild when simmered. Paired with some cheese and the meat from a rotisserie chicken, it cooks up quickly into a memorable pasta dish.

Active Minutes: 30

Total: 30 minutes

Per Serving: 463 calories; 12 g fat (3 g sat, 4 g mono); 60 mg cholesterol; 60 g carbohydrate; 30 g protein; 7 g fiber; 223 mg sodium.

Nutrition Bonus: Fiber (28% daily value).

High ↑ Fiber

- **1 pound whole-wheat penne**
- **1 head radicchio, torn into 1-inch pieces**
- **1/2 cup freshly grated Parmesan cheese, divided**
- **2 teaspoons extra-virgin olive oil**
- **1 2-pound roasted chicken, skin discarded, meat removed from bones and shredded (4 cups)**
- **1/4 cup balsamic vinegar**
- **Freshly ground pepper to taste**
- **1/4 cup chopped walnuts**

1. Cook pasta in a large pot of boiling water until just tender, 8 to 10 minutes or according to package directions.

2. Drain the pasta, reserving 1/4 cup of the cooking liquid. Place radicchio and the reserved liquid in the pot and cook over medium heat, stirring constantly, until wilted, 2 to 3 minutes. Stir in the pasta, 2 tablespoons Parmesan, oil, chicken, vinegar and pepper and continue cooking until the cheese starts to melt, 1 to 2 minutes. Serve the pasta garnished with walnuts and the remaining cheese.

Makes 6 servings, 1 1/2 cups each.

Chicken Stuffed with Golden Onions & Fontina

Active Minutes: 35

Total: 35 minutes

Per Serving: 258 calories; 12 g fat (5 g sat, 6 g mono); 88 mg cholesterol; 7 g carbohydrate; 32 g protein; 1 g fiber; 328 mg sodium.

Nutrition Bonus: Selenium (33% daily value), Calcium (13% dv).

Healthy Weight

Lower Carbs

A semi-firm cheese that's nonetheless quite creamy, fontina melts into pure heaven. Combined with caramelized onions, fontina becomes a nutty, gooey, irresistible filling for chicken breasts.

- **4 teaspoons extra-virgin olive oil, divided**
- **1 1/2 cups thinly sliced red onion**
- **2 teaspoons minced fresh rosemary, divided**
- **1/8 teaspoon salt**
- **Freshly ground pepper to taste**
- **2/3 cup shredded fontina cheese, preferably aged**
- **4 boneless, skinless chicken breasts (about 1 pound), trimmed of fat**
- **1/2 cup white wine**
- **1 cup reduced-sodium chicken broth**
- **4 teaspoons all-purpose flour**

1. Heat 2 teaspoons oil in a large nonstick skillet over medium-high heat. Add onion and 1 teaspoon rosemary; cook, stirring occasionally, until the onion is golden brown, 6 to 7 minutes. Season with salt and pepper. Let cool; stir in fontina.

2. Meanwhile, cut a horizontal slit along the thin, long edge of each chicken breast half, nearly through to the opposite side. Stuff each breast with 1/4 cup of the onion-cheese mixture.

3. Heat the remaining 2 teaspoons oil in the same skillet over medium-high heat. Add the chicken and cook until golden, about 5 minutes per side. Transfer to a plate and cover with foil to keep warm.

4. Add wine and the remaining 1 teaspoon rosemary to the pan. Cook over medium-high heat for 2 minutes. Whisk broth and flour in a bowl until smooth; add to the pan, reduce heat to low and whisk until the sauce thickens, about 1 minute. Return the chicken to the pan and coat with the sauce. Cook, covered, until the chicken is just cooked through, 2 to 4 minutes. Serve the chicken topped with the sauce.

Makes 4 servings.

Chicken & Spiced Apples

The buttery apples suit these chicken breasts, which are pounded thin so they cook evenly and quickly. You could also serve this compote with any roasted meat or vegetable.

Active Minutes: 20

Total: 20 minutes

Per Serving: 191 calories; 6 g fat (2 g sat, 2 g mono); 72 mg cholesterol; 6 g carbohydrate; 27 g protein; 1 g fiber; 351 mg sodium.

Nutrition Bonus: Niacin (65% daily value), Selenium (29% dv).

Healthy Weight

Lower Carbs

2 apples, preferably Braeburn, peeled and thinly sliced
1 tablespoon lemon juice
1/4 teaspoon ground cinnamon
3 teaspoons extra-virgin olive oil, divided
3 teaspoons unsalted butter, divided
1 1/8 teaspoons herbes de Provence (*see Note*), divided
1/2 teaspoon salt, or to taste
1/4 teaspoon freshly ground pepper
1 1/2 pounds boneless, skinless chicken breasts, trimmed of fat
1 cup reduced-sodium chicken broth
1 teaspoon freshly grated lemon zest

1. Toss apple slices with lemon juice and cinnamon in a small bowl. Heat 1 teaspoon oil and 1 teaspoon butter in a medium nonstick skillet over medium-high heat. Add the apples and cook, stirring occasionally, until tender, about 5 minutes. Keep warm.

2. Mix 1 teaspoon herbes de Provence, salt and pepper. Place chicken between sheets of plastic wrap and pound with a meat mallet or the bottom of a small saucepan to a 1/2-inch thickness. Sprinkle the chicken on both sides with the seasoning mixture.

3. Heat 1 teaspoon oil and 1 teaspoon butter in a large skillet over high heat. Add half the chicken and cook until no longer pink in the center, 2 to 3 minutes per side. Remove to a platter and keep warm. Add the remaining 1 teaspoon oil and 1 teaspoon butter to the skillet; heat over high heat. Cook the remaining chicken in the same manner.

4. Add broth, lemon zest, the remaining 1/8 teaspoon herbes and any accumulated juices from the chicken to the skillet. Cook, stirring to scrape up any browned bits, until slightly reduced, about 3 minutes. Spoon the sauce over the chicken and serve with the sautéed apples.

Makes 6 servings.

ingredient note:

- **Herbes de Provence is a mixture of dried herbs commonly used in the south of France. You can find commercial mixtures in specialty stores, but it is easy to make your own. Mix 1 tablespoon each (or equal proportions) dried thyme, rosemary, oregano, marjoram and savory in a small jar. If desired, add a pinch of dried lavender and crushed aniseed.**

Chicken Sausage with Quick Sauerkraut

Sauerkraut from a can, pale and puckery, is no match for this a flavorful cabbage sauté that goes well with savory chicken sausage. Serve this simple supper with assorted mustards and some toasted rye bread.

Active Minutes: 15

Total: 25 minutes

Per Serving: 194 calories; 6 g fat (0 g sat, 1 g mono); 60 mg cholesterol; 22 g carbohydrate; 13 g protein; 3 g fiber; 582 mg sodium.

Nutrition Bonus: Vitamin C (45% daily value).

Healthy Weight

Lower Carbs

- **1 12-ounce package chicken sausage**
- **1 teaspoon extra-virgin olive oil**
- **1 small onion, sliced**
- **1 Granny Smith apple, thinly sliced**
- **1 10-ounce package shredded cabbage, preferably finely shredded**
- **1/4 cup cider vinegar**
- **1/4 teaspoon salt**
- **1 cup apple cider**
- **1 teaspoon caraway seeds**

1. Cook sausages in a large skillet over medium-high heat until brown on all sides, 2 to 3 minutes. Transfer to a plate.

2. Heat oil in the pan over medium-high heat. Add onion and apple and cook, stirring constantly, until beginning to brown, 1 to 2 minutes. Add cabbage, vinegar and salt and cook, stirring often, until just wilted, about 2 minutes. Add cider and caraway seeds; bring to a boil. Return the sausages to the pan, cover, reduce heat to a simmer and cook until the sausages are heated through and cabbage is tender, about 10 minutes.

Makes 4 servings.

Japanese Chicken-Scallion Rice Bowl

Active Minutes: 15

Total: 20 minutes

Per Serving: 262 calories; 3 g fat (1 g sat, 1 g mono); 87 mg cholesterol; 34 g carbohydrate; 21 g protein; 2 g fiber; 395 mg sodium.

Here's the quintessence of Japanese home cooking: an aromatic, protein-rich broth served over rice. Admittedly, Japanese cooking leans heavily on sugar—for a less traditional taste, you could reduce or even omit the sugar.

- **1 1/2 cups instant brown rice**
- **1 cup reduced-sodium chicken broth**
- **1 1/2 tablespoons sugar**
- **2 tablespoons reduced-sodium soy sauce**
- **1 tablespoon mirin (*see Ingredient Note, page 243*)**
- **2 large egg whites**
- **1 large egg**
- **8 ounces boneless, skinless chicken breasts, cut into 1/2-inch pieces**
- **6 scallions, trimmed and thinly sliced**

1. Prepare instant brown rice according to package directions.

2. Pour broth into a heavy medium saucepan, along with sugar, soy sauce and mirin. Bring to a boil; reduce heat to medium-low.

3. Stir egg whites and whole egg in a small bowl until just mixed. Add chicken to the simmering broth. Gently pour in the egg mixture, without stirring. Sprinkle scallions on top. When the egg starts to firm up, after about 3 minutes, stir it with chopsticks or a knife. (The chicken will be cooked by now.) Divide the rice among 4 deep soup bowls and top with the chicken mixture.

Makes 4 servings, 1 1/2 cups each.

Sautéed Chicken Breasts with Creamy Chive Sauce

Active Minutes: 35

Total: 35 minutes

Per Serving: 242 calories; 9 g fat (3 g sat, 4 g mono); 72 mg cholesterol; 8 g carbohydrate; 26 g protein; 0 g fiber; 667 mg sodium.

Nutrition Bonus: Niacin (50% daily value), Selenium (31% dv).

Healthy Weight

Lower Carbs

Here's a sauce so creamy, it's missing only one thing: a little crunchy bread to dip in it. Serve with steamed cauliflower or asparagus, some orzo pasta and a glass of Vinho Verde.

- **4 boneless, skinless chicken breasts (about 1 pound), trimmed of fat**
- **1 teaspoon kosher salt, divided**
- **1/4 cup plus 1 tablespoon all-purpose flour, divided**
- **3 teaspoons extra-virgin olive oil, divided**
- **2 large shallots, finely chopped**
- **1/2 cup dry white wine**
- **1 14-ounce can reduced-sodium chicken broth**
- **1/3 cup reduced-fat sour cream**
- **1 tablespoon Dijon mustard**
- **1/2 cup chopped chives (about 1 bunch)**

1. Place chicken between sheets of plastic wrap and pound with a meat mallet or heavy skillet until flattened to an even thickness, about 1/2 inch. Season both sides of the chicken with 1/2 teaspoon salt. Place 1/4 cup flour in a shallow glass baking dish and dredge the chicken in it. Discard the remaining flour.

2. Heat 2 teaspoons oil in a large nonstick skillet over medium-high heat. Add the chicken and cook until golden brown, 1 to 2 minutes per side. Transfer to a plate, cover and keep warm.

3. Heat the remaining 1 teaspoon oil in the pan over medium-high heat. Add shallots and cook, stirring constantly and scraping up any browned bits, until golden brown, 1 to 2 minutes. Sprinkle with the remaining 1 tablespoon flour; stir to coat. Add wine, broth and the remaining 1/2 teaspoon salt; bring to a boil, stirring often. Return the chicken and any accumulated juices to the pan, reduce heat to a simmer, and cook until heated through and no longer pink in the center, about 6 minutes. Stir in sour cream and mustard until smooth; turn the chicken to coat with the sauce. Stir in chives and serve immediately.

Makes 4 servings.

Jerk Chicken Breasts

Jerk is a Jamaican seasoning blend the origins of which are fogged by time. Some say that it's a corruption of a Spanish word for "dried meat"; others, that the name refers to the way you quickly turn the meat over the fire. Whatever its meaning, it's a fiery blend that turns these chicken breasts into a five-alarm wonder. Have plenty of rice, potatoes or tortillas to pass on the side with tall glasses of herbal iced tea.

6 scallions, trimmed and coarsely chopped
2 tablespoons dry jerk seasoning (*see Tip*) *or* Jerk Seasoning Blend (*page 226*)
3 tablespoons lime juice
1 tablespoon dark brown sugar (optional)
2 teaspoons reduced-sodium soy sauce
2 teaspoons canola oil
4 boneless, skinless chicken breasts (about 1 pound), trimmed of fat

1. Combine scallions, jerk seasoning, lime juice, sugar (if using), soy sauce and oil in a blender or food processor; pulse to a coarse paste. Wearing gloves to protect your hands from the spice blend, spread the paste all over chicken. Cover and marinate in the refrigerator for at least 10 minutes or for up to 2 hours.

2. Lightly oil broiler rack and set it 5 inches from the heat source; preheat broiler.

3. Scrape most of the paste from the chicken and discard. Broil the chicken, turning once, until the juices run clear, 10 to 15 minutes. Let stand for 5 minutes before slicing.

Makes 4 servings.

Active Minutes: 15

Total: 40 minutes (including 10 minutes marinating time)

Per Serving: 154 calories; 5 g fat (1 g sat, 2 g mono); 63 mg cholesterol; 3 g carbohydrate; 23 g protein; 1 g fiber; 567 mg sodium.

Nutrition Bonus: Niacin (50% daily value), Selenium (28% dv), Vitamin C (15% dv).

Healthy Weight

Lower Carbs

tip:

- **If your dried jerk seasoning blend includes sugar as one of the first three ingredients, omit the brown sugar from this recipe.**

Almond-Crusted Chicken Fingers

Rather than a heavy coating, these chicken fingers are lightly covered in a spicy ground almond and whole-wheat flour mixture that'll have the kids forgetting about fast food and begging for this dinnertime treat.

Canola oil cooking spray
1/2 cup sliced almonds
1/4 cup whole-wheat flour
1 1/2 teaspoons paprika
1/2 teaspoon garlic powder
1/2 teaspoon dry mustard
1/4 teaspoon salt
1/8 teaspoon freshly ground pepper
1 1/2 teaspoons extra-virgin olive oil
4 egg whites (*see Note*)
1 pound chicken tenders

1. Preheat oven to 475°F. Set a wire rack on a foil-lined baking sheet and coat with cooking spray.

2. Place almonds, flour, paprika, garlic powder, dry mustard, salt and pepper in a food processor; process until the almonds are finely chopped and the paprika is mixed throughout, about 1 minute. With the motor running, drizzle in oil; process until combined. Transfer the mixture to a shallow dish.

3. Whisk egg whites in a second shallow dish. Add chicken tenders and turn to coat. Transfer each tender to the almond mixture; turn to coat evenly. (Discard any remaining egg white and almond mixture.) Place the tenders on the prepared rack and coat with cooking spray; turn and spray the other side.

4. Bake the chicken fingers until golden brown, crispy and no longer pink in the center, 20 to 25 minutes.

Makes 4 servings.

Active Minutes: 20

Total: 40 minutes

Per Serving: 147 calories; 4 g fat (1 g sat, 3 g mono); 49 mg cholesterol; 4 g carbohydrate; 21 g protein; 1 g fiber; 214 mg sodium.

Nutrition Bonus: Selenium (28% daily value).

Healthy Weight

Lower Carbs

ingredient note:

Dried egg whites are convenient in recipes like this one because you don't have to figure out what to do with 4 egg yolks. Look for powdered brands like Just Whites in the baking aisle or natural-foods section or fresh pasteurized whites in the dairy case of most supermarkets.

Peanut Noodles with Shredded Chicken & Vegetables

If you can't find a bagged vegetable medley for this easy noodle bowl, choose 12 ounces of cut vegetables from your market's salad bar and create your own mix.

Active Minutes: 30

Total: 30 minutes

To Make Ahead: Cover and refrigerate for up to 2 days. To serve, stir in 2 tablespoons warm water per portion; serve cold or reheat in microwave.

Per Serving: 363 calories; 12 g fat (2 g sat, 0 g mono); 44 mg cholesterol; 36 g carbohydrate; 29 g protein; 7 g fiber; 348 mg sodium.

Nutrition Bonus: Selenium (58% daily value), Fiber (27% dv), Vitamin C (25% dv), Magnesium (19% dv).

High ↑ Fiber

- **1 pound boneless, skinless chicken breasts**
- **1/2 cup smooth natural peanut butter**
- **2 tablespoons reduced-sodium soy sauce**
- **2 teaspoons minced garlic**
- **1 1/2 teaspoons chile-garlic sauce, or to taste (*see Note*)**
- **1 teaspoon minced fresh ginger**
- **8 ounces whole-wheat spaghetti**
- **1 12-ounce bag fresh vegetable medley, such as carrots, broccoli, snow peas**

1. Put a large pot of water on to boil for cooking pasta.

2. Meanwhile, place chicken in a skillet or saucepan and add enough water to cover; bring to a boil. Cover, reduce heat to low and simmer gently until cooked through and no longer pink in the middle, 10 to 12 minutes. Transfer the chicken to a cutting board. When cool enough to handle, shred into bite-size strips.

3. Whisk peanut butter, soy sauce, garlic, chile-garlic sauce and ginger in a large bowl.

4. Cook pasta in the boiling water until not quite tender, about 1 minute less than specified in the package directions. Add vegetables and cook until the pasta and vegetables are just tender, 1 minute more. Drain, reserving 1 cup of the cooking liquid. Rinse the pasta and vegetables with cool water to refresh. Stir the reserved cooking liquid into the peanut sauce; add the pasta, vegetables and chicken; toss well to coat. Serve warm or chilled.

Makes 6 servings, 1 1/2 cups each.

ingredient note:

- **Chile-garlic sauce (or chili-garlic sauce, or paste) is a blend of ground chiles, garlic and vinegar and is commonly used to add heat and flavor to Asian soups, sauces and stir-fries. It can be found in the Asian section of large supermarkets and keeps up to 1 year in the refrigerator.**

Barbecued Chicken Burritos

These burritos are something of a Tex-Mex wonder: tangy barbecue sauce, some roast chicken (or rotisserie chicken) and vegetables, all wrapped up in tortillas. For the best taste, look for a fiery barbecue sauce without added corn syrup.

Active Minutes: 15

Total: 15 minutes

Per Serving: 353 calories; 9 g fat (3 g sat, 3 g mono); 82 mg cholesterol; 40 g carbohydrate; 33 g protein; 5 g fiber; 579 mg sodium.

Nutrition Bonus: Fiber (24% daily value), Iron (20% dv).

High ↑ Fiber

- **1 2-pound roasted chicken, skin discarded, meat removed from bones and shredded (4 cups)**
- **1/2 cup prepared barbecue sauce**
- **1 cup canned black beans, rinsed**
- **1/2 cup frozen corn, thawed, *or* canned corn, drained**
- **1/4 cup reduced-fat sour cream**
- **4 leaves romaine lettuce**
- **4 10-inch whole-wheat tortillas**
- **2 limes, cut in wedges**

1. Place a large nonstick skillet over medium-high heat. Add chicken, barbecue sauce, beans, corn and sour cream; stir to combine. Cook until hot, 4 to 5 minutes.

2. Assemble the wraps by placing a lettuce leaf in the center of each tortilla and topping with one-fourth of the chicken mixture; roll as you would a burrito. Slice in half diagonally and serve warm, with lime wedges.

Makes 4 servings, 1 wrap each.

Chicken, Broccoli Rabe & Feta on Toast

Active Minutes: 35

Total: 35 minutes

Per Serving: 313 calories; 11 g fat (5 g sat, 5 g mono); 68 mg cholesterol; 26 g carbohydrate; 29 g protein; 4 g fiber; 613 mg sodium.

Nutrition Bonus: Vitamin C (160% daily value), Vitamin A (140% dv), Selenium (28% dv), Calcium (20% dv).

Healthy Weight

ingredient note:

- **Pleasantly pungent and mildly bitter, broccoli rabe, or rapini, is a member of the cabbage family and commonly used in Mediterranean cooking. Broccolini (a cross between broccoli and Chinese kale) is sweet and tender—the florets and stalks are edible.**

The assertive flavor of broccoli rabe can be a schoolyard bully in dishes. But here, the sweet tomatoes and briny feta stand up to its bite, rendering this dish a rustic but comforting favorite. Still, if broccoli rabe proves too strong for your taste, you can substitute broccolini or even tiny, trimmed broccoli florets.

- **4 thick slices whole-wheat country bread**
- **1 clove garlic, peeled (optional), plus 1/4 cup chopped garlic**
- **4 teaspoons extra-virgin olive oil, divided**
- **1 pound chicken tenders, cut crosswise into 1/2-inch pieces**
- **1 bunch broccoli rabe, stems trimmed, cut into 1-inch pieces, *or* 2 bunches broccolini, chopped (*see Note*)**
- **2 cups cherry tomatoes, halved**
- **1 tablespoon red-wine vinegar**
- **1/8 teaspoon salt**
- **Freshly ground pepper to taste**
- **3/4 cup crumbled feta cheese**

1. Grill or toast bread. Lightly rub with peeled garlic clove, if desired. Discard the garlic.

2. Heat 2 teaspoons oil in a large nonstick skillet over high heat until shimmering but not smoking. Add chicken; cook, stirring occasionally, until just cooked through and no longer pink in the middle, 4 to 5 minutes. Transfer the chicken and any juices to a plate; cover to keep warm.

3. Add the remaining 2 teaspoons oil to the pan. Add chopped garlic and cook, stirring constantly, until fragrant but not brown, about 30 seconds. Add broccoli rabe (or broccolini) and cook, stirring often, until bright green and just wilted, 2 to 4 minutes. Stir in tomatoes, vinegar, salt and pepper; cook, stirring occasionally, until the tomatoes are beginning to break down, 2 to 4 minutes. Return the chicken and juices to the pan, add feta cheese and stir to combine. Cook until heated through, 1 to 2 minutes. Serve warm over garlic toasts.

Makes 4 servings.

Stir-Fried Spicy Chicken Tenders

Active Minutes: 15

Total: 30 minutes (including 15 minutes marinating time)

To Make Ahead: Prepare through Step 1 up to 1 day ahead.

Per Serving: 196 calories; 5 g fat (1 g sat, 2 g mono); 66 mg cholesterol; 8 g carbohydrate; 28 g protein; 2 g fiber; 392 mg sodium.

Nutrition Bonus: Vitamin C (24% daily value).

Healthy Weight

Lower Carbs

variation:

- **Make Stir-Fried Spicy Beef by using 1 pound of stir-fry beef or thinly sliced top round steak instead of chicken in this dish.**

A bag of frozen peppers and onions can be a quick start to a stir-fry; here, it's combined with almost fat-free chicken tenders for a speedy dinner. Serve this dish with warm polenta rounds or brown rice.

1 teaspoon sugar
1 teaspoon paprika
1/2 teaspoon salt
1/2 teaspoon freshly ground pepper
1/4 teaspoon cayenne pepper
1 pound boneless, skinless chicken breast tenders, cut into 2-inch pieces (*see Variation*)
1 tablespoon canola oil
1 16-ounce package frozen bell pepper and onion mix

1. Combine sugar, paprika, salt, pepper and cayenne in a medium bowl. Add chicken and toss to coat. Cover and refrigerate for 15 minutes or overnight.

2. Heat oil in a large nonstick skillet over high heat. Add pepper-and-onion mix and cook, stirring occasionally, until the vegetables are soft, 5 to 7 minutes. Add the spice-rubbed chicken and cook, stirring, until no longer pink in the center, 3 to 5 minutes. Serve hot.

Makes 4 servings, 1 cup each.

Honey-Mustard Chicken

The honey-mustard sauce in this dish is so delicious, we bet you'll soon be finding lots of ways to use it—as a barbecue glaze, as a topper for baked potatoes or as a dip for fresh, cut-up vegetables.

3 tablespoons balsamic vinegar
3 tablespoons honey
2 tablespoons Dijon mustard
2 tablespoons capers, rinsed
2 cloves garlic, minced
4 boneless, skinless chicken breasts (about 1 pound), trimmed of fat
1/4 teaspoon salt, or to taste
Freshly ground pepper to taste
2 teaspoons extra-virgin olive oil

1. Whisk vinegar, honey, mustard, capers and garlic in a small bowl.

2. Place chicken between sheets of plastic wrap. Pound with a meat mallet or heavy skillet until flattened to an even thickness, about 1/2 inch. Season chicken with salt and pepper.

3. Heat oil in a large nonstick skillet over medium-high heat. Add the chicken and cook until the underside is well browned, about 5 minutes. Turn the chicken over and cook for 2 minutes more. Add the honey-mustard mixture to the skillet (it will bubble up and begin to boil quickly). Partially cover the pan; cook until the chicken is no longer pink in the center and the juices run clear, 2 to 4 minutes. Transfer the chicken to a platter or individual plates, top with the pan sauce and serve.

Makes 4 servings.

Active Minutes: 30

Total: 35 minutes

Per Serving: 205 calories; 4 g fat (1 g sat, 2 g mono); 66 mg cholesterol; 16 g carbohydrate; 26 g protein; 0 g fiber; 448 mg sodium.

Nutrition Bonus: Niacin (65% daily value), Selenium (30% dv).

Healthy Weight

Lower Carbs

Thai Chicken Satay with Spicy Peanut Sauce

Satay is Southeast Asian street food—strips of spiced meat, threaded on skewers and sold at carts all over the region. Although it's served with all sorts of condiments, peanut sauce has become the Western favorite. And why not? It's spicy, sweet, salty and the perfect match to the chicken strips.

- **3 tablespoons lime juice**
- **3 tablespoons canola oil**
- **2 teaspoons reduced-sodium soy sauce**
- **2 teaspoons fish sauce (*see Note*)**
- **1/2 teaspoon crushed red pepper**
- **1 pound chicken tenders**
- **Spicy Peanut Sauce (*page 227*)**

1. **To marinate chicken:** Whisk lime juice, oil, soy sauce, fish sauce and crushed red pepper in a shallow baking dish until combined; add chicken and turn to coat. Let marinate in the refrigerator for 15 minutes.

2. Preheat grill to high.

3. **To grill chicken & serve:** Thread each chicken tender onto a wooden skewer. Grill the chicken skewers until cooked through and no longer pink in the middle, about 3 minutes per side. Serve warm or chilled, with Spicy Peanut Sauce for dipping.

Makes 4 servings.

Active Minutes: 30

Total: 35 minutes

To Make Ahead: The peanut sauce will keep, covered, in the refrigerator for up to 2 days.

Equipment: 12 wooden skewers (*see Tip, page 242*)

Per Serving: 184 calories; 8 g fat (2 g sat, 2 g mono); 49 mg cholesterol; 4 g carbohydrate; 20 g protein; 1 g fiber; 330 mg sodium.

Nutrition Bonus: Selenium (28% daily value).

Healthy Weight

Lower Carbs

ingredient note:

- **Fish sauce is a pungent Southeast Asian sauce made from salted, fermented fish. You can find it in the Asian section of large supermarkets and in Asian specialty markets.**

Buffalo Chicken Wrap

Moms and Dads like wraps because they're neat and compact—so beware: ours is messy and spicy. This fiery combination of buffalo chicken in a modern wrap is guaranteed to drip. Get out the big napkins and have a ball!

Active Minutes: 35

Total: 35 minutes

Per Serving: 275 calories; 8 g fat (2 g sat, 2 g mono); 55 mg cholesterol; 29 g carbohydrate; 24 g protein; 4 g fiber; 756 mg sodium.

Nutrition Bonus: Vitamin A (35% daily value), Selenium (28% dv), Vitamin C (20% dv).

Healthy Weight

- **2 tablespoons hot pepper sauce, such as Frank's RedHot**
- **3 tablespoons white vinegar, divided**
- **1/4 teaspoon cayenne pepper**
- **2 teaspoons extra-virgin olive oil**
- **1 pound chicken tenders**
- **2 tablespoons reduced-fat mayonnaise**
- **2 tablespoons nonfat plain yogurt**
- **Freshly ground pepper to taste**
- **1/4 cup crumbled blue cheese**
- **4 8-inch whole-wheat tortillas**
- **1 cup shredded romaine lettuce**
- **1 cup sliced celery**
- **1 large tomato, diced**

1. Whisk hot pepper sauce, 2 tablespoons vinegar and cayenne pepper in a medium bowl.

2. Heat oil in a large nonstick skillet over medium-high heat. Add chicken tenders; cook until cooked through and no longer pink in the middle, 3 to 4 minutes per side. Add to the bowl with the hot sauce; toss to coat well.

3. Whisk mayonnaise, yogurt, pepper and the remaining 1 tablespoon vinegar in a small bowl. Stir in blue cheese.

4. To assemble wraps: Lay a tortilla on a work surface or plate. Spread with 1 tablespoon blue cheese sauce and top with one-fourth of the chicken, lettuce, celery and tomato. Drizzle with some of the hot sauce remaining in the bowl and roll into a wrap sandwich. Repeat with the remaining tortillas.

Makes 4 servings.

Roasted Chicken Tenders with Peppers & Onions

Active Minutes: 20

Total: 45 minutes

Per Serving: 172 calories; 7 g fat (1 g sat, 5 g mono); 49 mg cholesterol; 6 g carbohydrate; 19 g protein; 1 g fiber; 518 mg sodium.

Nutrition Bonus: Vitamin C (100% daily value), Selenium (28% dv), Vitamin A (20% dv).

Healthy Weight

Lower Carbs

Call this one an update of that favorite combo, sausage and peppers. Our healthy version can be served over rice or on a roll with a little shredded cheese for a new take on a Philly cheese steak sandwich.

- **1/2 teaspoon freshly grated lemon zest**
- **3 tablespoons lemon juice**
- **2 tablespoons finely chopped garlic**
- **2 tablespoons finely chopped fresh oregano *or* 1 teaspoon dried**
- **2 tablespoons finely chopped pickled jalapeño peppers**
- **2 tablespoons extra-virgin olive oil**
- **1/2 teaspoon salt**
- **1 pound chicken tenders**
- **1 red, yellow *or* orange bell pepper, seeded and thinly sliced**
- **1/2 medium onion, thinly sliced**

1. Preheat oven to 425°F. Whisk lemon zest, lemon juice, garlic, oregano, jalapeños, oil and salt in a 9-by-13-inch glass baking dish. Add tenders, bell pepper and onion; toss to coat. Spread the mixture out evenly; cover with foil. Bake until the chicken is cooked through and no longer pink in the middle, 25 to 30 minutes.

Makes 4 servings.

Fennel & Chicken Flatbread

Here's an easy, new take on pizza: pita rounds that hold a fennel and chicken sauté and that are then baked until the cheesy topping melts. Although great warm, they're just like pizza: a fabulous lunch out of the fridge the next day.

Active Minutes: 25

Total: 35 minutes

Per Serving (6 1/2-inch pita): 447 calories; 13 g fat (6 g sat, 4 g mono); 51 mg cholesterol; 53 g carbohydrate; 30 g protein; 10 g fiber; 660 mg sodium.

Nutrition Bonus: Vitamin C (160% daily value), Vitamin A (35% dv), Calcium (25% dv).

High ↑ Fiber

2 teaspoons extra-virgin olive oil
1 bulb fennel, quartered, cored and thinly sliced, plus 1 tablespoon chopped feathery tops for garnish
1 red bell pepper, thinly sliced
8 ounces boneless, skinless chicken breast, very thinly sliced crosswise
4 6 1/2-inch whole-wheat pitas *or* eight 4-inch whole-wheat pitas
1 cup shredded provolone cheese
Freshly ground pepper to taste

1. Preheat oven to 500°F.

2. Heat oil in a large nonstick skillet over medium heat. Add sliced fennel and bell pepper and cook, stirring often, until the vegetables begin to soften, about 5 minutes. Add chicken and cook another 5 minutes, stirring often, until the vegetables are tender and the chicken is cooked through.

3. Place pitas on a baking sheet and top each with an equal portion of the chicken and vegetable mixture; sprinkle with cheese and pepper. Bake until the cheese melts and turns golden, 10 to 15 minutes. Sprinkle with chopped fennel tops and serve warm.

Makes 4 servings.

Tandoori Chicken with Tomato-Cucumber Raita

Active Minutes: 40

Total: 40 minutes

Per Serving: 209 calories; 7 g fat (2 g sat, 3 g mono); 66 mg cholesterol; 8 g carbohydrate; 27 g protein; 1 g fiber; 396 mg sodium.

Nutrition Bonus: Calcium (15% daily value), Vitamin A (15% dv), Vitamin C (15% dv).

Healthy Weight

Lower Carbs

Associated with India, tandoori cooking, a high-heat process, is actually a Middle Eastern invention, originally done in ceramic ovens, which have been unearthed at Babylonian archeological digs. In 1948, a fashionable, jet-setter restaurant in New Delhi installed a tandoori oven, the media picked up the story, and the craze went around the world so fast that tandoori cooking is now almost exclusively associated with India. Here, a hot grill produces similar results.

- **1 teaspoon paprika**
- **1 teaspoon ground coriander**
- **1/2 teaspoon chili powder**
- **1/4 teaspoon cumin**
- **1/4 teaspoon salt**
- **1/4 teaspoon freshly ground pepper**
- **Pinch of ground nutmeg**
- **4 boneless, skinless chicken breasts (about 1 pound), trimmed of fat**
- **1 tablespoon canola oil**
- **Tomato-Cucumber Raita (*page 227*)**

1. Preheat grill to medium-high.

2. Combine paprika, coriander, chili powder, cumin, salt, pepper and nutmeg in a large sealable plastic bag. Place each chicken breast between sheets of plastic wrap. Pound with a meat mallet or heavy skillet until flattened to an even thickness, about 1/4 inch. Brush the chicken with oil; place in the bag, seal and turn to coat.

3. Oil the grill rack (*see Cooking Tip, page 242*). Grill the chicken until cooked through and no longer pink in the middle, 3 to 4 minutes per side. Serve warm with Tomato-Cucumber Raita.

Makes 4 servings.

Grilled Duck Quesadillas with Cilantro Cream

Active Minutes: 40

Total: 40 minutes

To Make Ahead: Grill the duck (Step 2), cover and refrigerate for up to 1 day.

Per Serving: 238 calories; 9 g fat (4 g sat, 3 g mono); 77 mg cholesterol; 23 g carbohydrate; 22 g protein; 2 g fiber; 587 mg sodium.

Nutrition Bonus: Selenium (23% daily value), Calcium (20% dv), Iron (15% dv).

Healthy Weight

Duck's gotten the unfortunate reputation of being both hard to cook and far too fatty. But duck breasts, with the skin removed, make a sophisticated, quick dinner, perfect for when company drops by. Still, you can substitute chicken breasts here, if you like. Serve these creamy quesadillas with a pitcher of Sangria or a fruit punch.

12 ounces boneless duck breast, skin removed
1 teaspoon extra-virgin olive oil
1/2 teaspoon kosher salt
1/4 teaspoon freshly ground pepper
1/4 cup chopped fresh cilantro
1/4 cup low-fat plain yogurt
3 tablespoons reduced-fat sour cream
4 10-inch whole-wheat tortillas
2 scallions, sliced
3/4 cup shredded reduced-fat pepper Jack cheese
4 lime wedges

1. Preheat grill to medium.

2. Rub duck breast with oil and sprinkle with salt and pepper. Grill, turning every 3 minutes, until an instant-read thermometer inserted into the center of the breast reads 145°F, about 12 minutes total. Allow to rest at least 5 minutes before slicing very thinly crosswise.

3. Meanwhile, mix cilantro, yogurt and sour cream in a small bowl until combined.

4. Cover one half of each tortilla with sliced duck, scallions and cheese. Fold the tortillas in half and carefully transfer them to the grill. Grill until the quesadillas are crispy and golden and the cheese is just melted, 1 1/2 to 3 minutes per side. Slice each quesadilla into 4 wedges and serve with the cilantro cream and lime wedges.

Makes 4 servings.

Thai Green Curry with Duck

Thai green curry paste is a quick trick for turning a simple dish into an exotic concoction. Go easy on the spice mixture at first—it's kickin' hot. Once you get the hang of it, you can adjust it to your taste. Enjoy this saucy curry with brown basmati rice.

12 ounces boneless duck breast, skin removed
2 teaspoons canola oil
1 pound eggplant, diced
2 red bell peppers, cut into 1-inch pieces
1 cup "lite" coconut milk
1 cup reduced-sodium chicken broth
2 tablespoons brown sugar
1 tablespoon green curry paste (*see Note*)
1 tablespoon fish sauce (*see Note, page 243*), optional
1 tablespoon lime juice
1/2 cup sliced fresh basil

1. Cut duck breast crosswise into 1/4-inch-thick strips. Heat oil in a Dutch oven or large straight-sided skillet over high heat until shimmering but not smoking. Cook the duck, in a single layer, stirring once, until beginning to brown, 1 to 3 minutes. Transfer to a plate.

2. Add eggplant, bell peppers, coconut milk, broth, brown sugar, curry paste, fish sauce (if using) and lime juice to the pan. Bring to a boil, stirring. Reduce heat to a simmer, cover and cook, stirring occasionally, until the vegetables are tender, 8 to 10 minutes.

3. Return the duck to the pan; stir to coat with sauce and cook until heated through, about 1 minute. Remove from heat; stir in basil and serve immediately.

Makes 4 servings, 1 1/2 cups each.

Active Minutes: 35

Total: 35 minutes

Per Serving: 273 calories; 9 g fat (4 g sat, 2 g mono); 103 mg cholesterol; 26 g carbohydrate; 24 g protein; 7 g fiber; 200 mg sodium.

Nutrition Bonus: Vitamin C (480% daily value), Vitamin A (100% dv), Iron (25% dv), Potassium (19% dv).

Healthy Weight

High Fiber

ingredient note:

Green curry paste, a fiery and moist mixture of green chiles and Thai seasonings, such as lemongrass and galangal, is available in the Asian section of large supermarkets. Red curry paste can be substituted.

Turkey & Balsamic Onion Quesadillas

Active Minutes: 15

Total: 20 minutes

Per Serving: 261 calories; 10 g fat (5 g sat, 0 g mono); 56 mg cholesterol; 25 g carbohydrate; 23 g protein; 2 g fiber; 702 mg sodium.

Nutrition Bonus: Calcium (22% daily value), Magnesium (12% dv).

Healthy ⟩⟨ Weight

Soaking onions in balsamic vinegar brings out their sweetness. Just don't use an expensive aged balsamic for this quick treat. To make these easy tortilla sandwiches into a meal, serve them with simple sautéed vegetables or a tossed green salad.

- **1 small red onion, thinly sliced**
- **1/4 cup balsamic vinegar**
- **4 10-inch whole-wheat tortillas**
- **1 cup shredded sharp Cheddar cheese**
- **8 slices deli turkey, preferably smoked (8 ounces)**

1. Combine onion and vinegar in a bowl; let marinate for 5 minutes. Drain, reserving the vinegar for another use, such as salad dressing.

2. Place 2 tortillas in a large nonstick skillet over medium-high heat (they will overlap); warm for about 45 seconds, then flip. Pull the tortillas up the edges of the pan so they are no longer overlapping. Working on one half of each tortilla, sprinkle one-fourth of the cheese, cover with 2 slices of turkey and top with one-fourth of the onion. Fold the tortillas in half, press gently with a spatula to flatten and cook until the cheese starts to melt, about 2 minutes. Flip and continue cooking until the second side is golden, 1 to 2 minutes more. Transfer to a plate and cover with foil to keep warm. Make two more quesadillas with the remaining ingredients. Serve warm.

Makes 4 servings.

Turkey Cutlets with Peas & Spring Onions

Peas and baby onions are harbingers of spring, the first sign that warm weather's on its way. With turkey cutlets and a simple white wine sauce, they pair up in this flavorful dish that calls out for mashed roots or steamed asparagus on the side.

Active Minutes: 30

Total: 30 minutes

Per Serving: 302 calories; 8 g fat (1 g sat, 5 g mono); 46 mg cholesterol; 19 g carbohydrate; 34 g protein; 3 g fiber; 471 mg sodium.

Nutrition Bonus: Iron (20% daily value), Vitamin A (20% dv), Vitamin C (20% dv), Folate (14% dv).

Healthy Weight

Lower Carbs

- **1/2 cup all-purpose flour**
- **1/2 teaspoon salt, divided**
- **1/4 teaspoon freshly ground pepper**
- **1 pound 1/4-inch-thick turkey breast cutlets *or* steaks**
- **2 tablespoons extra-virgin olive oil, divided**
- **4 ounces shiitake mushrooms, stemmed and sliced (about 1 1/2 cups)**
- **1 bunch spring onions *or* scallions, sliced, whites and greens separated**
- **1 cup reduced-sodium chicken broth**
- **1/2 cup dry white wine**
- **1 cup peas, fresh *or* frozen, thawed**
- **1 teaspoon freshly grated lemon zest**

1. Whisk flour, 1/4 teaspoon salt and pepper in a shallow dish. Dredge each turkey cutlet (or steak) in the flour mixture. Heat 1 tablespoon oil in a large nonstick skillet over medium-high heat. Add the turkey and cook until lightly golden, 2 to 3 minutes per side. Transfer to a plate; cover with foil to keep warm.

2. Add the remaining 1 tablespoon oil to the pan and heat over medium-high heat. Add mushrooms and onion (or scallion) whites and cook, stirring often, until the mushrooms are browned and the whites are slightly softened, 2 to 3 minutes. Add broth, wine and the remaining 1/4 teaspoon salt; cook, stirring occasionally, until the sauce is slightly reduced, 2 to 3 minutes. Stir in peas and onion (or scallion) greens and cook, stirring, until heated through, about 1 minute. Stir in lemon zest. Nestle the turkey into the vegetables along with any accumulated juices from the plate. Cook, turning the cutlets once, until heated through, 1 to 2 minutes.

Makes 4 servings.

Rigatoni with Turkey Sausage, Cheese & Pepper

Active Minutes: 25

Total: 25 minutes

Per Serving: 356 calories; 12 g fat (5 g sat, 3 g mono); 34 mg cholesterol; 44 g carbohydrate; 19 g protein; 5 g fiber; 506 mg sodium.

Nutrition Bonus: Calcium (20% daily value), Fiber (20% dv).

High Fiber

This supper is a study in simplicity. A little pasta, some cheese and a dash of pepper—suddenly, it's just right for after a date at the movies. For more substantial fare, throw in some broccoli rabe, broccolini or stemmed and chopped chard.

12 ounces whole-wheat rigatoni *or* penne
6 ounces sweet Italian-style turkey sausage, casings removed
1/2 cup freshly grated Pecorino Romano *or* Parmesan cheese, divided
2 teaspoons coarsely ground black pepper
1 tablespoon extra-virgin olive oil

1. Bring a large pot of water to a boil. Cook pasta until just tender, 9 to 11 minutes, or according to package directions.

2. Meanwhile, cook sausage in a nonstick skillet over medium-low heat, breaking it into small chunks, until cooked through but not crisp, about 6 minutes. Blot with a paper towel.

3. Combine 1/4 cup cheese and pepper in a large pasta bowl. Measure out 1/2 cup of the cooking liquid; drain the pasta. Add to the bowl along with the sausage, the reserved cooking water and oil; toss well. Serve immediately, sprinkled with the remaining 1/4 cup cheese.

Makes 6 servings, generous 1 cup each.

Turkey Tetrazzini

We've taken the fuss and the excess fat out of this one-time favorite, a retro supper that still can please a family. Rather than a stuffy casserole, we're revamped it into a quick sauté with a creamy pan-gravy that's sure to be a comforting, cold-weather warmer. Soak up the sauce with whole-wheat egg noodles.

2 tablespoons extra-virgin olive oil, divided
1 pound 1/4-inch-thick turkey breast cutlets
8 ounces sliced mushrooms (about 2 1/2 cups)
3 tablespoons all-purpose flour
1 cup reduced-sodium chicken broth
1/4 cup dry sherry (*see Note*)
1 cup low-fat milk
2/3 cup frozen peas, thawed
1/2 cup chopped jarred roasted red peppers
1/4 cup shredded Parmesan cheese
Freshly ground pepper to taste

1. Heat 1 tablespoon oil in a large nonstick skillet over medium-high heat. Add turkey and cook until lightly golden, 2 to 3 minutes per side. Transfer to a plate, cover and keep warm.

2. Heat the remaining 1 tablespoon oil in the pan. Add mushrooms and cook, stirring often, until browned, 4 to 6 minutes. Sprinkle with flour; stir to coat. Stir in broth and sherry; bring to a simmer. Continue simmering, stirring constantly, until the mixture is slightly reduced, 1 to 2 minutes. Add milk, peas and peppers; return to a simmer, stirring often. Cook until thick and slightly reduced, about 2 minutes. Stir in Parmesan and pepper. Return the turkey and any accumulated juices to the pan, turn to coat with sauce and cook until heated through, 1 to 2 minutes.

Makes 4 servings.

Active Minutes: 35

Total: 35 minutes

Per Serving: 340 calories; 11 g fat (3 g sat, 6 g mono); 56 mg cholesterol; 17 g carbohydrate; 38 g protein; 2 g fiber; 529 mg sodium.

Nutrition Bonus: Vitamin A (20% daily value), Calcium (15% dv), Iron (15% dv).

Healthy Weight

Lower Carbs

ingredient note:

Don't use the "cooking sherry" sold in many supermarkets—it can be surprisingly high in sodium. Instead, purchase dry sherry that's sold with other fortified wines in your wine or liquor store.

Turkey with Blueberry Pan Sauce

Active Minutes: 35

Total: 40 minutes

Per Serving: 215 calories; 5 g fat (1 g sat, 3 g mono); 45 mg cholesterol; 16 g carbohydrate; 29 g protein; 2 g fiber; 288 mg sodium.

Nutrition Bonus: Vitamin C (15% daily value).

Healthy Weight

Lower Carbs

ingredient note:

- **A turkey tenderloin is an all-white piece that comes from the rib side of the breast. Tenderloins typically weigh between 7 and 14 ounces each and can be found with other turkey products in the meat section of most supermarkets.**

Blueberries have just the right mix of acid and pectin so that they're terrific in both sweet and savory dishes. They work especially well with thyme—and so this easy turkey sauté can be a delight whenever the berries are in season. To make this dish into a meal, dress some quick-cooking barley with lemon and pepper and offer steamed green beans on the side.

1/4 cup all-purpose flour
3/4 teaspoon salt, divided
1/2 teaspoon freshly ground pepper
1 pound turkey tenderloin (*see Note*)
1 tablespoon extra-virgin olive oil
1/4 cup chopped shallots
1 tablespoon chopped fresh thyme
2 cups blueberries
3 tablespoons balsamic vinegar

1. Preheat oven to 450°F. Whisk flour, 1/2 teaspoon salt and pepper in a shallow dish. Dredge turkey in the mixture. (Discard any leftover flour.)

2. Heat oil in a large ovenproof skillet over high heat. Add the turkey; cook until golden brown on one side, 3 to 5 minutes. Turn the turkey over and transfer the pan to the oven. Roast until the turkey is just cooked through and no longer pink in the middle, 15 to 20 minutes. Transfer the turkey to a plate and tent with foil to keep warm.

3. Place the skillet over medium heat. (Take care, the handle will still be very hot.) Add shallots and thyme and cook, stirring constantly, until the shallots begin to brown, 30 seconds to 1 minute. Add blueberries, vinegar and the remaining 1/4 teaspoon salt; continue cooking, stirring occasionally and scraping up any brown bits, until the blueberries burst and release their juices and the mixture becomes thick and syrupy, 4 to 5 minutes. Slice the turkey and serve with the blueberry pan sauce.

Makes 4 servings.

Turkey with Cherries & Port

A combination of dried cherries and rosemary give this sauté character. You can substitute red wine for the port, but increase the pepper to give the dish a little more bite.

Active Minutes: 35

Total: 35 minutes

Per Serving: 378 calories; 6 g fat (1 g sat, 4 g mono); 48 mg cholesterol; 32 g carbohydrate; 31 g protein; 2 g fiber; 275 mg sodium.

Nutrition Bonus: Niacin (40% daily value), Selenium (40% dv).

- **1 cup ruby port *or* cherry juice**
- **1/2 cup dried cherries**
- **1 pound 1/4-inch-thick turkey breast cutlets**
- **1/4 teaspoon salt**
- **1/4 teaspoon freshly ground pepper**
- **1/3 cup all-purpose flour**
- **4 teaspoons extra-virgin olive oil, divided**
- **1 teaspoon unsalted butter**
- **1/3 cup chopped red onion**
- **1 tablespoon minced fresh rosemary**
- **1/2 cup reduced-sodium chicken broth**
- **1 tablespoon cornstarch**
- **1/4 cup balsamic vinegar**

1. Combine port (or cherry juice) and dried cherries in a small saucepan. Bring to a boil, reduce heat to low and simmer gently for 5 minutes. Cover and set aside.

2. Season cutlets on both sides with salt and pepper. Place flour on a large plate and dredge the cutlets, shaking off excess flour.

3. Heat 2 teaspoons oil in a large nonstick skillet over medium heat. Add half the cutlets and cook until golden brown and just cooked through, 2 to 3 minutes per side. Transfer to a platter, cover and keep warm. Add the remaining 2 teaspoons oil to the pan and cook the remaining cutlets. Transfer to the platter and cover.

4. Heat butter in the skillet over medium heat. Add onion and rosemary and cook, stirring often, until the onion is tender, 3 to 4 minutes. Whisk broth and cornstarch in a small bowl until smooth; stir into the pan along with the reserved cherry mixture and vinegar. Reduce heat to low, return the turkey and any juices to the pan and cook, turning to coat, until heated through, 1 to 2 minutes. Serve with the cherry sauce.

Makes 4 servings.

Turkey Mini Meatloaves

While turkey can too often lend a depressingly gummy texture to meatloaf, we've improved on the standard by adding couscous, zucchini and lots of spices. The best thing of all? They cook in half the time of a full-size meatloaf and you can have left-overs for a sandwich the next day on toasted whole-grain bread.

Active Minutes: 20

Total: 45 minutes

Per Serving: 196 calories; 6 g fat (2 g sat, 0 g mono); 79 mg cholesterol; 18 g carbohydrate; 19 g protein; 3 g fiber; 368 mg sodium.

Nutrition Bonus: Vitamin C (90% daily value), Selenium (24% dv), Vitamin A (20% dv).

Healthy Weight

Lower Carbs

- **1 pound 93%-lean ground turkey**
- **1 medium zucchini, shredded**
- **1 cup finely chopped onion**
- **1 cup finely chopped red bell pepper**
- **1/3 cup uncooked whole-wheat couscous**
- **1 large egg, lightly beaten**
- **2 tablespoons Worcestershire sauce**
- **1 tablespoon Dijon mustard**
- **1/2 teaspoon freshly ground pepper**
- **1/4 teaspoon salt**
- **1/4 cup barbecue sauce (optional)**

1. Preheat oven to 400°F. Generously spray a nonstick muffin pan with cooking spray.

2. Gently mix turkey, zucchini, onion, bell pepper, couscous, egg, Worcestershire, mustard, pepper and salt in a large bowl, preferably with your hands, without overworking. Equally divide the mixture among the muffin cups. Spread barbecue sauce on top of each loaf, if using.

3. Bake until the meatloaves are cooked through or an instant-read thermometer inserted into the center registers 165°F, about 25 minutes. Let the loaves stand in the pan for 5 minutes before serving.

Makes 6 servings, 2 loaves each.

Chapter 5: Fish & Seafood

Cajun Pecan-Crusted Catfish

Crunchy, battered catfish fillets have jumped out of the Louisiana backwaters to become a national favorite, thanks in large part to the Cajun cooking craze that started in the '80s. Here, the fillets are coated in a spicy melange of cornflakes and pecans and baked for a traditional yet surprisingly healthy take on this bayou favorite.

Active Minutes: 15

Total: 40 minutes

Per Serving: 307 calories; 18 g fat (3 g sat, 9 g mono); 54 mg cholesterol; 15 g carbohydrate; 21 g protein; 2 g fiber; 171 mg sodium.

Nutrition Bonus: Selenium (21% daily value).

Healthy Weight

Lower Carbs

1/2 cup nonfat buttermilk
1/4 teaspoon hot sauce, such as Tabasco, *or* 1/8 teaspoon cayenne pepper, *or* to taste
1/2 teaspoon dried oregano
1/2 teaspoon chili powder
1/4 teaspoon garlic salt
2 cups cornflakes
1/2 cup pecan pieces
1 pound catfish fillets, about 1 inch thick, cut into 4 portions

1. Preheat oven to 375°F. Line a baking sheet with foil.

2. Blend buttermilk, hot sauce (or cayenne), oregano, chili powder and garlic salt in a shallow dish. Pulse cornflakes in a food processor until coarse crumbs form. Transfer to a large plate. Pulse pecans in the food processor until coarsely chopped; mix the pecans with the cornflake crumbs. (*Alternatively, place cornflakes in a sealable bag and crush with a rolling pin; chop nuts with a knife.*)

3. Dip each catfish fillet in the buttermilk mixture, then dredge in the cornflake mixture, coating both sides. Transfer to the prepared baking sheet.

4. Bake the catfish for 25 minutes, or until it flakes easily with a fork. Serve immediately.

Makes 4 servings.

Roasted Cod with Warm Tomato-Olive-Caper Tapenade

A tapenade is perhaps the easiest way to perk up roasted fish fillets. Here, the forthright flavors of this quick-cook tapenade, reminiscent of the Mediterranean, match well with cod, the pride of the Atlantic. You could also serve this simple condiment with grilled chicken or pork.

Active Minutes: 20

Total: 25 minutes

Per Serving: 168 calories; 8 g fat (1 g sat, 6 g mono); 43 mg cholesterol; 4 g carbohydrate; 19 g protein; 1 g fiber; 373 mg sodium.

Nutrition Bonus: Selenium (42% daily value), Vitamin C (15% dv).

Healthy Weight

Lower Carbs

- **1 pound cod fillet**
- **3 teaspoons extra-virgin olive oil, divided**
- **1/4 teaspoon freshly ground pepper**
- **1 tablespoon minced shallot**
- **1 cup halved cherry tomatoes**
- **1/4 cup chopped cured olives**
- **1 tablespoon capers, rinsed and chopped**
- **1 1/2 teaspoons chopped fresh oregano**
- **1 teaspoon balsamic vinegar**

1. Preheat oven to 450°F. Coat a baking sheet with cooking spray.

2. Rub cod with 2 teaspoons oil. Sprinkle with pepper. Place on the prepared baking sheet. Transfer to the oven and roast until the fish flakes easily with a fork, 15 to 20 minutes, depending on the thickness of the fillet.

3. Meanwhile, heat the remaining 1 teaspoon oil in a small skillet over medium heat. Add shallot and cook, stirring, until beginning to soften, about 20 seconds. Add tomatoes and cook, stirring, until softened, about 1 1/2 minutes. Add olives and capers; cook, stirring, for 30 seconds more. Stir in oregano and vinegar; remove from heat. Spoon the sauce over the cod to serve.

Makes 4 servings.

Cod with Grapefruit

Cod is a rich fish, so this citrus dressing enlivens the flavor yet mellows the taste a bit. While this recipe calls for relatively inexpensive white grapefruit, sweeter pink ones work too.

Active Minutes: 30

Total: 35 minutes

To Make Ahead: The dressing (Step 1) will keep, covered, in the refrigerator for up to 2 days. Bring to room temperature before using.

Per Serving: 449 calories; 31 g fat (4 g sat, 24 g mono); 57 mg cholesterol; 14 g carbohydrate; 26 g protein; 3 g fiber; 397 mg sodium.

Nutrition Bonus: Vitamin C (80% daily value), Selenium (57% dv), Vitamin A (50% dv), Potassium (18% dv).

Lower Carbs

variation:

- **Pink grapefruit will result in a slightly sweeter and more subtle dish. You can also substitute oranges, but the resulting taste will be even less bold.**

2 white grapefruit (*see Variation*), scrubbed
1/2 cup plus 2 teaspoons mild extra-virgin olive, grapeseed *or* canola oil, divided
1/4 teaspoon salt, or to taste
Freshly ground pepper to taste
1 1/3 pounds cod *or* other firm white fish, cut into 4 portions
1/4 teaspoon salt, or to taste
Freshly ground pepper to taste
2 tablespoons finely chopped shallot
1/4 cup dry white wine
2 tablespoons reduced-sodium chicken broth *or* water
6 cups mixed salad greens
3 tablespoons chopped fresh chives for garnish

1. Cut long strips of zest from one grapefruit. Blanch the zest in boiling water for 30 seconds. Pat dry. Segment both grapefruit (*see Tip, page 242*); cut the segments in half. Place one-fourth of them in a food processor or blender. Add the blanched zest and 1/2 cup oil; process until very smooth and thick, about 2 minutes. Stir in salt and pepper.

2. Season fish on both sides with salt and pepper. Heat the remaining 2 teaspoons oil in a large nonstick skillet over medium-high heat. Add the fish and cook until golden, about 2 minutes per side. Place shallots and half the remaining grapefruit around the fish, then add wine and broth (or water). Cover, reduce heat to low and cook until the fish is opaque and flakes easily with a fork, 2 to 3 minutes. Keep warm.

3. Put greens in a large bowl. Add 2 tablespoons of the reserved dressing and toss gently. Divide the greens and remaining grapefruit among 4 plates. Top with a piece of fish, spooning some of the cooking liquid over the greens. Drizzle about 2 tablespoons of the dressing over each serving. Garnish with chives.

Makes 4 servings.

Mustard-Crusted Salmon

Active Minutes: 10

Total: 20 minutes

Per Serving: 290 calories; 18 g fat (4 g sat, 6 g mono); 89 mg cholesterol; 2 g carbohydrate; 29 g protein; 0 g fiber; 389 mg sodium.

Nutrition Bonus: Selenium (74% daily value), Potassium (26% dv), omega-3s.

Healthy Weight

Lower Carbs

This updated French bistro dish makes a simple dinner any night of the week. You might want to consider doubling the batch and using the remaining salmon in a tossed salad the next day, or even as the salmon topper in the Warm Salmon Salad with Crispy Potatoes (*page 32*).

- **1 1/4 pounds center-cut salmon fillets, cut into 4 portions**
- **1/4 teaspoon salt, or to taste**
- **Freshly ground pepper to taste**
- **1/4 cup reduced-fat sour cream**
- **2 tablespoons stone-ground mustard**
- **2 teaspoons lemon juice**
- **Lemon wedges**

1. Preheat broiler. Line a broiler pan or baking sheet with foil, then coat it with cooking spray.

2. Place salmon pieces, skin-side down, on the prepared pan. Season with salt and pepper. Combine sour cream, mustard and lemon juice in a small bowl. Spread evenly over the salmon.

3. Broil the salmon 5 inches from the heat source until it is opaque in the center, 10 to 12 minutes. Serve with lemon wedges.

Makes 4 servings.

Pan-Seared Salmon with Fennel & Dill Salsa

Crunchy fennel gives great texture to this tomato-based salsa, which is itself a zippy, slightly sour complement to sweet, seared salmon. Make this dish a meal by serving it with some whole-wheat couscous and a glass of rosé.

- **1 large tomato, chopped**
- **1 cup finely chopped fennel (about 1/2 bulb, stalks trimmed)**
- **2 tablespoons minced red onion**
- **2 tablespoons minced dill**
- **1 tablespoon red-wine vinegar**
- **1/2 teaspoon salt, divided**
- **1 pound salmon fillet, skinned (*see Tip*)**
- **Freshly ground pepper to taste**
- **2 tablespoons extra-virgin olive oil**

1. Combine tomato, fennel, onion, dill, vinegar and 1/4 teaspoon salt in a medium bowl.

2. Cut salmon into 4 equal portions, sprinkle with the remaining 1/4 teaspoon salt and pepper. Heat oil in a large nonstick pan over high heat until shimmering but not smoking. Cook the salmon, skinned-side up, until golden brown, 3 to 5 minutes. Turn the salmon over and remove the pan from the heat. Allow the salmon to finish cooking off the heat until just cooked through, 3 to 5 minutes more. Serve immediately with the salsa.

Makes 4 servings.

Active Minutes: 30

Total: 30 minutes

Per Serving: 289 calories; 20 g fat (3 g sat, 10 g mono); 67 mg cholesterol; 4 g carbohydrate; 23 g protein; 1 g fiber; 373 mg sodium.

Nutrition Bonus: Selenium (60% daily value), Vitamin C (32% dv), omega-3s.

Healthy Weight

Lower Carbs

to skin a salmon fillet:

- **Place it on a clean cutting board, skin-side down. Starting at the tail end, slip the blade of a long, sharp knife between the fish flesh and the skin, holding the skin down firmly with your other hand. Gently push the blade along at a 30° angle, separating the fillet from the skin without cutting through either. Or have your fishmonger do it for you.**

Midori Salmon

Miso sauces have recently moved out of Japan and into the global culinary landscape—and why not? Here, the fermented bean paste, familiar as a soup base, becomes a sweet, delicious glaze, turning a simple roast salmon into an international sensation.

Active Minutes: 10

Total: 25 minutes

To Make Ahead: Prepare through Step 1, cover and refrigerate for up to 2 days.

Per Serving: 211 calories; 10 g fat (2 g sat, 4 g mono); 82 mg cholesterol; 8 g carbohydrate; 18 g protein; 0 g fiber; 465 mg sodium.

Nutrition Bonus: Selenium (47% daily value), omega-3s.

Healthy Weight

Lower Carbs

1/3 cup white miso (*see Ingredient Note, page 243*)
1 large egg yolk
1 tablespoon sugar
1 tablespoon sake (*see Ingredient Note, page 244*)
1 tablespoon mirin
1 teaspoon matcha (*see Note*), optional
3 tablespoons water
1 1/2 pounds salmon fillet (about 1 inch thick), cut into 6 portions
Lemon wedges

1. Place miso in a small double boiler. Whisk in egg yolk, sugar, sake, mirin and matcha, if using, until smooth. Cook over simmering water, whisking, until the mixture begins to thicken, about 2 minutes. Gradually whisk in water and continue whisking until the sauce is thick enough to coat the back of a spoon, about 4 minutes. Scrape into a bowl and set aside.

2. Preheat broiler. Line a baking sheet with foil and coat with cooking spray.

3. Arrange salmon, skin-side down, on the prepared baking sheet. Dip your fingers into cold water and lightly moisten the top of the fish. Broil the salmon 4 to 6 inches from the heat source until just cooked through, 6 to 8 minutes, depending on the thickness of the fish.

4. Remove the salmon from the broiler. Put 1 tablespoon of the miso sauce over each portion, spreading evenly. Return the salmon to the broiler and continue cooking, shifting the baking sheet as necessary, until the salmon is cooked through and the topping is lightly browned, about 1 minute. Serve with lemon wedges.

Makes 6 servings.

ingredient note:

- **Matcha is an emerald-green powder made by grinding the older, carefully protected leaves of a Japanese tea plantation's oldest bushes. Some online sources are www.uptontea.com and www.edenfoods.com.**

Wasabi Salmon Burgers

Bring out the flavors of salmon with a Japanese-inspired infusion of ginger, sesame oil and wasabi. If you serve these patties on whole-wheat buns, consider reduced-fat mayonnaise and sliced cucumbers as condiments. Or skip the buns and set the patties atop a vinegary salad of greens, carrots, radishes and sprouts.

Active Minutes: 30

Total: 30 minutes

Per Serving: 184 calories; 7 g fat (1 g sat, 2 g mono); 117 mg cholesterol; 3 g carbohydrate; 27 g protein; 0 g fiber; 369 mg sodium.

Nutrition Bonus: Selenium (84% daily value), omega-3s.

Healthy Weight

Lower Carbs

2 tablespoons reduced-sodium soy sauce
1 1/2 teaspoons wasabi powder (*see Note*)
1/2 teaspoon honey
1 pound salmon fillet, skinned (*see Tip, page 157*)
2 scallions, finely chopped
1 egg, lightly beaten
2 tablespoons minced peeled fresh ginger
1 teaspoon toasted sesame oil

1. Whisk soy sauce, wasabi powder and honey in a small bowl until smooth. Set aside.

2. With a large chef's knife, chop salmon using quick, even, straight-up-and-down motions (do not rock the knife through the fish or it will turn mushy). Continue chopping, rotating the knife, until you have a mass of roughly 1/4-inch pieces. Transfer to a large bowl. Add scallions, egg, ginger and oil; stir to combine. Form the mixture into 4 patties. The mixture will be moist and loose, but holds together nicely once the first side is cooked.

3. Coat a large nonstick skillet with cooking spray and heat over medium heat for 1 minute. Add the patties and cook for 4 minutes. Turn and continue to cook until firm and fragrant, about 3 minutes. Spoon the reserved wasabi glaze evenly over the burgers and cook for 15 seconds more. Serve immediately.

Makes 4 servings.

ingredient note:

- **Wasabi powder, when mixed with water, becomes the green paste most of us know from sushi restaurants. The powder is available in jars in the Asian aisle of most supermarkets or in almost all Asian markets. Store at room temperature for up to 1 year.**

Pacific Sole with Oranges & Pecans

Active Minutes: 20

Total: 20 minutes

Per Serving: 234 calories; 9 g fat (3 g sat, 3 g mono); 70 mg cholesterol; 11 g carbohydrate; 28 g protein; 2 g fiber; 401 mg sodium.

Nutrition Bonus: Vitamin C (70% daily value); Calcium (20% dv).

Healthy Weight

Lower Carbs

ingredient note:

- **The term "sole" is widely used for many types of flatfish from both the Atlantic and Pacific. Flounder and Atlantic halibut are included in the group that is often identified as sole or grey sole. The best choices are Pacific, Dover or English sole. Other sole and flounder are overfished.**

Not so long ago, Dover sole meant an overcooked fillet swimming in butter, dotted with tasteless dried herbs and soaked in too much lemon juice. But sole deserves a comeback: it can become a satisfying, sophisticated, one-skillet dinner with very little effort. The recipe can easily be doubled.

- **1 orange**
- **10 ounces Pacific sole (*see Note*) *or* tilapia fillets**
- **1/4 teaspoon salt**
- **1/4 teaspoon freshly ground pepper**
- **2 teaspoons unsalted butter**
- **1 medium shallot, minced**
- **2 tablespoons white-wine vinegar**
- **2 tablespoons chopped pecans, toasted (*see Cooking Tip, page 242*)**
- **2 tablespoons chopped fresh dill**

1. Using a sharp paring knife, remove the skin and white pith from orange. Hold the fruit over a medium bowl and cut between the membranes to release individual orange sections into the bowl, collecting any juice as well. Discard membranes, pith and skin.

2. Sprinkle both sides of fillets with salt and pepper. Coat a large nonstick skillet with cooking spray and place over medium heat. Add the fillets and cook 1 minute for sole or 3 minutes for tilapia. Gently flip and cook until the fish is opaque in the center and just cooked through, 1 to 2 minutes for sole or 3 to 5 minutes for tilapia. Divide between 2 serving plates; tent with foil to keep warm.

3. Add butter to the pan and melt over medium heat. Add shallot and cook, stirring, until soft, about 30 seconds. Add vinegar and the orange sections and juice; loosen any browned bits on the bottom of the pan and cook for 30 seconds. Spoon the sauce over the fish and sprinkle each portion with pecans and dill. Serve immediately.

Makes 2 servings.

Beer-Battered Tilapia with Mango Salsa

Lovers of fried fish get the taste without all the calories in this recipe. Seasoned whole-wheat flour improves the usual fish-and-chips batter. A good pilsner or lager makes this dish taste best—and since you only need 1/2 cup, there's some left over for the cook to enjoy.

Active Minutes: 20

Total: 35 minutes

Per Serving: 242 calories; 7 g fat (1 g sat, 4 g mono); 48 mg cholesterol; 21 g carbohydrate; 23 g protein; 2 g fiber; 234 mg sodium.

Nutrition Bonus: Selenium (77% daily value), Vitamin C (35% dv), Calcium (13% dv).

Healthy Weight

Lower Carbs

- **3 tablespoons whole-wheat flour**
- **2 tablespoons all-purpose flour**
- **1/4 teaspoon ground cumin**
- **1/4 teaspoon salt, or to taste**
- **1/8-1/4 teaspoon cayenne pepper**
- **1/2 cup beer**
- **1 pound tilapia fillets (about 3), cut in half lengthwise**
- **4 teaspoons canola oil, divided**
- **Mango Salsa (*page 226*)**

1. Combine whole-wheat flour, all-purpose flour, cumin, salt and cayenne in a medium bowl. Whisk in beer to create a batter.

2. Coat half the tilapia pieces in the batter. Heat 2 teaspoons oil in a large nonstick skillet over medium-high heat. Letting excess batter drip back into the bowl, add the fish to the pan; cook until crispy and golden, 2 to 4 minutes per side. Transfer to a plate and loosely cover with foil. Coat the remaining fish with batter and cook in the remaining 2 teaspoons oil; adjust heat as necessary for even browning. Serve immediately with Mango Salsa.

Makes 4 servings.

Chili-Rubbed Tilapia with Asparagus & Lemon

Tilapia, a relatively plentiful fish, has the unfortunate reputation of being dull. All it needs is a spice rub, a familiar barbecuing technique that works just as well indoors. You could also use this rub on chicken breasts or toss it with lightly oiled shrimp before cooking.

Active Minutes: 20

Total: 20 minutes

Per Serving: 210 calories; 10 g fat (1 g sat, 6 g mono); 48 mg cholesterol; 8 g carbohydrate; 24 g protein; 4 g fiber; 418 mg sodium.

Nutrition Bonus: Vitamin C (37% daily value), Folate (33% dv), Iron (33% dv), Fiber (24% dv).

Healthy Weight

Lower Carbs

- **2 pounds asparagus, tough ends trimmed, cut into 1-inch pieces**
- **2 tablespoons chili powder**
- **1/2 teaspoon garlic powder**
- **1/2 teaspoon salt, divided**
- **1 pound tilapia, Pacific sole *or* other firm white fish fillets**
- **2 tablespoons extra-virgin olive oil**
- **3 tablespoons lemon juice**

1. Bring 1 inch of water to a boil in a large saucepan. Put asparagus in a steamer basket, place in the pan, cover and steam until tender-crisp, about 4 minutes. Transfer to a large plate, spreading out to cool.

2. Combine chili powder, garlic powder and 1/4 teaspoon salt on a plate. Dredge fillets in the spice mixture to coat. Heat oil in a large nonstick skillet over medium-high heat. Add the fish and cook until just opaque in the center, gently turning halfway, 5 to 7 minutes total. Divide among 4 plates. Immediately add lemon juice, the remaining 1/4 teaspoon salt and asparagus to the pan and cook, stirring constantly, until the asparagus is coated and heated through, about 2 minutes. Serve the asparagus with the fish.

Makes 4 servings.

The EatingWell Tuna Melt

Here's our updated version of the classic—and great proof that you can have your, well, melt and eat it, too, even if you're building a healthy lifestyle. How about a tossed green salad (*page 228*) on the side?

Active Minutes: 10

Total: 15 minutes

Per Serving: 264 calories; 7 g fat (3 g sat, 1 g mono); 68 mg cholesterol; 19 g carbohydrate; 31 g protein; 3 g fiber; 403 mg sodium.

Nutrition Bonus: Vitamin A (20% daily value), Vitamin C (20% dv).

Healthy Weight

Lower Carbs

- **4 slices whole-wheat bread**
- **2 6-ounce cans chunk light tuna (*see Note, page 246*), drained**
- **1 medium shallot, minced (2 tablespoons)**
- **2 tablespoons reduced-fat mayonnaise**
- **1 tablespoon lemon juice**
- **1 tablespoon minced flat-leaf parsley**
- **1/8 teaspoon salt**
- **Dash of hot sauce, such as Tabasco**
- **Freshly ground pepper to taste**
- **2 tomatoes, sliced**
- **1/2 cup shredded sharp Cheddar cheese**

1. Preheat the broiler.

2. Toast bread in a toaster.

3. Combine tuna, shallot, mayonnaise, lemon juice, parsley, salt, hot sauce and pepper in a medium bowl. Spread 1/4 cup of the tuna mixture on each slice of toast; top with tomato slices and 2 tablespoons cheese. Place sandwiches on a baking sheet and broil until the cheese is bubbling and golden brown, 3 to 5 minutes. Serve immediately.

Makes 4 servings.

Spaghetti with Caramelized Onions & Anchovies

Active Minutes: 35

Total: 35 minutes

Per Serving: 447 calories; 10 g fat (2 g sat, 6 g mono); 12 mg cholesterol; 77 g carbohydrate; 18 g protein; 13 g fiber; 544 mg sodium.

Nutrition Bonus: Selenium (104% daily value), Iron (25% dv), Folate (19% dv), Zinc (17% dv), Vitamin C (15% dv).

High Fiber

ingredient note:

- **Before you think "Hold the anchovies" because of their sodium content, realize that a small quantity delivers a depth of flavor along with a few good omega-3s.**

Anchovies have gotten a bad rap in North America, probably because most of us are introduced to them right out of the tin. But when cooked in a dish, they mellow dramatically, melting into the sauce for a salty, briny taste that can't be beat—as in this Venetian specialty.

2 tablespoons extra-virgin olive oil, divided
4 cups thinly sliced onions (2-3 medium)
2 cloves garlic, minced
1 2-ounce can anchovy fillets, rinsed and minced, *or* 5 teaspoons anchovy paste
Freshly ground pepper to taste
12 ounces whole-wheat spaghetti
2 tablespoons coarsely chopped flat-leaf parsley
1 tablespoon plain dry breadcrumbs

1. Put a large pot of water on to boil.

2. Heat 1 tablespoon oil in a large skillet over medium-high heat. Add onions and cook, stirring often, until golden and slightly caramelized, 10 to 15 minutes. Stir in garlic and anchovies (or anchovy paste); continue cooking, stirring often, for 2 to 3 minutes. Season with pepper.

3. Meanwhile, cook pasta until just tender, 9 to 11 minutes, or according to package directions. Reserving 1/3 cup of the cooking water, drain the pasta and add to the onion mixture. Add the remaining 1 tablespoon oil and reserved cooking water; toss well. Serve immediately, sprinkled with parsley and breadcrumbs.

Makes 4 servings, about 1 3/4 cups each.

Tuna Pomodoro

Inspired by the Italian dish *spaghetti al tonno e pomodoro*, this quick and healthy pasta became a staff favorite at EatingWell. If you keep canned tuna and whole-wheat pasta on hand, you'll do what we did: return to this quick meal again and again.

Active Minutes: 25

Total: 25 minutes

Per Serving: 349 calories; 8 g fat (1 g sat, 6 g mono); 27 mg cholesterol; 50 g carbohydrate; 22 g protein; 9 g fiber; 33 mg sodium.

Nutrition Bonus: Selenium (60% daily value), Magnesium (21% dv).

High Fiber

- **8 ounces whole-wheat spaghetti**
- **2 tablespoons extra-virgin olive oil**
- **1 tablespoon minced garlic**
- **2 anchovies, minced (optional)**
- **1/4 teaspoon crushed red pepper, or to taste**
- **1 28-ounce can diced tomatoes**
- **1 6-ounce can chunk light tuna, drained and flaked**
- **2 tablespoons thinly sliced fresh basil**

1. Bring a large pot of water to a boil. Cook spaghetti, stirring occasionally, until just tender, 9 to 11 minutes or according to package directions. Drain.

2. Meanwhile, heat oil in a large nonstick skillet over medium-high heat. Add garlic and cook, stirring, until fragrant, about 1 minute. Add anchovies (if using) and crushed red pepper and cook for 30 seconds more. Add tomatoes, reduce heat to medium and cook, stirring occasionally, for 8 minutes. Stir in tuna and cook until it is incorporated into the sauce and heated through, 2 minutes more. Divide the spaghetti evenly among 4 plates, top with sauce and garnish with basil. Serve hot.

Makes 4 servings, about 1 cup each.

Muffin-Tin Crab Cakes

We've taken the frying (and the guilt) out of crab cakes by shaping and baking them in muffin tins. For the best taste, look for pasteurized crabmeat in the refrigerator case at your market's fish counter, a better choice than canned varieties. Try these cakes with Creamy Coleslaw (*page 228*).

- **1 pound crabmeat**
- **2 cups fresh whole-wheat breadcrumbs (*see Tip*)**
- **1/2 red bell pepper, minced**
- **3 scallions, sliced**
- **1/4 cup reduced-fat mayonnaise**
- **2 large eggs**
- **1 large egg white**
- **10 dashes hot sauce, such as Tabasco**
- **1/2 teaspoon celery salt**
- **1/4 teaspoon freshly ground pepper**
- **1/2 cup Tangy Tartar Sauce (*page 227*)**
- **6 lemon wedges for garnish**

1. Preheat oven to 450°F. Generously coat a nonstick muffin pan with cooking spray.

2. Mix crab, breadcrumbs, bell pepper, scallions, mayonnaise, eggs, egg white, hot sauce, celery salt and pepper in a large bowl until well combined. Divide mixture evenly among muffin cups. Bake until crispy and cooked through, 20 to 25 minutes. Serve with Tangy Tartar Sauce and lemon wedges.

Makes 6 servings.

Active Minutes: 20

Total: 40 minutes

To Make Ahead: Cover and refrigerate for up to 2 days. Reheat in the microwave or serve cold.

Per Serving: 222 calories; 7 g fat (1 g sat, 1 g mono); 127 mg cholesterol; 20 g carbohydrate; 22 g protein; 6 g fiber; 656 mg sodium.

Nutrition Bonus: Vitamin C (70% daily value), Calcium (20% dv), Zinc (17% dv), Vitamin A (15% dv).

Healthy Weight

Lower Carbs

High Fiber

to make fresh breadcrumbs:

- **Trim crusts from firm sandwich bread. Tear bread into pieces and process in a food processor until a coarse crumb forms. One slice of bread makes about 1/3 cup crumbs.**

Miso-Glazed Scallops with Soba Noodles

This Japanese-inspired dish uses one sauce—a sweet/salt combination of mirin and miso—to make both the marinade for the scallops and the caramelized pan sauce for the noodles. A good pairing would be a simple green salad dressed with a citrus vinaigrette.

- **8 ounces soba noodles *or* whole-wheat spaghetti**
- **3 tablespoons white miso (*see Ingredient Note, page 243*)**
- **2 tablespoons mirin (*see Ingredient Note, page 243*)**
- **2 tablespoons rice vinegar**
- **2 tablespoons canola oil**
- **1 teaspoon minced fresh ginger**
- **1 teaspoon minced garlic**
- **1 pound dry sea scallops (*see Note*), tough muscle removed**
- **2 teaspoons extra-virgin olive oil**
- **1 cup sliced scallions**

1. Bring a large pot of water to a boil. Cook noodles, stirring occasionally, until just tender, 6 to 8 minutes or according to package directions. Drain and transfer to a large bowl.

2. Meanwhile, whisk miso, mirin, vinegar, canola oil, ginger and garlic in a medium bowl. Add scallops and stir gently to coat. Let marinate for 5 minutes (scallops will begin to break down if marinated longer). Using a slotted spoon, remove the scallops, reserving the marinade for the sauce.

3. Heat olive oil in a large nonstick skillet over medium-high heat. Add the scallops and cook until golden brown, about 3 minutes per side. Transfer to a plate and cover with foil to keep warm. Add the reserved marinade to the pan and cook over medium-high heat until brown, about 1 minute. Pour the sauce over the noodles, add scallions and toss to coat. Top with scallops and serve immediately.

Makes 4 servings.

Active Minutes: 25

Total: 30 minutes

Per Serving: 440 calories; 12 g fat (1 g sat, 6 g mono); 37 mg cholesterol; 51 g carbohydrate; 29 g protein; 3 g fiber; 611 mg sodium.

Nutrition Bonus: Selenium (35% daily value), Iron (17% dv).

ingredient note:

- **Be sure to request "dry" sea scallops, which have not been treated with sodium tripolyphosphate (STP). They are more flavorful and will brown the best.**

Chile-Crusted Scallops with Cucumber Salad

Active Minutes: 40

Total: 40 Minutes

To Make Ahead: Prepare through Step 2. Cover the salad and scallop skewers separately and refrigerate for up to 8 hours.

Equipment: Four 12-inch skewers (*see Tip, page 242*)

Per Serving: 326 calories; 22 g fat (3 g sat, 15 g mono); 37 mg cholesterol; 11 g carbohydrate; 22 g protein; 2 g fiber; 587 mg sodium.

Nutrition Bonus: Selenium (38% daily value), Magnesium (29% dv), Vitamin C (25% dv).

Lower Carbs

A refreshing salad of cucumbers and roasted cashews makes a nice contrast to these smoky scallops. You can make the salad and scallop skewers up to 8 hours in advance; cover separately and store in the refrigerator until you're ready to grill.

Salad

- **2 medium cucumbers**
- **1/2 cup salted roasted cashews, coarsely chopped (2 ounces)**
- **2 scallions (white and light green parts), thinly sliced**
- **2 teaspoons lemon juice**
- **1/4 cup extra-virgin olive oil**
- **1/4 cup coarsely chopped flat-leaf parsley**
- **1/8 teaspoon salt**

Scallops

- **1 teaspoon cumin seeds**
- **2 tablespoons minced seeded serrano chile**
- **1 teaspoon freshly cracked black pepper**
- **1/2 teaspoon kosher salt**
- **1-1 1/4 pounds dry sea scallops (*see Note, page 171*), tough muscle removed**

1. **To prepare salad:** Peel and seed cucumbers; quarter lengthwise and slice 1/4 inch thick. Combine the cucumbers, cashews, scallions, lemon juice, oil, parsley and salt in a large bowl.

2. **To prepare scallops:** Toast cumin seeds in a small skillet over medium heat until fragrant, about 1 minute. Transfer to a cutting board and let cool, then coarsely chop. Combine the cumin seeds, chile, pepper and salt in a small bowl. Rinse scallops, pat dry and rub with the spice mixture. Thread the scallops onto four 12-inch skewers.

3. Preheat grill to medium-high. Oil the grill rack (*see Cooking Tip, page 242*). Grill the scallops until cooked through, about 4 minutes per side. Carefully remove the scallops from the skewers. Serve warm with the cucumber salad.

Makes 4 servings.

Mussels with Saffron & Leeks

Active Minutes: 40

Total: 45 minutes

Per Serving: 350 calories; 12 g fat (2 g sat, 7 g mono); 64 mg cholesterol; 21 g carbohydrate; 29 g protein; 2 g fiber; 652 mg sodium.

Nutrition Bonus: Selenium (147% daily value), Iron (50% dv), Vitamin C (50% dv), Folate (32% dv), Zinc (22% dv), Vitamin A (20% dv).

Healthy Weight

Lower Carbs

kitchen tip:

- **To clean mussels, scrub them with a stiff brush under cold running water. Scrape off any barnacles using the shell of another mussel. Just before cooking, pull off the fuzzy "beard" from each one (some mussels may not have a beard). Discard any mussels with broken shells or any that do not close when tapped.**

Mussels are an excellent fast, healthy dinner. Look for them on ice in mesh bags at your fish counter; the individual mollusks should be mostly closed, or they should close when tapped. The only other thing you need with this aromatic dinner? A couple of crunchy rolls that just might happen to fall into the sauce.

- **2 tablespoons extra-virgin olive oil**
- **1 large onion, finely diced**
- **1 bunch leeks, white and pale green parts only, sliced and washed**
- **4 cloves garlic, crushed and peeled**
- **1/4 teaspoon salt**
- **1/4 teaspoon freshly ground pepper**
- **1 cup white wine**
- **1/4 cup bottled clam juice**
- **1/2 teaspoon saffron (*see Ingredient Note, page 244*)**
- **3 pounds mussels, cleaned (*see Tip*)**
- **1/2 cup coarsely chopped fresh parsley**

1. Heat oil in a Dutch oven over medium-high heat. Add onion, leeks, garlic, salt and pepper and cook, stirring often, until the onion and leeks are softened and just starting to brown, 4 to 6 minutes. Add wine, clam juice and saffron, increase heat to high and bring to a boil. Stir in mussels. Reduce heat to a simmer. Cover and steam until all the mussels have opened, 4 to 5 minutes. (Discard any unopened mussels.) Stir in parsley.

Makes 4 servings.

Shrimp with Broccoli

Here's an example of international cooking at its fastest and best: a speedy Asian take-out favorite given an update with the Italian sparkle of basil, garlic and lemon.

- **2/3 cup bottled clam juice *or* reduced-sodium chicken broth**
- **1 teaspoon cornstarch**
- **1 tablespoon minced garlic, divided**
- **3 teaspoons extra-virgin olive oil, divided**
- **1/4-1/2 teaspoon crushed red pepper**
- **1 pound raw shrimp (21-25 per pound), peeled and deveined**
- **1/4 teaspoon salt, divided**
- **4 cups broccoli florets**
- **2/3 cup water**
- **2 tablespoons chopped fresh basil *or* parsley**
- **1 teaspoon lemon juice**
- **Freshly ground pepper to taste**
- **Lemon wedges**

1. Combine clam juice (or broth), cornstarch and half the garlic in a small bowl; whisk until smooth. Set aside.

2. Heat 1 1/2 teaspoons oil in a large nonstick skillet over medium-high heat. Add the remaining garlic and crushed red pepper to taste; cook, stirring, until fragrant but not browned, about 30 seconds. Add shrimp and 1/8 teaspoon salt. Sauté until the shrimp are pink, about 3 minutes. Transfer to a bowl.

3. Add the remaining 1 1/2 teaspoons oil to the pan. Add broccoli and the remaining 1/8 teaspoon salt; cook, stirring, for 1 minute. Add water, cover and cook until the broccoli is crisp-tender, about 3 minutes. Transfer to the bowl with the shrimp.

4. Add the reserved clam juice mixture to the pan and cook, stirring, over medium-high heat, until thickened, 3 to 4 minutes. Stir in basil (or parsley) and season with lemon juice and pepper. Add the shrimp and broccoli; heat through. Serve immediately, with lemon wedges.

Makes 4 servings, 1 1/2 cups each.

Active Minutes: 25

Total: 25 minutes

Per Serving: 178 calories; 6 g fat (1 g sat, 3 g mono); 172 mg cholesterol; 6 g carbohydrate; 25 g protein; 2 g fiber; 520 mg sodium.

Nutrition Bonus: Vitamin C (120% daily value), Selenium (65% dv), Vitamin A (50% dv), Iron (20% dv).

Healthy Weight

Lower Carbs

shopping tip:

- **Shrimp are sold by the number needed to make one pound—for example, "21-25 count" or "31-40 count"—and by more generic size names, such as "large" or "extra large." Size names don't always correspond to the actual "count size." To be sure you're getting the size you want, order by the count (or number) per pound.**

Sichuan-Style Shrimp

Chinese cooks typically stir-fry shrimp in their shells for a more flavorful dish. You can do the same, but we recommend first removing the tiny legs. While rice may seem like the logical side, braised greens, such as chard or spinach (*page 236*), are actually just as traditional.

1 pound raw shrimp (21-25 per pound), peeled and deveined
2 tablespoons canola oil, divided
1 tablespoon minced garlic
1 tablespoon minced fresh ginger
1 large green bell pepper, cut into 1-inch dice
1/4 teaspoon salt
Sichuan Sauce (*page 227*)

1. Place shrimp in a colander and rinse under cold water. Drain and pat dry with paper towels.

2. Heat a 14-inch flat-bottomed wok or large skillet over high heat until a bead of water vaporizes within 1 to 2 seconds of contact. Swirl in 1 tablespoon oil; add garlic and ginger and stir-fry for 10 seconds. Add the remaining 1 tablespoon oil and the shrimp and stir-fry until the shrimp just begin to turn color, 1 minute. Add bell pepper and salt and stir-fry for 30 seconds. Swirl in Sichuan Sauce and stir-fry until the shrimp is just cooked, 1 to 2 minutes. Serve immediately.

Makes 4 servings, about 3/4 cup each.

Active Minutes: 25

Total: 25 minutes

To Make Ahead: Prepare the shrimp through Step 1, cover with paper towels and refrigerate for several hours before cooking.

Per Serving: 175 calories; 9 g fat (1 g sat, 5 g mono); 168 mg cholesterol; 5 g carbohydrate; 19 g protein; 1 g fiber; 415 mg sodium.

Nutrition Bonus: Vitamin C (61% daily value).

Healthy Weight

Lower Carbs

Shrimp & Snow Pea Stir-Fry

A stir-fry is all about preparation: you need to have everything ready to go before you start the cooking, which actually takes place in a matter of minutes. Serve this stir-fry over brown rice—or for a more traditional take, over wilted mustard greens splashed with a little rice vinegar.

Active Minutes: 35

Total: 35 minutes

Per Serving: 305 calories; 10 g fat (1 g sat, 5 g mono); 173 mg cholesterol; 23 g carbohydrate; 31 g protein; 4 g fiber; 574 mg sodium.

Nutrition Bonus: Vitamin C (130% daily value), Selenium (64% dv), Iron (40% dv), Folate (25% dv), Potassium (17% dv).

Healthy ⟩⟨ Weight

2 tablespoons canola oil, divided
1 pound raw shrimp (21-25 per pound), peeled and deveined
3 cups snow peas, trimmed
8 ounces shiitake mushrooms, stemmed, sliced
2 tablespoons minced fresh ginger
1/4 cup dry sherry (*see Ingredient Note, page 246*)
2 tablespoons hoisin sauce (*see Note*)
2 tablespoons reduced-sodium soy sauce
2 teaspoons cornstarch
1/2 teaspoon freshly ground pepper
3 cups mung bean sprouts

1. Heat 1 tablespoon oil in a wok or large nonstick skillet over high heat. Add shrimp and cook, stirring, until pink and beginning to curl, about 1 minute. Transfer the shrimp to a plate (it will finish cooking later).

2. Heat the remaining 1 tablespoon oil in the pan over high heat. Add snow peas, shiitakes and ginger and cook, stirring occasionally, until the vegetables are softened, 5 to 7 minutes.

3. Meanwhile, whisk sherry, hoisin, soy sauce, cornstarch and pepper in a small bowl.

4. Stir bean sprouts, the cooked shrimp and the sherry mixture into the snow pea mixture and cook, stirring constantly, until the sauce is slightly thickened and the shrimp are cooked through, 1 to 2 minutes.

Makes 4 servings, 1 1/2 cups each.

ingredient note:

- **Hoisin sauce is a dark brown, thick, spicy-sweet sauce made with soybeans and a complex mix of spices. Look for it in the Chinese section of your supermarket, and in Asian markets.**

Grilled Shrimp Rémoulade

An updated and untraditional rémoulade makes a tangy sauce for these spice-rubbed shrimp. While this is a warm-weather favorite on the grill, you can also cook the shrimp under a preheated broiler. Cook shrimp on a lightly sprayed broiler rack, about 4 inches from the heat, for a winter warmer any night of the week.

Rémoulade Sauce

- **1/4 cup reduced-fat mayonnaise**
- **1/4 cup low-fat plain yogurt**
- **1 tablespoon chopped flat-leaf parsley**
- **1 teaspoon Dijon mustard**
- **1/4 teaspoon hot sauce, such as Tabasco**

Shrimp

- **2 teaspoons ground cumin**
- **2 teaspoons paprika**
- **1 teaspoon ground coriander**
- **1/2 teaspoon garlic powder**
- **1/4 teaspoon salt**
- **1/8 teaspoon freshly ground pepper**
- **36 raw shrimp, peeled and deveined (about 1 pound)**

1. **To prepare sauce:** Mix mayonnaise, yogurt, parsley, mustard and hot sauce in a small bowl. Cover and refrigerate.

2. Preheat grill to high.

3. **To prepare shrimp:** Combine cumin, paprika, coriander, garlic powder, salt and pepper in a large bowl. Add shrimp and toss to coat with spices. Thread the shrimp onto four 12-inch skewers. Oil the grill rack (*see Cooking Tip, page 242*). Grill the shrimp until just cooked through, about 3 minutes per side. Carefully remove the shrimp from the skewers. Serve immediately, with the sauce.

Makes 4 servings.

Active Minutes: 25

Total: 25 Minutes

To Make Ahead: Cover the rémoulade sauce and refrigerate for up to 1 day.

Equipment: Four 12-inch skewers (*see Tip, below*)

Per Serving: 114 calories; 5 g fat (1 g sat, 1 g mono); 101 mg cholesterol; 4 g carbohydrate; 12 g protein; 1 g fiber; 379 mg sodium.

Nutrition Bonus: Selenium (28% daily value), Vitamin A (15% dv).

Healthy Weight

Lower Carbs

grilling tip:

When using wooden skewers, wrap the exposed parts with foil to keep them from burning. (Contrary to conventional wisdom, soaking skewers in water doesn't protect them.)

Paprika Shrimp & Green Bean Sauté

Crisp-tender beans add snap and color to the garlicky melange of shrimp and creamy butter beans in this Spanish-inspired sauté. Prepeeled shrimp can be worth their weight in gold for the amount of time they'll save on a harried weeknight.

4 cups green beans, trimmed (about 12 ounces)
1/4 cup extra-virgin olive oil
1/4 cup minced garlic
2 teaspoons paprika
1 pound raw shrimp (21-25 per pound), peeled and deveined
2 16-ounce cans large butter beans *or* cannellini beans, rinsed
1/4 cup sherry vinegar *or* red-wine vinegar
1/2 cup chopped fresh parsley, divided
Freshly ground pepper to taste

1. Bring 1 inch of water to a boil in a large saucepan. Put green beans in a steamer basket, place in the pan, cover and steam until tender-crisp, 4 to 6 minutes.

2. Meanwhile, heat oil in a large skillet over medium-high heat. Add garlic and paprika and cook, stirring constantly, until just fragrant but not browned, about 20 seconds. Add shrimp and cook until pink and opaque, about 2 minutes per side. Stir in butter beans (or cannellini) and vinegar; cook, stirring occasionally, until heated through, about 2 minutes. Stir in 1/4 cup parsley.

3. Divide the green beans among 4 plates. Top with the shrimp mixture. Sprinkle with pepper and the remaining 1/4 cup parsley.

Makes 4 servings.

Active Minutes: 30

Total: 30 minutes

Per Serving: 423 calories; 16 g fat (2 g sat, 11 g mono); 172 mg cholesterol; 45 g carbohydrate; 36 g protein; 14 g fiber; 697 mg sodium.

Nutrition Bonus: Selenium (63% daily value), Vitamin C (45% dv), Potassium (41% dv), Iron (40% dv), Vitamin A (35% dv), Calcium (20% dv).

High ↑ Fiber

Shrimp with Mango & Basil

This one-pan stir-fry is an Indian feast of sweet shrimp, perfumy mangoes and spicy basil. It's guaranteed to evoke dinnertime oohs and ahhs. Carbs are a time-tested way to take the pop out of the heat, so make sure you have plenty of aromatic jasmine rice to go with this fiery dish. Use prepeeled shrimp to make preparation a breeze.

Active Minutes: 15 (if using peeled shrimp)

Total: 45 minutes

Per Serving: 183 calories; 5 g fat (1 g sat, 3 g mono); 168 mg cholesterol; 16 g carbohydrate; 20 g protein; 3 g fiber; 352 mg sodium.

Nutrition Bonus: Vitamin C (57% daily value), Vitamin A (30% dv), Iron (20% dv).

Healthy Weight

Lower Carbs

- **1 pound raw shrimp (21-25 per pound), peeled and deveined, tails left on**
- **1/4 teaspoon salt**
- **1/4-1/2 teaspoon cayenne pepper**
- **1/4 teaspoon ground turmeric**
- **1 tablespoon extra-virgin olive oil**
- **1 large ripe, firm mango, peeled and cut into 1/2-inch cubes** (***see Tip, page 242***)
- **1 bunch scallions, green tops only, thinly sliced**
- **1/4 cup firmly packed fresh basil leaves, finely chopped**

1. Toss shrimp with salt, cayenne to taste and turmeric in a medium bowl. Cover; refrigerate for about 30 minutes.

2. Heat oil in a large nonstick skillet over medium-high heat; place the shrimp in a single layer and cook until the undersides turn salmon-pink, about 1 minute. Flip them over and cook for 1 minute more.

3. Add mango, scallion greens and basil and cook, stirring, until the shrimp is just cooked and starts to barely curl, 1 to 2 minutes.

Makes 4 servings, 1 cup each.

tip:

- **Always use spoons and spatulas approved for nonstick surfaces when cooking on nonstick cookware. One nick compromises the surface irredeemably.**

Indian Spiced Shrimp

The magic in this dish happens in the spice grinder, where all the layers of flavor are brought together before cooking even begins. Serve with brown basmati rice.

- **1 tablespoon yellow split peas**
- **1 tablespoon coriander seeds**
- **1 teaspoon cumin seeds**
- **1/4 teaspoon black peppercorns**
- **1 dried red chile, such as Thai, cayenne *or* chile de arbol**
- **2 tablespoons finely chopped fresh cilantro**
- **1 teaspoon tamarind concentrate (*see Note*) *or* 2 tablespoons lime juice**
- **1/2 teaspoon salt, or to taste**
- **1 pound raw shrimp (16-20 per pound), peeled and deveined**
- **1 tablespoon canola oil**
- **1 teaspoon black *or* yellow mustard seeds**
- **1/4 cup minced shallots**
- **1/2 cup water**

1. Toast split peas, coriander, cumin, peppercorns and chile in a large skillet over medium heat, shaking the pan occasionally, until the peas turn reddish brown, the spices become fragrant and the chile blackens slightly, 2 to 3 minutes. Transfer to a plate to cool for 3 to 5 minutes. Grind in a spice grinder or mortar and pestle until the mixture is the texture of finely ground black pepper.

2. Combine cilantro, tamarind concentrate (or lime juice), salt and the spice blend in a medium bowl. Add shrimp and turn to coat. Cover and refrigerate for 30 minutes. (Do not marinate for more than 2 hours or the acidity in the tamarind will affect the shrimp's texture.)

3. Heat oil in the skillet over medium-high heat; add mustard seeds. When the seeds begin to pop, cover the skillet. As soon as the popping stops, add shallots and the shrimp in a single layer and cook until the undersides of the shrimp turn salmon-pink, 1 to 2 minutes. Turn the shrimp and cook until the other side is pink, 1 to 2 minutes. Add water and continue cooking for 1 minute. Serve immediately.

Makes 4 servings, 3/4 cup each.

Active Minutes: 10
(if using peeled shrimp)

Total: 45 minutes (including 30 minutes marinating time)

Per Serving: 180 calories; 6 g fat (1 g sat, 3 g mono); 172 mg cholesterol; 7 g carbohydrate; 24 g protein; 2 g fiber; 463 mg sodium.

Nutrition Bonus: Selenium (64% daily value), Iron (20% dv).

Healthy Weight

Lower Carbs

ingredient note:

- **Highly acidic, tart and complex-tasting tamarind fruit is used extensively in southern Indian cooking. The pulp is extracted and stored in paste form as tamarind concentrate. It is widely available in Indian grocery stores and other ethnic supermarkets. It will keep in a covered container in the refrigerator for up to 1 year. Lime juice is an acceptable substitute.**

Shrimp Banh Mi

French colonial rule in Vietnam influenced the country's cooking profoundly, as here with this street-food sandwich (*bahn mi*), usually served on a baguette. The spicy mayo melange really adds tartness and spice. You could also use it for dressing a Vietnamese-inspired coleslaw.

- **1 large carrot, peeled and shredded**
- **2 tablespoons rice vinegar**
- **1/3 cup chopped fresh cilantro**
- **2 1/2 tablespoons reduced-fat mayonnaise**
- **2 1/2 tablespoons low-fat plain yogurt**
- **3/4 teaspoon fish sauce (*see Ingredient Note, page 243*)**
- **1 tablespoon lime juice**
- **1/4 teaspoon cayenne pepper**
- **3 12-inch baguettes, halved lengthwise**
- **1 pound peeled cooked shrimp (21-25 per pound; thawed if frozen), tails removed**
- **18 thin slices cucumber**
- **3 scallions, thinly sliced lengthwise and cut into 2-inch pieces**

1. Place carrot and vinegar in a small bowl; stir to combine. Let marinate while preparing the rest of the ingredients.

2. Place cilantro, mayonnaise, yogurt, fish sauce, lime juice and cayenne in a medium bowl; stir to combine. Spread 2 teaspoons of this sauce on the bottom half of each baguette. Add shrimp to the remaining sauce; toss to coat. Using a slotted spoon, divide carrot among the baguettes (discard vinegar). Top with shrimp, cucumber and scallions. Cut each baguette into two 6-inch sandwiches.

Makes 6 sandwiches.

Active Minutes: 25

Total: 25 minutes

Per Serving: 247 calories; 4 g fat (1 g sat, 1 g mono); 153 mg cholesterol; 30 g carbohydrate; 24 g protein; 5 g fiber; 504 mg sodium.

Nutrition Bonus: Vitamin A (50% daily value), Vitamin C (25% dv), Folate (20% dv), Magnesium (17% dv).

Healthy Weight

High Fiber

kitchen tip:

- **To defrost frozen shrimp, place in a colander under cold running water until thawed.**

Shrimp Enchiladas Verde

Shrimp with spicy tomatillo-and-cilantro sauce, a common combination in coastal Mexican cuisine, make bright-tasting enchiladas. Precooked shrimp help get them on your table in a hurry.

- **1 pound peeled cooked shrimp (21-25 per pound; thawed if frozen), tails removed, diced**
- **1 cup frozen corn, thawed**
- **2 4-ounce cans chopped green chiles (*not* drained)**
- **2 cups canned green enchilada sauce *or* green salsa, divided**
- **12 corn tortillas**
- **1 15-ounce can nonfat refried beans**
- **1 cup reduced-fat shredded cheese, such as Mexican-style, Monterey Jack *or* Cheddar**
- **1/2 cup chopped fresh cilantro**
- **1 lime, cut into wedges**

1. Preheat oven to 425°F. Coat a 9-by-13-inch glass baking dish with cooking spray.

2. Combine shrimp, corn, chiles and 1/2 cup enchilada sauce (or salsa) in a microwave-safe medium bowl. Cover and microwave on High until heated through, 2 1/2 minutes.

3. Spread 1/4 cup enchilada sauce (or salsa) in the prepared baking dish. Top with an overlapping layer of 6 tortillas. Spread refried beans evenly over the tortillas. Top the beans with the shrimp mixture, followed by the remaining 6 tortillas. Pour the remaining sauce (or salsa) over the tortillas. Cover with foil.

4. Bake the enchiladas until they begin to bubble on the sides, about 20 minutes. Remove the foil; sprinkle cheese on top. Continue baking until heated through and the cheese is melted, about 5 minutes more. Top with cilantro and serve with lime wedges.

Makes 8 servings.

Active Minutes: 20

Total: 45 minutes

To Make Ahead: Prepare through Step 2, cover and refrigerate for up to 1 day. Allow the cold baking dish to warm slightly before placing in a hot oven.

Per Serving: 320 calories; 9 g fat (4 g sat, 1 g mono); 136 mg cholesterol; 37 g carbohydrate; 26 g protein; 7 g fiber; 538 mg sodium.

Nutrition Bonus: Fiber (28% daily value), Vitamin C (25% dv), Calcium (20% dv), Iron (20% dv).

High ↑ Fiber

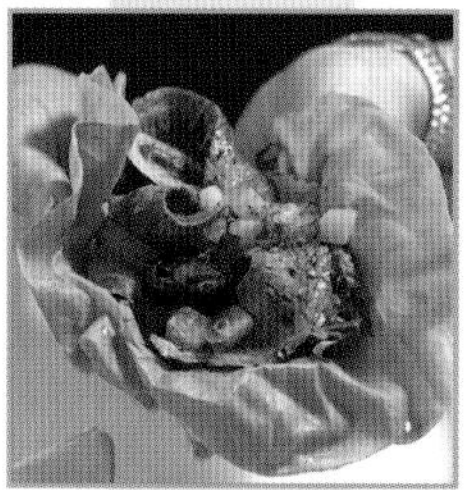

Chapter 6: Beef, Pork & Lamb

Beef

Pork

Lamb

Spicy Beef with Shrimp & Bok Choy

Like fish sauce or anchovies, pungent oyster sauce mellows brilliantly in sauce, creating a salty back taste that works well with greens (here, bok choy) and especially with beef. If you want to forgo rice, try shredded jícama, carrots and zucchini as a bed for this easy supper.

- **1/4 cup Shao Hsing rice wine (*see Note*)**
- **1 1/2 tablespoons oyster-flavored sauce**
- **2 teaspoons cornstarch**
- **4 teaspoons canola oil, divided**
- **3/4 pound sirloin steak, trimmed of fat, cut in half lengthwise and thinly sliced**
- **1/4-1/2 teaspoon crushed red pepper**
- **10 raw shrimp (21-25 per pound), peeled, deveined and chopped**
- **1 pound bok choy, preferably baby bok choy, trimmed and sliced into 1-inch pieces**

1. Whisk rice wine, oyster sauce and cornstarch in a small bowl until the cornstarch is dissolved.

2. Heat 2 teaspoons oil in a large nonstick skillet or wok over medium-high heat. Add beef and crushed red pepper; cook, stirring, until the beef begins to brown, 1 to 2 minutes. Add shrimp and continue to cook, stirring, until the shrimp is opaque and pink, 1 to 2 minutes. Transfer the beef, shrimp and any juices to a plate.

3. Heat the remaining 2 teaspoons oil over medium-high heat in the same pan. Add bok choy and cook, stirring, until it begins to wilt, 2 to 4 minutes. Stir in the cornstarch mixture. Return the beef-shrimp mixture to the pan and cook, stirring, until heated through and the sauce has thickened slightly, about 1 minute.

Makes 4 servings, about 1 cup each.

Active Minutes: 25

Total: 25 minutes

Per Serving: 207 calories; 8 g fat (2 g sat, 4 g mono); 58 mg cholesterol; 6 g carbohydrate; 22 g protein; 1 g fiber; 388 mg sodium.

Nutrition Bonus: Vitamin A (100% daily value), Vitamin C (50% dv), Zinc (23% dv), Iron (15% dv).

Healthy Weight

Lower Carbs

ingredient note:

Shao Hsing (or Shaoxing) is a seasoned rice wine. It is available in most Asian specialty markets and some larger supermarkets in the Asian section. If unavailable, dry sherry is an acceptable substitute.

Korean-Style Steak & Lettuce Wraps

Active Minutes: 35

Total: 40 Minutes

To Make Ahead: The steak mixture will keep, covered, in the refrigerator for up to 1 day.

Per Serving: 199 calories; 7 g fat (3 g sat, 3 g mono); 45 mg cholesterol; 9 g carbohydrate; 24 g protein; 1 g fiber; 465 mg sodium.

Nutrition Bonus: Vitamin A (35% daily value), Vitamin C (20% dv), Iron (15% dv).

Healthy Weight

Lower Carbs

These wraps should be served with lots of condiments: kimchee, for sure, but also nonfat yogurt and shredded carrots dressed with rice vinegar. Serve the various components of the dish separately and let your family or guests build their own wraps to taste.

- **1 pound flank steak**
- **1/4 teaspoon salt**
- **1/4 teaspoon freshly ground pepper**
- **1 cup diced peeled cucumber**
- **6 cherry tomatoes, halved**
- **1/4 cup thinly sliced shallot**
- **1 tablespoon finely chopped fresh mint**
- **1 tablespoon finely chopped fresh basil**
- **1 tablespoon finely chopped fresh cilantro**
- **1 tablespoon brown sugar**
- **2 tablespoons reduced-sodium soy sauce**
- **2 tablespoons lime juice**
- **1/2 teaspoon crushed red pepper**
- **1 head Bibb lettuce, leaves separated**

1. Preheat grill to medium-high.

2. Sprinkle steak with salt and pepper. Oil the grill rack (*see Cooking Tip, page 242*). Grill the steak for 6 to 8 minutes per side for medium. Transfer to a cutting board and let rest for 5 minutes. Cut across the grain into thin slices.

3. Combine the sliced steak, cucumber, tomatoes, shallot, mint, basil and cilantro in a large bowl. Mix sugar, soy sauce, lime juice and crushed red pepper in a small bowl. Drizzle over the steak mixture; toss well to coat. To serve, spoon a portion of the steak mixture into a lettuce leaf and roll into a "wrap."

Makes 4 servings.

Beef Stroganoff with Portobello Mushrooms

Active Minutes: 40

Total: 40 minutes

Per Serving: 329 calories; 16 g fat (5 g sat, 7 g mono); 56 mg cholesterol; 14 g carbohydrate; 26 g protein; 2 g fiber; 383 mg sodium.

Nutrition Bonus: Selenium (42% daily value), Zinc (31% dv), Potassium (18% dv), Iron (15% dv).

Healthy Weight

Lower Carbs

Meaty portobello mushrooms add to the richness of this meal without adding a lot of fat and calories. Ensure the tenderness of the flank steak by slicing it against the grain.

- **2 teaspoons plus 1 tablespoon canola oil, divided**
- **1 pound flank steak, trimmed**
- **4 large portobello mushrooms, stemmed, halved and thinly sliced**
- **1 large onion, sliced**
- **3/4 teaspoon dried thyme leaves**
- **1/2 teaspoon salt**
- **1/2 teaspoon freshly ground pepper**
- **3 tablespoons all-purpose flour**
- **1 14-ounce can reduced-sodium beef broth**
- **2 tablespoons cognac *or* brandy**
- **1 tablespoon red-wine vinegar**
- **1/2 cup reduced-fat sour cream**
- **4 tablespoons chopped fresh chives *or* parsley, divided**

1. Heat 2 teaspoons oil in a large skillet over high heat until shimmering but not smoking. Add steak and cook until browned on both sides, 3 to 4 minutes per side. (The meat will be rare, but will continue to cook as it rests.) Transfer to a cutting board and let rest for 5 minutes. Cut lengthwise into 2 long pieces then crosswise, across the grain, into 1/4-inch-thick slices.

2. Heat the remaining 1 tablespoon oil in the skillet over medium heat. Add mushrooms, onion, thyme, salt and pepper and cook, stirring often, until the vegetables are very tender and lightly browned, 8 to 12 minutes. Sprinkle flour over the vegetables; stir to coat. Stir in broth, cognac (or brandy) and vinegar and bring to a boil, stirring often. Reduce heat to a simmer, and continue cooking, stirring often, until the mixture is thickened, about 3 minutes. Stir in sour cream, chives (or parsley), the sliced steak and any accumulated juices. Bring to a simmer and cook, stirring, until heated through, 1 to 2 minutes more.

Makes 4 servings, 1 1/2 cups each.

Chipotle Flank Steak Tacos with Pineapple Salsa

Who says tacos are just kids' fare? Here's a sophisticated weeknight dinner that combines a charred steak and a bright, fresh salsa. (Best of all, the kids will like it too.)

- **12 soft corn tortillas**
- **1 teaspoon extra-virgin olive oil**
- **1 teaspoon powdered chipotle chile plus 1 pinch, divided**
- **1 teaspoon kosher salt, divided**
- **1 pound flank steak, trimmed of fat**
- **1 fresh pineapple, peeled, cored and cut into 1/2-inch-thick rings (*see Tip*)**
- **1 red bell pepper, finely diced**
- **1/2 cup minced red onion**
- **1/4 cup chopped fresh cilantro**
- **2 tablespoons red-wine vinegar**

1. Preheat grill to high. Stack tortillas and wrap in heavy-duty foil.

2. Combine oil, 1 teaspoon powdered chipotle and 1/2 teaspoon salt in a small dish. Rub into both sides of steak. Place the tortilla stack on the coolest part of the grill or upper warming rack, if possible, and heat, flipping once, until warmed through and very pliable. Meanwhile, grill the steak for 4 to 6 minutes per side for medium, or until desired doneness. Grill pineapple rings until moderately charred, 1 to 2 minutes per side. Remove the tortillas, steak and pineapple from the grill. Let the steak rest for at least 5 minutes before very thinly slicing crosswise into strips.

3. Meanwhile, dice the pineapple and transfer to a medium bowl. Add bell pepper, onion, cilantro, vinegar, the remaining pinch of chipotle and the remaining 1/2 teaspoon salt; toss to combine. Serve the sliced steak in the warm tortillas with the pineapple salsa.

Makes 6 servings.

Active Minutes: 35

Total: 35 minutes

Per Serving: 283 calories; 8 g fat (3 g sat, 3 g mono); 29 mg cholesterol; 36 g carbohydrate; 19 g protein; 5 g fiber; 378 mg sodium.

Nutrition Bonus: Vitamin C (110% daily value), Selenium (28% dv), Zinc (24% dv), Vitamin A (20% dv).

High ↑ Fiber

shopping tip:

- **Prepeeled and cored fresh pineapple is commonly available in the produce section of supermarkets.**

Grilled Steak with Fresh Corn Salad

Active Minutes: 40

Total: 40 minutes

Per Serving: 383 calories; 12 g fat (3 g sat, 6 g mono); 52 mg cholesterol; 39 g carbohydrate; 34 g protein; 6 g fiber; 379 mg sodium.

Nutrition Bonus: Vitamin C (90% daily value), Zinc (40% dv), Potassium (30% dv), Vitamin A (30% dv), Folate (27% dv), Iron (15% dv).

High ↑ Fiber

Prepare the ingredients for this easy salad before you head to the grill with the steak. That way, you can mix together the corn salad and serve it at once, while the taste is still bright and summery.

- **1 tablespoon minced garlic**
- **3 teaspoons extra-virgin olive oil, divided**
- **1/2 teaspoon salt, divided**
- **2 boneless strip (top loin) steaks, trimmed (about 1 1/4 pounds)**
- **5 large ears corn, husked**
- **2 medium tomatoes, chopped**
- **1 small orange *or* red bell pepper, diced**
- **2 tablespoons chopped fresh basil**
- **2 tablespoons red-wine vinegar**

1. Preheat grill to high.

2. Combine garlic, 1 teaspoon oil and 1/4 teaspoon salt in a small bowl. Rub the mixture on both sides of steaks. Place the steaks and corn on the grill. Grill the steaks 2 to 4 minutes per side for medium-rare. Let them rest while the corn finishes cooking. (The steaks will continue to cook while resting.) Grill the corn, turning to cook all sides, until some of the kernels are slightly charred, 8 minutes total. Let stand until cool enough to handle, about 5 minutes.

3. Remove the kernels from the cobs using a sharp knife. Combine the corn, tomatoes and bell pepper in a medium bowl; stir in basil, vinegar, the remaining 2 teaspoons oil and 1/4 teaspoon salt. Slice the steaks and serve with the corn salad.

Makes 4 servings.

Grilled Filet Mignon with Vegetable Kebabs

Active Minutes: 20

Total: 30 minutes

Equipment: Eight 10-inch skewers (*see Tip, page 242*)

Per Serving: 291 calories; 17 g fat (4 g sat, 9 g mono); 70 mg cholesterol; 10 g carbohydrate; 27 g protein; 3 g fiber; 363 mg sodium.

Nutrition Bonus: Vitamin C (45% daily value), Zinc (33% dv), Iron (25% dv).

Healthy Weight

Lower Carbs

You might be tempted to save beef filet for special occasions, but this low-fat cut is actually perfect weekday fare: it cooks up fast, stays juicy and carries other flavors perfectly. The kebabs are a wonderful mix of lemon, herbs and fresh vegetables.

- **1 lemon, zested and juiced**
- **2 tablespoons extra-virgin olive oil**
- **1 tablespoon dried oregano**
- **1/2 teaspoon salt**
- **1/4 teaspoon freshly ground pepper**
- **16 cherry tomatoes**
- **10 ounces white mushrooms, stemmed**
- **1 medium zucchini, halved lengthwise and sliced into 1-inch pieces**
- **1 small red onion, cut into wedges**
- **1 pound filet mignon steak, 1 1/2 to 2 inches thick, cut into 4 pieces**

1. Preheat grill to high.

2. Combine lemon zest, lemon juice, oil, oregano, salt and pepper in a large bowl. Reserve 2 tablespoons of the marinade in a small bowl. Add tomatoes, mushrooms, zucchini and onion to the remaining marinade; toss well to coat. Thread the vegetables onto eight 10-inch skewers. Drizzle the vegetables and steak with the reserved marinade.

3. Grill the steak 4 to 6 minutes per side for medium. Grill the vegetable kebabs, turning frequently, until tender and lightly charred, 8 to 12 minutes total. Remove the vegetables from the skewers and serve with the steak.

Makes 4 servings.

Loaded Twice-Baked Potatoes

Active Minutes: 30

Total: 40 minutes

To Make Ahead: Prepare and stuff potatoes. Cover and refrigerate for up to 2 days. Microwave just before serving.

Per Serving: 366 calories; 12 g fat (6 g sat, 4 g mono); 54 mg cholesterol; 41 g carbohydrate; 24 g protein; 5 g fiber; 535 mg sodium.

Nutrition Bonus: Vitamin C (70% daily value), Potassium (37% dv), Calcium (20% dv).

High ↑ Fiber

Baked potatoes are nature's mini casseroles: an edible dish that can hold (and hold up to) a hearty stuffing. Russets have just the right balance to make a perfect twice-baked potato: enough starch to hold structure, enough moisture to endure the double cooking.

- **4 medium russet potatoes**
- **8 ounces 90%-lean ground beef**
- **1 cup broccoli florets, finely chopped**
- **1 cup water**
- **1 cup reduced-fat Cheddar cheese, divided**
- **1/2 cup reduced-fat sour cream**
- **1/2 teaspoon salt**
- **1/4 teaspoon freshly ground pepper**
- **3 scallions, sliced**

1. Pierce potatoes all over with a fork. Place in the microwave and cook at 50% power, turning once or twice, until the potatoes are soft, about 20 minutes. (Or, use the "potato setting" on your microwave and cook according to the manufacturer's instructions.)

2. Meanwhile, brown meat in a large skillet over medium-high heat, stirring often, about 3 minutes. Transfer to a large bowl. Increase heat to high, add broccoli and water to the skillet, cover, and cook until tender, 4 to 5 minutes. Drain the broccoli; add to the meat.

3. Carefully, cut off the top third of the cooked potatoes; reserve the tops for another use. Scoop the insides out into a medium bowl. Place the potato shells in a small baking dish. Add 1/2 cup Cheddar, sour cream, salt and pepper to the potato insides and mash with a fork or potato masher. Add scallions and the potato mixture to the broccoli mixture; stir to combine.

4. Evenly divide the potato mixture among the potato shells and top with the remaining 1/2 cup cheese. Microwave on high until the filling is hot and the cheese is melted, 2 to 4 minutes.

Makes 4 servings.

Stuffed Chard with Fresh Marinara

Like an updated version of stuffed cabbage, these rolls are a satisfying, hearty dinner—but light enough to be served year-round. They can also be made ahead.

- **1 pound 90%-lean ground beef**
- **1/2 cup plain dry breadcrumbs**
- **2 medium shallots, minced, divided**
- **1 1/2 teaspoons Italian seasoning, divided**
- **1 teaspoon garlic powder**
- **1/2 teaspoon freshly ground pepper, divided**
- **8 large Swiss chard leaves, stems removed (*see Tip*)**
- **1 14-ounce can reduced-sodium chicken broth**
- **1 tablespoon extra-virgin olive oil**
- **1/4 teaspoon crushed red pepper**
- **1 28-ounce can crushed tomatoes**
- **1/2 cup freshly shredded Parmesan cheese (optional)**

1. Gently mix beef, breadcrumbs, 1 tablespoon shallot, 1/2 teaspoon Italian seasoning, garlic powder and 1/4 teaspoon pepper in a large bowl until just combined. Divide the mixture into 8 oblong 3-inch portions.

2. Overlap the two sides of a chard leaf where the stem was removed and place a portion of beef there. Tightly roll the chard around the beef. Place each roll, seam-side down, in a large nonstick skillet. Pour in broth, cover and bring to a boil over high heat. Reduce heat to a simmer; cook until an instant-read thermometer inserted into the center of a roll reads 165°F, 8 to 10 minutes. Discard any remaining broth.

3. Meanwhile, heat oil in a medium saucepan over medium heat. Add the remaining shallot, 1 teaspoon Italian seasoning, 1/4 teaspoon pepper and crushed red pepper. Cook, stirring often, until the shallot is soft, 1 to 2 minutes. Stir in tomatoes and cook, stirring occasionally, until slightly reduced and thickened, about 8 minutes. Serve the chard rolls topped with sauce and Parmesan cheese, if desired.

Makes 4 servings, 2 rolls each.

Active Minutes: 35

Total: 40 minutes

To Make Ahead: Cover and refrigerate the chard rolls in the sauce; reheat in a covered baking dish at 350°F for about 10 minutes.

Per Serving: 388 calories; 16 g fat (5 g sat, 7 g mono); 43 mg cholesterol; 32 g carbohydrate; 32 g protein; 6 g fiber; 720 mg sodium.

Nutrition Bonus: Vitamin A (150% daily value), Vitamin C (80% dv), Iron (45% dv), Zinc (42% dv), Potassium (40% dv).

High ↑ Fiber

kitchen tip:

- **Remove chard stems, including the widest section of the rib at the base of the leaf, by making narrow, triangular cuts.**

Inside-Out Cheeseburgers

Why put the cheese on top of the burger when half of it just melts off? Instead, form the burger around the cheese so you can char the meat and safeguard the more delicate flavors. Use any mixture of hard or semihard cheeses—Emmentaler and Gouda or Asiago and Parmigiano-Reggiano also pair well.

1/4 cup shredded Cheddar cheese
1/4 cup shredded Gruyère cheese
1 pound 90%-lean ground beef
1 tablespoon Worcestershire sauce
1 1/2 teaspoons paprika
1/4 teaspoon freshly ground pepper

1. Preheat grill to medium-high or preheat the broiler.

2. Combine Cheddar and Gruyère in a small bowl.

3. Gently mix beef, Worcestershire, paprika and pepper in a large bowl, preferably with your hands, without overworking. Shape into 8 thin, 4-inch-wide patties. Mound 2 tablespoons of the cheese mixture on each of 4 patties, leaving a 1/2-inch border. Cover each with one of the remaining patties. Crimp and seal the edges closed.

4. **To grill:** Lightly oil the grill rack (*see Tip, page 242*). Grill the stuffed patties over medium-high heat, about 4 minutes per side for medium-well. (Be sure not to press the burgers as they cook or they'll split open and the cheese will ooze out.) **To broil:** Cover a broiler pan with foil and coat with cooking spray. Broil the stuffed patties in the upper third of the oven, about 4 minutes per side for medium-well. In either case, let the burgers stand for 5 minutes before serving.

Makes 4 servings.

Active Minutes: 20

Total: 35 minutes

Per Serving: 250 calories; 16 g fat (7 g sat, 6 g mono); 74 mg cholesterol; 1 g carbohydrate; 24 g protein; 0 g fiber; 164 mg sodium.

Nutrition Bonus: Zinc (37% daily value), Calcium (15% dv), Iron (15% dv).

Healthy Weight

Lower Carbs

EatingWell Sloppy Joes

There's no reason not to serve family favorites, even retro ones, just because you're "eating well." Our delicious retake of the popular sandwich will keep the family at the table. Serve steamed corn or broccoli on the side.

Active Minutes: 35

Total: 45 minutes

To Make Ahead: The filling will keep in the refrigerator for up to 3 days and in the freezer for up to 1 month.

Per Serving: 237 calories; 6 g fat (2 g sat, 2 g mono); 15 mg cholesterol; 34 g carbohydrate; 14 g protein; 5 g fiber; 438 mg sodium.

Nutrition Bonus: Selenium (36% daily value), Zinc (20% dv), Iron (15% dv), Vitamin C (15% dv).

High ↑ Fiber

- **12 ounces 90%-lean ground beef**
- **1 large onion, finely diced**
- **2 cups finely chopped cremini mushrooms (about 4 ounces)**
- **5 plum tomatoes, diced**
- **2 tablespoons all-purpose flour**
- **1/2 cup water**
- **1/4 cup cider vinegar**
- **1/4 cup chili sauce, such as Heinz**
- **1/4 cup ketchup**
- **8 whole-wheat hamburger buns, toasted if desired**

1. Crumble beef into a large nonstick skillet; cook over medium heat until it starts to sizzle, about 1 minute. Add onion and mushrooms and cook, stirring occasionally, breaking up the meat with a wooden spoon, until the vegetables are soft and the moisture has evaporated, 8 to 10 minutes.

2. Add tomatoes and flour; stir to combine. Stir in water, vinegar, chili sauce and ketchup and bring to a simmer, stirring often. Reduce heat and simmer, stirring occasionally, until the sauce is thickened and the onion is very tender, 8 to 10 minutes. Serve warm on buns.

Makes 8 servings, generous 1/2 cup filling each.

Tangerine Veal Medallions

A bright, tasty citrus sauce matches perfectly with veal, especially in this easy sauté. If you like, spike the dish with a few dashes of bottled red pepper sauce. In any case, serve it with wilted chard or steamed asparagus.

- **2 tablespoons pink peppercorns, crushed, *or* 1 tablespoon black peppercorns, crushed**
- **1 pound boneless veal loin, trimmed of fat and cut into eight 1/2-inch-thick medallions**
- **Salt to taste**
- **1 tablespoon extra-virgin olive oil, divided**
- **1 large shallot, minced**
- **1 cup fresh tangerine juice *or* fresh orange juice**
- **2 tablespoons balsamic vinegar**
- **1 teaspoon tomato paste**
- **2 scallions, chopped**

1. Press peppercorns into both sides of veal medallions. (They will not completely coat the veal.) Season with salt.

2. Heat 1 1/2 teaspoons oil in a large skillet over medium-high heat. Add the veal and cook until golden outside and faintly pink inside, about 2 minutes per side. Transfer to a plate and tent with foil to keep warm.

3. Add the remaining 1 1/2 teaspoons oil to the pan. Add shallot and cook, stirring, until softened, about 1 minute. Add juice, vinegar and tomato paste. Bring to a boil, scraping up any browned bits. Cook until the liquid is reduced by half, about 4 minutes. Stir in scallions and any accumulated juices from the veal. Season with salt. Divide the veal among 4 plates and top with the sauce. Serve immediately.

Makes 4 servings.

Active Minutes: 30

Total: 30 minutes

Per Serving: 222 calories; 9 g fat (3 g sat, 5 g mono); 85 mg cholesterol; 11 g carbohydrate; 22 g protein; 1 g fiber; 168 mg sodium.

Nutrition Bonus: Vitamin C (35% daily value), Zinc (18% dv).

Healthy Weight

Lower Carbs

shopping tip

Ask your butcher for the boneless veal; as an alternative, you can use pork tenderloin.

Veal Scaloppine with Lemon, Capers & Leeks

Active Minutes: 45

Total: 45 minutes

Per Serving: 253 calories; 9 g fat (2 g sat, 6 g mono); 119 mg cholesterol; 15 g carbohydrate; 28 g protein; 1 g fiber; 513 mg sodium.

Nutrition Bonus: Zinc (21% daily value), Iron (20% dv), Vitamin A (20% dv), Vitamin C (20% dv), Folate (16% dv).

Healthy Weight

Lower Carbs

This dish is elegant enough for company, yet easy enough to serve on a weeknight. Chicken or turkey cutlets could easily substitute for the veal, if you like.

1 pound veal cutlets (4-6 cutlets), 1/8-1/4 inch thick
1/2 teaspoon salt, divided
1/2 teaspoon freshly ground pepper, divided
1/3 cup all-purpose flour
6 teaspoons extra-virgin olive oil, divided
2 large leeks, trimmed, washed and thinly sliced
1 cup reduced-sodium chicken broth
3 cloves garlic, minced
2 tablespoons capers, rinsed
1 teaspoon freshly grated lemon zest
1 tablespoon lemon juice
3 tablespoons chopped flat-leaf parsley

1. Season cutlets on both sides with 1/4 teaspoon each salt and pepper. Place flour on a large plate; dredge the cutlets, shaking off excess.

2. Heat 2 teaspoons oil in a large nonstick skillet over medium heat. Add half the cutlets and cook until golden brown and just cooked through, 1 to 3 minutes per side. Transfer to a platter; tent with foil to keep warm. Add 2 more teaspoons oil to the pan and cook the remaining cutlets. Transfer to the platter.

3. Add the remaining 2 teaspoons oil to the pan. Add leeks and cook, stirring occasionally, until soft and light brown, 6 to 8 minutes. Stir in broth and garlic; bring to a boil, scraping up any brown bits, and simmer for 2 minutes. Stir in capers, lemon zest, lemon juice, parsley and the remaining 1/4 teaspoon each salt and pepper. Return the veal and any accumulated juices to the pan. Cook, turning the veal to coat with the sauce, until heated through, 1 to 2 minutes. To serve, divide veal among 4 plates and top with the leek mixture.

Makes 4 servings.

Curried Burgers with Chutney Sauce

Burgers are a backyard passion, but—dare we admit it?—sometimes the passion wears a little thin. But once the patties are spiked with curry powder and topped with a creamy chutney sauce, the old spark is back and everyone's happy at the table.

Active Minutes: 15

Total: 25 minutes

Per Serving: 385 calories; 13 g fat (4 g sat, 4 g mono); 62 mg cholesterol; 40 g carbohydrate; 31 g protein; 6 g fiber; 660 mg sodium.

Nutrition Bonus: Calcium (25% daily value), Iron (25% dv), Folate (24% dv), Selenium (24% dv).

High ↑ Fiber

Sauce

- **2 tablespoons low-fat plain yogurt,**
- **2 tablespoons reduced-fat mayonnaise**
- **1 tablespoon prepared mango chutney**
- **1/2 teaspoon curry powder, divided**

Burgers

- **1/2 pound lean ground pork**
- **1/2 pound lean ground turkey**
- **1/2 cup fresh breadcrumbs (*see Tip, page 242*)**
- **1/4 cup low-fat plain yogurt**
- **2 tablespoons curry powder**
- **1/2 teaspoon salt**
- **1/2 teaspoon freshly ground pepper**
- **4 whole-wheat hamburger buns, toasted**
- **1 cup stemmed watercress leaves**

1. **To prepare sauce:** Mix 2 tablespoons yogurt, mayonnaise, chutney and 1/2 teaspoon curry powder in a small bowl. Cover and chill.

2. **To prepare burgers:** Preheat grill to medium-high or preheat broiler.

3. Combine pork, turkey, breadcrumbs, 1/4 cup yogurt, 2 tablespoons curry powder, salt and pepper in a medium bowl. Shape into four 3/4-inch-thick patties.

4. Grill or broil the patties until no longer pink inside and an instant-read thermometer reads at least 160°F, about 5 minutes per side. Serve the burgers on buns, topped with the sauce and watercress.

Makes 4 servings.

Spiced Pork Chops & Peaches

An exquisite blend of cardamom and curry dresses up pork and spotlights peaches in this easy favorite, perfect even for a family meal. Round out supper with brown rice and sugar snap peas.

Active Minutes: 35

Total: 45 minutes (including 10 minutes marinating time)

Per Serving: 274 calories; 9 g fat (3 g sat, 5 g mono); 67 mg cholesterol; 23 g carbohydrate; 25 g protein; 2 g fiber; 318 mg sodium.

Nutrition Bonus: Selenium (49% daily value), Vitamin C (40% dv), Potassium (18% dv).

Healthy Weight

2 tablespoons brown sugar
2 tablespoons plus 1/3 cup orange juice
2 tablespoons reduced-sodium soy sauce
3/4 teaspoon ground cardamom
1/2 teaspoon mild curry powder
1/8 teaspoon freshly ground pepper
4 boneless pork loin chops (1-1 1/4 pounds), trimmed of fat
2 teaspoons extra-virgin olive oil
3 cups thickly sliced peeled peaches (about 3 medium peaches)
2 tablespoons chopped fresh cilantro for garnish (optional)

1. Stir brown sugar, 2 tablespoons orange juice, soy sauce, cardamom, curry powder and pepper in a small bowl until the sugar dissolves. Lay pork chops in a 7-by-11-inch (or similar) shallow glass dish. Pour the spice mixture over the chops and turn to coat both sides. Let marinate for 10 to 15 minutes or cover and refrigerate for up to 2 hours.

2. Heat oil in a large nonstick skillet over medium-high heat. Shake off excess marinade and place the chops in the pan (reserve marinade). Cook until the chops are browned, 1 1/2 to 2 minutes per side. Meanwhile, add peaches to the reserved marinade and stir to coat.

3. Add the remaining 1/3 cup orange juice to the pan and bring to a simmer, stirring. Reduce heat to medium-low and simmer, turning occasionally, until the chops are just cooked through, 4 to 5 minutes. Transfer to a plate and cover loosely with foil.

4. Add the peaches and marinade to the pan; increase heat to medium-high and bring to a simmer. Cook, stirring often, until the liquid is reduced to a light sauce, 2 to 3 minutes. Stir in any juices from the pork chops. To serve, spoon the sauce and peaches over the chops. Sprinkle with cilantro, if desired.

Makes 4 servings.

kitchen tip:

- **To peel peaches, bring a medium saucepan of water to a boil. Immerse peaches in boiling water for 1 minute. Remove with a slotted spoon and plunge into a bowl of ice water to cool slightly. Transfer to a cutting board. Remove the skins with a paring knife.**

Pork Chops with Apricot-Tomato Chutney

Active Minutes: 30

Total: 35 minutes

Per Serving: 242 calories; 10 g fat (3 g sat, 6 g mono); 65 mg cholesterol; 11 g carbohydrate; 25 g protein; 2 g fiber; 414 mg sodium.

Nutrition Bonus: Selenium (55% daily value), Vitamin C (25% dv), Vitamin A (20% dv).

Healthy Weight

Lower Carbs

Roasted tomatoes have a bright taste that's perfect with apricots—which are themselves a traditional bistro pairing with pork. Altogether, here's a meal that only needs couscous and some steamed cauliflower or green beans on the side.

- **4 boneless, center-cut pork loin chops (1-1 1/4 pounds), trimmed of fat**
- **1/4 teaspoon salt**
- **1/8 teaspoon freshly ground pepper**
- **1 tablespoon extra-virgin olive oil**
- **1 14-ounce can diced fire-roasted tomatoes**
- **1/4 cup chopped dried apricots**
- **1 tablespoon lemon juice**
- **1/8 teaspoon crushed red pepper**
- **1 tablespoon chopped fresh thyme for garnish**

1. Preheat oven to 350°F.

2. Sprinkle pork chops with salt and pepper. Heat oil in a large skillet over medium heat. Add the pork chops and cook until browned, 1 to 2 minutes per side. Transfer to an 8-inch-square glass baking dish. Add tomatoes, apricots, lemon juice and crushed red pepper to the skillet and increase heat to medium-high. Bring to a boil and cook, scraping up any browned bits, until the sauce thickens into chutney, 4 to 5 minutes. Pour the chutney over the pork chops.

3. Bake the pork chops until just cooked through, 8 to 10 minutes. Divide the chops and chutney among 4 plates and sprinkle with thyme.

Makes 4 servings.

Pork Chops with Orange-Soy Sauce

This dish uses a very traditional French technique: you first brown meat in a skillet, then roast it in the oven. Make sure you use cookware that's oven-safe, preferably cast iron or stainless steel.

- **1 cup fresh orange juice**
- **1 tablespoon reduced-sodium soy sauce**
- **2 cloves garlic, minced**
- **1/2 teaspoon dried thyme**
- **4 bone-in pork chops (1 1/2-1 3/4 pounds), trimmed of fat**
- **1/4 teaspoon salt, or to taste**
- **Freshly ground pepper to taste**
- **2 teaspoons canola oil**

1. Preheat oven to 400°F. Combine orange juice, soy sauce, garlic and thyme in a small bowl. Set aside.

2. Season pork chops with salt and pepper. Heat oil in a large ovenproof skillet, preferably cast-iron, over high heat. Add the pork chops and sear until browned, 1 to 2 minutes per side.

3. Transfer the pan to the oven and bake the chops until just cooked through, about 5 minutes. Transfer the chops to a plate and keep warm.

4. Add the reserved orange juice mixture to the pan (take care, the handle will still be hot); cook over high heat until the sauce is reduced by half, 3 to 5 minutes. Return the chops to the skillet; heat through, turning to coat. Serve with the pan sauce.

Makes 4 servings.

Active Minutes: 20

Total: 30 minutes

Per Serving: 176 calories; 8 g fat (2 g sat, 4 g mono); 49 mg cholesterol; 7 g carbohydrate; 18 g protein; 0 g fiber; 325 mg sodium.

Nutrition Bonus: Vitamin C (50% daily value), Selenium (36% dv).

Healthy Weight

Lower Carbs

Adobo Pork & Potato Packets

Active Minutes: 30

Total: 30 minutes

To Make Ahead: Prepare adobo sauce (Step 2), cover and refrigerate for up to 5 days.

Per Serving: 373 calories; 18 g fat (4 g sat, 11 g mono); 69 mg cholesterol; 24 g carbohydrate; 28 g protein; 3 g fiber; 350 mg sodium.

Nutrition Bonus: Vitamin A (120% daily value), Selenium (57% dv), Vitamin C (35% dv).

To make these packets, slice the potatoes very thinly, no thicker than 1/8 inch. Use a mandoline or the 2mm slicing blade on a food processor—or cut them slowly with a very sharp knife.

3 tablespoons extra-virgin olive oil
2 tablespoons sherry vinegar *or* red-wine vinegar
2 teaspoons paprika
2 teaspoons chopped garlic
1/2 teaspoon salt, divided
1 small sweet potato, peeled and very thinly sliced
1 medium yellow-fleshed potato, peeled and very thinly sliced
1 medium red onion, halved and thinly sliced
4 bone-in pork loin chops (1 1/2-1 3/4 pounds), trimmed of fat

1. Preheat grill to high.

2. Combine oil, vinegar, paprika, garlic and 1/4 teaspoon salt in a blender; process until creamy, scraping down the sides as needed. Place sweet potato, potato and onion in a medium bowl. Add the remaining 1/4 teaspoon salt and 3 tablespoons of the sauce; toss well to coat. Rub both sides of pork chops with the remaining sauce.

3. To make a packet, lay two 24-inch sheets of foil on top of each other (the double layers will help protect the contents from burning); generously coat the top piece with cooking spray. Spread half the potato mixture in the center of the foil in a thin layer. Bring the short ends of foil together, fold over and pinch to seal. Pinch the seams together along the sides to seal the packet. Make a second packet in the same fashion with the remaining potato mixture.

4. Place the packets on the hottest part of the grill and the pork chops in the front or back. Cook the pork for 3 to 4 minutes per side and the packets for 5 minutes per side. Transfer the chops to plates and let rest while the packets finish cooking. Open the packets (be careful of steam) and serve the pork chops with the vegetables.

Makes 4 servings.

Boneless Pork Chops with Mushrooms & Thyme

Active Minutes: 25

Total: 25 minutes

Per Serving: 350 calories; 16 g fat (5 g sat, 8 g mono); 83 mg cholesterol; 4 g carbohydrate; 31 g protein; 1 g fiber; 420 mg sodium.

Nutrition Bonus: Selenium (71% daily value); Potassium (17% dv), Zinc (17% dv).

Healthy Weight

Lower Carbs

tip:

To pound the chops flat, place them between two sheets of plastic wrap, then set them on a stable counter. Pound steadily with the smooth side of a meat mallet or the bottom of a heavy saucepan until 1/4 inch thick. Remove plastic wrap before cooking.

Although this supper is made to serve two, you can double or triple the recipe so it becomes a family meal that's big on taste but still very healthy. If you'd rather not use vermouth, substitute unsweetened apple juice.

- **2 5-ounce boneless, center-cut pork loin chops, trimmed and pounded to 1/4 inch thick (*see Tip*)**
- **1/4 teaspoon salt**
- **1/4 teaspoon freshly ground pepper**
- **1 teaspoon extra-virgin olive oil**
- **1 medium shallot, minced**
- **1 1/2 cups sliced mushrooms (about 4 ounces)**
- **1/2 cup dry vermouth**
- **1 teaspoon Dijon mustard**
- **1 teaspoon chopped fresh thyme**

1. Sprinkle pork chops with salt and pepper. Coat a large nonstick skillet with cooking spray and place over medium heat. Add the pork chops and cook until browned on both sides and cooked through, 2 to 3 minutes per side. Transfer to 2 serving plates; tent with foil to keep warm.

2. Swirl oil into the pan, add shallot and cook, stirring, until soft, about 30 seconds. Add mushrooms and cook, stirring occasionally, until they soften and begin to brown, about 2 minutes. Add vermouth and cook for 15 seconds. Stir in mustard, thyme and any juices that have accumulated from the pork; cook until the sauce is thickened and slightly reduced, 1 to 2 minutes more. Spoon the sauce over the pork chops and serve immediately.

Makes 2 servings.

Easy Pork Chop Sauté with Cranberries

Cranberries can be momentary pleasures, just around for late autumn—that is, unless you think to stock ahead. Buy a packet or two for the freezer so you can make this quick supper all year long. (Or out of season, look for frozen whole cranberries in the freezer case of your local market.)

Active Minutes: 30

Total: 30 minutes

Per Serving: 301 calories; 10 g fat (3 g sat, 5 g mono); 81 mg cholesterol; 21 g carbohydrate; 30 g protein; 1 g fiber; 207 mg sodium.

Nutrition Bonus: Selenium (67% daily value), Vitamin C (30% dv), Zinc (16% dv).

Healthy Weight

Lower Carbs

- **1/4 teaspoon dried thyme leaves**
- **1/4 teaspoon salt, divided**
- **1/4 teaspoon freshly ground pepper, divided**
- **4 boneless pork loin chops (1-1 1/4 pounds), trimmed of fat**
- **2/3 cup cranberry juice cocktail *or* orange juice**
- **2 1/2-3 tablespoons honey**
- **2 teaspoons canola oil**
- **1/4 cup chopped onion**
- **1 cup cranberries, fresh *or* frozen, thawed, coarsely chopped (*see Tip*)**

1. Mix thyme and 1/8 teaspoon each salt and pepper in a small bowl. Sprinkle both sides of pork chops with the thyme mixture.

2. Stir juice and 2 1/2 tablespoons honey in a 1-cup glass measure until well blended.

3. Heat oil in a large nonstick skillet over medium-high heat until hot but not smoking. Add the chops and cook until browned on both sides, 2 to 3 minutes per side. Push the chops to one side of the pan, add onion to the empty half and cook, stirring, until the onion is soft and beginning to brown, 1 to 2 minutes. Pour half the juice mixture into the pan. Add cranberries. Reduce heat to medium and cook, turning the chops occasionally, until cooked through, 2 to 4 minutes. Transfer the chops to a serving plate and tent with foil to keep warm. Add the remaining juice mixture to the pan. Increase heat to high and cook until the mixture reduces to form a syrupy sauce, about 2 minutes. Season with the remaining 1/8 teaspoon salt and pepper and up to an additional 1/2 tablespoon honey to taste. Spoon the sauce over the chops.

Makes 4 servings.

kitchen tip:

- **To make quick work of chopping cranberries, place whole berries in a food processor and pulse a few times until the berries are chopped into smaller pieces.**

Vegetable & Sausage Skillet Supper

Active Minutes: 35

Total: 35 minutes

Per Serving: 355 calories; 6 g fat (1 g sat, 3 g mono); 20 mg cholesterol; 58 g carbohydrate; 17 g protein; 10 g fiber; 861 mg sodium

Nutrition Bonus: Vitamin C (180% daily value), Vitamin A (30% dv), Iron (20% dv), Potassium (16% dv).

High ↑ Fiber

This satisfying supper is a great way to use up leftover rice and those pesky bits of leftover vegetables that always manage to clog the crisper. Serve with some grated cheese on top and some warm cornbread alongside.

- **8 ounces low-fat kielbasa, cut into 1/2-inch-thick slices**
- **1 tablespoon extra-virgin olive oil**
- **2 medium onions, finely chopped**
- **2 medium zucchini, cut into 1/2-inch dice**
- **1 large red bell pepper, seeded and diced**
- **2 jalapeño peppers, seeded and minced**
- **2 cloves garlic, minced**
- **1/2 teaspoon ground cumin**
- **1/2 teaspoon dried oregano**
- **1/2 teaspoon salt, or to taste**
- **2 cups cooked brown rice (*see page 238*)**
- **1 15-ounce can black beans, rinsed**
- **1/2 cup water**
- **Hot sauce, to taste**

1. Cook kielbasa in a large nonstick skillet over high heat, turning from time to time, until lightly browned, about 2 minutes. Transfer to a plate.

2. Add oil to the pan. Add onions, zucchini, bell pepper, jalapeños, garlic, cumin, oregano and salt; cook, stirring, until the onions are tender, 4 to 5 minutes. Stir in rice, beans and water; cook, stirring, until heated through, about 4 minutes. Add the reserved kielbasa and season with hot sauce. Serve hot.

Makes 4 servings, about 1 1/2 cups each.

Pork Tenderloin with Grilled Peach-Ginger Chutney

Active Minutes: 35

Total: 35 minutes

Per Serving: 249 calories; 10 g fat (2 g sat, 6 g mono); 79 mg cholesterol; 11 g carbohydrate; 29 g protein; 1 g fiber; 275 mg sodium.

Nutrition Bonus: Selenium (68% daily value), Zinc (20% dv).

Healthy Weight

Lower Carbs

Fruit on the grill is a wonderful pleasure—the natural sugars caramelize as the juices are seared inside. Combined in a ginger sauce, grilled peaches are a fantastic condiment for pork.

- **2 medium peaches**
- **4 teaspoons extra-virgin olive oil, divided**
- **1-1 1/4 pounds pork tenderloin, trimmed of fat**
- **1/4 teaspoon plus 1/8 teaspoon salt, divided**
- **1/4 teaspoon freshly ground pepper**
- **1 teaspoon finely chopped fresh ginger**
- **1 tablespoon light brown sugar**
- **2 tablespoons rice vinegar**

1. Preheat grill to high.

2. Peel peaches (*see Tip, page 206*). Cut in half and remove the pits. Brush the cut sides with 2 teaspoons oil.

3. Brush pork with the remaining 2 teaspoons oil; sprinkle with 1/4 teaspoon salt and pepper. Grill the pork, turning occasionally, until an instant-read thermometer inserted into the center registers 160°F, 14 to 18 minutes.

4. Meanwhile, place the peaches, cut-side down, on the grill rack. Grill, turning occasionally, until tender, 6 to 8 minutes. Transfer the pork and peaches to a cutting board. Let the peaches cool slightly while the pork rests.

5. Whisk ginger, brown sugar, vinegar and the remaining 1/8 teaspoon salt in a medium bowl. Chop the peaches and add them to the ginger sauce; stir to combine. Slice the pork on the diagonal into 8 pieces. Serve topped with the peach chutney.

Makes 4 servings.

Pork Tenderloin with Sweet Onion-Rhubarb Sauce

Rhubarb is a natural with pork: its sourness complements the sweet tenderloin. If you can't find fresh rhubarb, use frozen right out of the freezer. Serve this dish with Zucchini Noodles (*page 231*) for the consummate spring dinner—any time of year.

Active Minutes: 35

Total: 40 minutes

Per Serving: 261 calories; 8 g fat (2 g sat, 5 g mono); 68 mg cholesterol; 23 g carbohydrate; 23 g protein; 2 g fiber; 538 mg sodium.

Nutrition Bonus: Selenium (45% daily value), Potassium (20% dv), Vitamin C (20% dv), Zinc (16% dv).

Healthy Weight

- **4 teaspoons extra-virgin olive oil, divided**
- **1 1/2 teaspoons ground coriander**
- **1 teaspoon kosher salt, divided**
- **1/4 teaspoon freshly ground pepper**
- **1-1 1/4 pounds pork tenderloin, trimmed**
- **1 large sweet onion, sliced**
- **2-4 tablespoons water**
- **2 cups diced rhubarb**
- **1/4 cup red-wine vinegar**
- **1/4 cup brown sugar**
- **1/4 cup minced fresh chives**

1. Preheat oven to 450°F.

2. Mix 1 teaspoon oil, coriander, 1/2 teaspoon salt and pepper in a small bowl. Rub the mixture into pork. Heat 1 teaspoon oil in a large ovenproof skillet over medium-high heat. Add the pork and cook, turning occasionally, until brown on all sides, 5 to 7 minutes. Transfer the skillet to the oven and roast the pork until an instant-read thermometer registers 155°F, 15 to 17 minutes. Let rest 5 minutes before slicing.

3. Meanwhile, heat the remaining 2 teaspoons oil in a large nonstick skillet over medium heat. Add onion and the remaining 1/2 teaspoon salt and cook, stirring occasionally, until browned, 7 to 8 minutes. Add 2 tablespoons water; continue cooking, stirring often, until the onion is soft, 5 to 7 minutes more, adding water a tablespoon at a time, if necessary, to prevent burning. Stir in rhubarb, vinegar and brown sugar and cook, stirring often, until the rhubarb has broken down, about 5 minutes. Spoon the sauce over the sliced pork and sprinkle with chives.

Makes 4 servings.

Pork Medallions with Miso-Mushroom Sauce

Active Minutes: 45

Total: 45 minutes

Per Serving: 300 calories; 11 g fat (2 g sat, 7 g mono); 70 mg cholesterol; 17 g carbohydrate; 29 g protein; 2 g fiber; 312 mg sodium.

Nutrition Bonus: Selenium (51% daily value), Iron (20% dv), Potassium (20% dv), Vitamin C (15% dv).

Healthy Weight

Lower Carbs

There are as many varieties of sake, a rice wine, as there are of, well, wine. Try a Junmai sake in this hearty but simple sauce; the added fruitiness will work well against the woody shiitake mushrooms.

- **1/4 cup plus 2 tablespoons all-purpose flour, divided**
- **1 pound trimmed pork tenderloin, cut into 1-inch-thick slices**
- **2 tablespoons extra-virgin olive oil, divided**
- **6 cups sliced stemmed shiitake mushrooms (about 14 ounces before stemming)**
- **3 cups sliced white mushrooms (8 ounces)**
- **1 14-ounce can reduced-sodium chicken broth**
- **1/4 cup sake (*see Ingredient Note, page 244*)**
- **2 teaspoons rice vinegar**
- **1/2 teaspoon freshly ground pepper**
- **4 scallions, sliced**
- **1 tablespoon miso (*see Ingredient Note, page 243*)**

1. Place 1/4 cup flour on a large plate and dredge pork slices in it, shaking off the excess.

2. Heat 1 tablespoon oil in a large nonstick skillet over medium-high heat. Add the pork and cook until golden and crispy and just barely pink in the center, 2 to 3 minutes per side. Transfer the pork to a plate; tent with foil to keep warm.

3. Heat the remaining 1 tablespoon oil in the skillet over medium-high heat. Add mushrooms and cook, stirring often, until softened and beginning to brown, 5 to 7 minutes. Sprinkle the remaining 2 tablespoons flour over the mushrooms; stir to coat. Add broth, sake, vinegar and pepper and bring to a simmer over high heat, stirring often. Reduce heat and continue simmering, stirring occasionally, until the sauce is thickened and slightly reduced, 4 to 6 minutes. Stir in scallions and miso. Return the pork to the pan, turn to coat with the sauce and simmer until heated through, about 1 minute. Serve the pork topped with the sauce.

Makes 4 servings.

Canadian Bacon & Scallion Mini Quiches

Real men do eat quiche—or will when it's stuffed with Canadian bacon and cheese. Served over salad, these quiches make an elegant lunch or a quick, healthy dinner. You can also make them in advance, store them in the refrigerator, and let the kids have one or two for a healthy after-school snack.

5 eggs
3 egg whites
1 cup low-fat buttermilk *or* low-fat milk
1 bunch scallions, sliced
1 1/2 cup shredded reduced-fat Swiss cheese
6 ounces Canadian bacon, diced
1/2 teaspoon freshly ground pepper, plus more to taste
2 tablespoons lemon juice
2 tablespoons extra-virgin olive oil
2 teaspoons Dijon mustard
12 cups mixed salad greens
2 large tomatoes, cut into wedges

1. Preheat oven to 350°F. Coat a nonstick 12-cup muffin pan with cooking spray.

2. Whisk eggs, egg whites and buttermilk (or milk) in a large bowl. Stir in scallions, cheese, bacon and 1/2 teaspoon pepper. Divide the egg mixture evenly among the prepared muffin cups.

3. Bake until the eggs are cooked and beginning to brown on top, 25 to 28 minutes. Run a knife around edges to loosen the quiches from the cups.

4. Meanwhile, whisk lemon juice, oil, mustard and pepper to taste in a large bowl. Add salad greens to the bowl; toss to coat with the dressing. To serve, divide the salad among 6 plates and top with tomato wedges and 2 quiches each.

Makes 6 servings.

Active Minutes: 30

Total: 40 minutes

To Make Ahead: Wrap each quiche in plastic and refrigerate for up to 3 days or freeze for up to 1 month. To reheat, remove plastic, wrap in a paper towel and microwave on High for 30 to 60 seconds.

Per Serving: 268 calories; 13 g fat (4 g sat, 7 g mono); 202 mg cholesterol; 13 g carbohydrate; 25 g protein; 4 g fiber; 677 mg sodium.

Nutrition Bonus: Vitamin A (90% daily value), Vitamin C (60% dv), Folate (46% dv), Calcium (40% dv).

Healthy Weight

Lower Carbs

Fusilli with Walnuts & Prosciutto

Active Minutes: 25

Total: 25 minutes

Per Serving: 322 calories; 11 g fat (4 g sat, 2 g mono); 22 mg cholesterol; 47 g carbohydrate; 11 g protein; 7 g fiber; 261 mg sodium.

Nutrition Bonus: Vitamin A (20% daily value).

High ↑ Fiber

Prosciutto is an air-dried ham, originally from Parma but now made domestically as well. Have your deli slice it paper-thin; keep the slices sealed in wax paper in your refrigerator until you're ready to use them.

- **12 ounces whole-wheat fusilli *or* rotini**
- **1/2 cup shelled walnuts**
- **3/4 cup reduced-sodium chicken broth**
- **1/2 cup reduced-fat sour cream**
- **2 tablespoons slivered fresh sage *or* 1 teaspoon crumbled dried**
- **Freshly ground pepper to taste**
- **2 ounces sliced prosciutto, finely chopped**
- **6 cups baby spinach**
- **1 tablespoon butter**

1. Bring a large pot of water to a boil. Cook pasta until just tender, 9 to 11 minutes, or according to package directions.

2. Meanwhile, place walnuts in a sealable bag and crush with a rolling pin. Transfer the walnuts to a large dry skillet and toast over medium-high heat, stirring constantly, until fragrant, about 3 minutes. Add broth, sour cream, sage, pepper, prosciutto, spinach and butter to the pan. Bring to a boil, stirring. Cook just until the spinach wilts and the butter melts.

3. Drain the pasta. Add to the pan with the sauce and toss well. Serve immediately.

Makes 6 servings, about 1 1/3 cups each.

North African Orange & Lamb Kebabs

Active Minutes: 20

Total: 40 minutes

Equipment: Eight 10-inch skewers (*see Tip, page 242*)

Per Serving: 199 calories; 5 g fat (2 g sat, 2 g mono); 73 mg cholesterol; 12 g carbohydrate; 25 g protein; 2 g fiber; 377 mg sodium.

Nutrition Bonus: Vitamin C (90% daily value), Selenium (39% dv), Zinc (30% dv), Vitamin A (25% dv), Folate (16% dv).

Healthy Weight

Lower Carbs

This spicy yogurt marinade tenderizes lamb beautifully—but it's not a long process, as with some marinades. Twenty minutes does the trick. Here, the lamb is paired with orange sections, which sear and turn slightly bitter, a bracing complement to the meat.

- **1/2 cup loosely packed fresh cilantro leaves**
- **1/2 cup loosely packed fresh parsley leaves**
- **3 cloves garlic, crushed and peeled**
- **1 teaspoon paprika**
- **1 teaspoon ground cumin**
- **1/2 teaspoon salt**
- **1/4 teaspoon freshly ground pepper**
- **1/4 cup nonfat plain yogurt**
- **2 tablespoons lemon juice**
- **1 pound lean leg of lamb, trimmed of fat and cut into 1-inch cubes**
- **2 seedless oranges, unpeeled, quartered and cut into 1/4-inch-thick slices**

1. Preheat grill to high.

2. Combine cilantro, parsley, garlic, paprika, cumin, salt and pepper in a food processor; process until the herbs are finely chopped. Add yogurt and lemon juice; process until smooth. Scrape into a medium bowl, add lamb and toss to coat. Cover with plastic wrap and marinate in the refrigerator for 20 minutes.

3. Thread lamb and orange slices alternately onto 8 skewers. Discard marinade.

4. Oil the grill rack (*see Cooking Tip, page 242*). Grill the kebabs, turning occasionally, until cooked to desired doneness, 7 to 10 minutes for medium-rare. Serve immediately.

Makes 4 servings.

Garam Masala Lamb Chops with Apricot Couscous

Visit an Indian market to find various blends of garam masala, a popular spice mix. You'll also find it in the specialty-spice section at the supermarket or at Indian markets on the Web like www.kalustyans.com.

1 1/4 cups water
1 teaspoon kosher salt, divided
1 tablespoon garam masala
4 teaspoons extra-virgin olive oil, divided
1/2 teaspoon freshly ground pepper
1 rack of lamb, exterior fat trimmed
3/4 cup whole-wheat couscous (*see Ingredient Note, page 243*)
1/4 cup chopped dried apricots
1/4 cup golden raisins
2 tablespoons pine nuts, toasted if desired
1/4 cup sliced fresh mint
1/4 cup lemon juice

1. Preheat oven to 450°F. Bring water and 1/2 teaspoon salt to a boil in a small saucepan.

2. Mix garam masala, 1 teaspoon oil, the remaining 1/2 teaspoon salt and pepper in a small bowl. Rub into lamb. Heat 1 teaspoon oil in a large, ovenproof, nonstick skillet over high heat. Cook the lamb, skin-side down, until browned on one side, 3 to 5 minutes. Turn it over and transfer the skillet to the oven. Roast the lamb until an instant-read thermometer inserted into the center reaches 145°F for medium-rare, 6 to 12 minutes. Transfer to a cutting board and let rest 5 minutes before slicing into chops.

3. Meanwhile, stir couscous, apricots and raisins into the boiling water. Return to a boil, reduce heat to a low simmer, cover and cook for 2 minutes. Remove from the heat and let stand, covered, for 5 minutes. Stir in pine nuts, mint, lemon juice and the remaining 2 teaspoons oil. Serve the couscous with the lamb.

Makes 4 servings.

Active Minutes: 35

Total: 40 minutes

Per Serving: 435 calories; 15 g fat (3 g sat, 7 g mono); 62 mg cholesterol; 51 g carbohydrate; 27 g protein; 7 g fiber; 530 mg sodium.

Nutrition Bonus: Selenium (31% daily value), Zinc (20% dv), Vitamin C (15% dv).

High ↑ Fiber

Herbed Lamb Chops with Greek Couscous Salad

Active Minutes: 25

Total: 30 minutes

To Make Ahead: The salad (Step 3) will keep, covered, in the refrigerator for 1 day.

Per Serving: 333 calories; 14 g fat (6 g sat, 5 g mono); 121 mg cholesterol; 18 g carbohydrate; 36 g protein; 3 g fiber; 386 mg sodium.

Nutrition Bonus: Vitamin C (43% daily value), Iron (17% dv).

Healthy Weight

Lower Carbs

Lamb loin chops are a healthy alternative to the more popular and more fatty lamb shoulder chops. The loin chops have quite enough flavor to stand up to this herbaceous couscous.

- **1 cup water**
- **1 tablespoon minced garlic**
- **1 tablespoon finely chopped fresh parsley**
- **1/4 teaspoon salt**
- **2 1/2 pounds lamb loin chops (about 8), trimmed of fat**
- **2 teaspoons extra-virgin olive oil**
- **1/2 cup whole-wheat couscous**
- **2 medium tomatoes, chopped**
- **1 medium cucumber, peeled and chopped**
- **1/2 cup crumbled feta**
- **3 tablespoons lemon juice**
- **2 tablespoons finely chopped fresh dill**

1. Put water on to boil in a medium saucepan.

2. Combine garlic, parsley and salt in a small bowl. Press the garlic mixture into both sides of lamb chops. Heat oil in a large nonstick skillet over medium-high heat. Add the lamb chops and cook to desired doneness, 5 to 6 minutes per side for medium. Keep warm.

3. Meanwhile, stir couscous into the boiling water. Return to a boil, reduce heat to a low simmer, cover and cook for 2 minutes. Remove from the heat and let stand, covered, for 5 minutes; fluff with a fork. Transfer to a medium bowl. Add tomatoes, cucumber, feta, lemon juice and dill. Stir to combine. Serve the couscous with the lamb chops.

Makes 4 servings.

Sauces in a Hurry

Basic Basil Pesto

Place 2 cups packed fresh basil leaves, 1/4 cup toasted walnut pieces, 1/4 cup grated Parmesan cheese, 3 tablespoons extra-virgin olive oil, 2 tablespoons water, 1 large quartered clove garlic, 1/2 teaspoon each salt and freshly ground pepper in a food processor; pulse a few times, then process until fairly smooth, or to the desired consistency, scraping down the sides occasionally.

Makes about 1 cup.

Per 2-Tablespoon Serving: 83 calories; 8 g fat (1 g sat, 5 g mono); 2 mg cholesterol; 1 g carbohydrate; 2 g protein; 1 g fiber; 176 mg sodium.

Blue Cheese Dressing

Whisk 1/4 cup crumbled blue cheese, 2 tablespoons reduced-fat sour cream and 2 tablespoons reduced-fat mayonnaise in a small bowl. Stir in 1/4 cup buttermilk, 1 tablespoon white-wine vinegar, 1 tablespoon chopped fresh parsley and 1 tablespoon chopped scallions. Season with salt and pepper.

Makes about 3/4 cup.

Per Tablespoon: 20 calories; 1 g fat (1 g sat, 0 g mono); 2 mg cholesterol; 1 g carbohydrate; 1 g protein; 0 g fiber; 92 mg sodium.

Fresh Tomato Vinaigrette

Halve and seed 2 vine-ripened tomatoes. Set a box grater over a shallow bowl. Rub the cut side of a tomato half against the coarse holes to squeeze out tomato flesh. Discard skin. Repeat with remaining tomato halves. Skewer a garlic clove with a fork and use it to vigorously mix 1 tablespoon red-wine vinegar into the grated tomato. Still mixing, slowly drizzle in 1 tablespoon extra-virgin olive oil. Add 1 tablespoon finely chopped parsley (or basil) and season with salt and pepper. Discard the garlic.

Makes about 1/2 cup.

Per Tablespoon: 23 calories; 2 g fat (0 g sat, 1 g mono); 0 mg cholesterol; 2 g carbohydrate; 0 g protein; 0 g fiber; 39 mg sodium.

Jerk Seasoning Blend

Mix 3-5 seeded and coarsely chopped Scotch bonnet peppers (*or* 1-2 tablespoons hot pepper sauce), a 1-inch piece fresh ginger, peeled and minced, 1 large minced clove garlic, 1 teaspoon ground allspice, 1/2 teaspoon dried thyme, 1/2 teaspoon salt, 1/4 teaspoon ground nutmeg in a small bowl.

Makes about 2 tablespoons.

Lemon-Tahini Dressing

Whisk 3 tablespoons lemon juice, 2 tablespoons water, 2 tablespoons tahini, 1 small minced garlic clove, 1/2 teaspoon salt and 1/8 teaspoon cayenne pepper in a small bowl until smooth. Spoon over cooked broccoli, green beans, salad or poached fish.

Makes about 1/3 cup.

Per Tablespoon: 40 calories; 4 g fat (1 g sat, 1 g mono); 0 mg cholesterol; 2 g carbohydrate; 1 g protein; 1 g fiber; 234 mg sodium.

Mango Salsa

Combine 1 diced ripe mango (*see Cooking Tip, page 242*), 1/4 cup finely chopped red onion, 2 tablespoons lime juice, 2 tablespoons rice vinegar and 1 tablespoon chopped fresh cilantro in a medium bowl. Let stand for 15 minutes; stir before serving.

Makes 4 servings, about 1/3 cup each.

Per Serving: 50 calories; 0 g fat (0 g sat, 0 g mono); 0 mg cholesterol; 13 g carbohydrate; 0 g protein; 1 g fiber; 2 mg sodium.

Mint Pesto

Place 1 1/2 cups packed fresh basil leaves, 3/4 cup packed fresh mint leaves, 1/4 cup toasted sliced almonds, 3 tablespoons extra-virgin olive oil, 1 tablespoon lemon zest, 2 tablespoons lemon juice, 1 large quartered clove garlic and 1/4 teaspoon salt in a food processor; pulse a few times, then process until fairly smooth, or to the desired consistency.

Makes about 1 cup.

Per 2-Tablespoon Serving: 70 calories; 7 g fat (1 g sat, 5 g mono); 0 mg cholesterol; 2 g carbohydrate; 1 g protein; 1 g fiber; 75 mg sodium

Moroccan-Spiced Lemon Dressing

Whisk 1/4 cup lemon juice, 2 tablespoons nonfat plain yogurt, 1 1/2 teaspoons honey, 1/4 teaspoon each ground cumin, ground cinnamon and ground ginger in a small bowl until blended. Slowly whisk in 1/4 cup extra-virgin olive oil so the dressing becomes smooth and emulsified. Season with 1/4 teaspoon salt and freshly ground pepper to taste.

Makes about 2/3 cup.

Per Tablespoon: 54 calories; 5 g fat (1 g sat, 4 g mono); 0 mg cholesterol; 2 g carbohydrate; 0 g protein; 0 g fiber; 56 mg sodium.

Sichuan Sauce

Whisk 3 tablespoons reduced-sodium chicken broth, 1 tablespoon tomato paste, 2 teaspoons Chinkiang vinegar (*see Ingredient Note, page 243*) *or* balsamic vinegar, 1 teaspoon sugar, 1 teaspoon reduced-sodium soy sauce, 1/2 teaspoon sesame oil, 1/4 teaspoon cornstarch and 1/4 teaspoon crushed red pepper to taste in a small bowl.

Makes 1/3 cup, for 4 servings.

Per Serving: 15 calories; 1 g fat (0 g sat, 0 g mono); 0 mg cholesterol; 2 g carbohydrate; 0 g protein; 0 g fiber; 75 mg sodium.

Spicy Peanut Sauce

Whisk 2 tablespoons smooth natural peanut butter, 2 tablespoons "lite" coconut milk, 1 tablespoon lime juice, 2 teaspoons reduced-sodium soy sauce, 1 teaspoon brown sugar, 1/2 teaspoon crushed red pepper, (or to taste) in a small bowl until smooth.

Makes 1/3 cup.

Per Tablespoon: 50 calories; 4 g fat (1 g sat, 0 g mono); 0 mg cholesterol; 0 g carbohydrate; 2 g protein; 0 g fiber; 97 mg sodium.

Tangy Tartar Sauce

Whisk 1/4 cup reduced-fat mayonnaise, 1/4 cup low-fat *or* nonfat plain yogurt and 1 tablespoon lemon juice in a small bowl until smooth. Stir in 1 teaspoon finely chopped capers, 1 teaspoon sweet pickle relish, 1/2 teaspoon freshly grated lemon zest, 1/2 teaspoon Dijon mustard and 1 clove minced garlic.

Makes 1/2 cup.

Per Tablespoon: 29 calories; 2 g fat (0 g sat, 0 g mono); 2 mg cholesterol; 2 g carbohydrate; 0 g protein; 0 g fiber; 70 mg sodium.

Tomato-Cucumber Raita

Combine 1 cup low-fat plain yogurt, 1/2 cup finely chopped seeded peeled cucumber, 1/2 cup chopped seeded tomato, 1/4 cup minced red onion, 2 tablespoons chopped fresh mint, 1 teaspoon ground cumin and 1/4 teaspoon salt in a small bowl; mix well. Cover and refrigerate until ready to serve.

Makes 1 3/4 cup, for 4 servings.

Per Serving: 53 calories; 1 g fat (1 g sat, 0 g mono); 4 mg cholesterol; 7 g carbohydrate; 4 g protein; 1 g fiber; 193 mg sodium.

Sides in a Hurry

These recipes all make 4 servings.

SALADS

Asian Salad

Toss an 8-ounce can of drained sliced water chestnuts with 8 ounces blanched snow peas. For a dressing, puree 2 jarred roasted red peppers or pimientos with 2 teaspoons each reduced-sodium soy sauce and toasted sesame oil.

Basic Green Salad with Vinaigrette

Whisk together 3 tablespoons extra-virgin olive oil, 2 tablespoons red-wine vinegar, 1 tablespoon chopped flat-leaf parsley and 1/2 teaspoon each finely chopped garlic and Dijon mustard. Season with salt and freshly ground pepper. Toss with 8 cups mixed salad greens.

Black-Eyed Pea & Artichoke Salad

Thaw a 9-ounce package of frozen artichoke hearts. Cut each artichoke in half. Combine with two 15-ounce cans of black-eyed peas, rinsed, 1/2 cup chopped red onion, 2 tablespoons balsamic vinegar, 1 1/2 tablespoons extra-virgin olive oil, 1 teaspoon Worcestershire sauce and 1/2 teaspoon caraway seeds. Season with salt and freshly ground pepper.

Carrot-Cumin Salad

Peel and coarsely grate 6 carrots. Toss with 1/2 cup chopped fresh parsley, 1 tablespoon each lemon juice and extra-virgin olive oil, 1 finely chopped garlic clove, 1 teaspoon ground cumin, and salt and freshly ground pepper to taste.

Chopped Salad

Whisk together 1 minced shallot and 2 tablespoons each extra-virgin olive oil and red-wine vinegar. Combine 4 cups chopped romaine lettuce, 1 chopped red bell pepper and 1 cup chopped carrots. Toss the vegetables with the dressing and 2 ounces crumbled blue cheese.

Chopped Tomato Salad

Chop 4 large tomatoes and combine with 1/4 cup chopped fresh basil, 1 tablespoon extra-virgin olive oil and 1 teaspoon lemon juice. Season with salt and freshly ground pepper just before serving.

Creamy Coleslaw

Whisk together 3 tablespoons each reduced-fat mayonnaise and nonfat plain yogurt, 1 tablespoon Dijon mustard, 2 teaspoons cider vinegar, 1 teaspoon sugar and 1/2 teaspoon caraway seeds. Season with salt and freshly ground pepper. Toss the dressing with 2 cups each shredded red and green cabbage and 1 cup grated carrots.

Cucumber Salad

Whisk together 1 tablespoon rice-wine vinegar, 1/4 teaspoon sugar and a pinch of cayenne pepper. Season with salt and freshly ground pepper. Peel 2 cucumbers, halve lengthwise and seed; cut into 1/4-inch thick slices. Toss with the dressing. Chill until ready to serve.

Endive & Watercress Salad

Trim 2 heads of Belgian endive. Separate leaves and break into 1 1/2-inch lengths. Thinly slice 1/2 small red onion. Whisk together 2 tablespoons apple cider, 1 tablespoon each extra-virgin olive oil and white-wine vinegar, and salt and freshly ground pepper to taste. Toss with 2 cups watercress leaves, the endive and the red onion.

Fresh Fruit Salsa

Combine 2 cups chopped fresh fruit (mango, melon, pineapple, figs), 1/4 cup chopped fresh cilantro, 1 small red onion, minced, 1 small serrano chile, minced, and 2 teaspoons lime juice. Season with salt and freshly ground pepper just before serving.

Greens with Gorgonzola Dressing

Mash 1 ounce Gorgonzola cheese with a whisk in a large bowl. Whisk in 2 tablespoons strong brewed tea (such as Earl Grey), 1 tablespoon each white-wine vinegar, extra-virgin olive oil and finely chopped shallot, 1 teaspoon Dijon mustard, and salt and freshly ground pepper to taste. Toss with 6 cups mixed salad greens.

Greens with Parmesan Vinaigrette

Whisk together 1/3 cup freshly grated Parmesan cheese, 3 tablespoons extra-virgin olive oil, 2 tablespoons white-wine vinegar, 1/2 teaspoon finely chopped garlic and 1/2 teaspoon Dijon mustard. Season with salt and freshly ground pepper. Toss with 8 cups mixed salad greens.

Napa Cabbage Slaw

Shred 8 ounces each napa cabbage, peeled carrots and peeled jicama using the large-hole side of a box grater. Mix with 1/4 cup low-fat creamy salad dressing and 1 tablespoon Dijon mustard. Season with salt and freshly ground pepper.

Sliced Tomato Salad

Slice 4 tomatoes and arrange on a platter. Top with thinly sliced red onion, anchovies, dried oregano, salt and freshly ground pepper. Drizzle with 2 tablespoons extra-virgin olive oil and 1 tablespoon white-wine vinegar.

Three-Bean Salad

Whisk together 1 minced shallot, 1/4 cup extra-virgin olive oil, 2 tablespoons red-wine vinegar, 1/2 teaspoon sugar, and salt and freshly ground pepper to taste. Toss with one 15-ounce can (rinsed) each of white beans, kidney beans and chickpeas.

TriColor Salad

Combine 2 cups each sliced radicchio and endive with 4 cups sliced arugula; toss with a little extra-virgin olive oil and balsamic vinegar. Season with salt and freshly ground pepper.

Watercress Salad

Trim 2 bunches watercress. Whisk together 2 tablespoons each reduced-sodium soy sauce and white vinegar and 1 tablespoon sesame oil. Toss with watercress and season with freshly ground pepper.

GRAINS

Barley-Black Bean Salad

Cook 1 cup barley (*see page 238*). When done, combine with one 15-ounce can of black beans, rinsed, 1/2 cup corn (thawed if frozen), 1/3 cup chopped fresh cilantro, 2 tablespoons lime juice, 1 tablespoon extra-virgin olive oil, a pinch of cayenne pepper, and salt and freshly ground pepper to taste.

Brown Rice & Greens

Cook 1 cup brown rice (*see page 238*). Stir 2 cups baby spinach or arugula into the hot rice, cover and let stand for 5 minutes. Season with salt and freshly ground pepper.

Dressed-Up Rice

Cook 1 cup brown rice (*see page 238*) with a handful of dried fruit of your choice. When done, stir in 1/4 cup chopped nuts (walnuts, pecans, almonds or pine nuts), cover and let stand for 5 minutes. Fluff with a fork.

Golden Couscous with Currants & Scallions

Place 2 cups water, 2 tablespoons lemon juice, 1 tablespoon extra-virgin olive oil, 1/2 teaspoon salt and 1/8 teaspoon turmeric in a medium saucepan; bring to a boil. Stir in 1 1/3 cups couscous and 1/2 cup currants. Remove from heat; cover and let stand for 5 minutes. Uncover, fluff with a fork and stir in 1 bunch chopped scallions. Season with salt.

Herbed Couscous with Tomatoes

Bring 1 1/2 cups broth or water to a boil, add 1 cup whole-wheat couscous, 1 tablespoon extra-virgin olive oil or infused oil, 1/2 cup chopped tomatoes and 2 tablespoons minced fresh tarragon, parsley or thyme. Stir, remove from the heat, cover and let stand for 5 minutes. Uncover, fluff with a fork and season with salt and freshly ground pepper.

BREAD, PASTA, POTATOES...

Bruschetta with Tomatoes

Preheat grill. Chop and seed 2 large tomatoes. Combine the tomatoes with 2 tablespoons chopped fresh basil, 2 teaspoons extra-virgin olive oil, 1 teaspoon red-wine vinegar, 1/2 teaspoon finely chopped garlic, and salt and freshly ground pepper to taste. Brush eight 3/4-inch-thick slices of crusty Italian bread on both sides with extra-virgin olive oil and grill, flipping once, until lightly toasted on both sides. Top with the tomato mixture.

Cold Soba Noodles

Cook 8 ounces soba noodles according to package directions. Drain the noodles in a colander and rinse under cold running water until cool. Transfer to a bowl and toss with 2 trimmed and sliced scallions, and 2 teaspoons each sesame oil, reduced-sodium soy sauce and toasted sesame seeds.

New Potatoes & Sugar Snap Peas

Scrub 1 pound new potatoes. Place in a small saucepan, cover with water and add 1 teaspoon salt. Bring to a boil; cook over medium heat until tender, 5 to 6 minutes. Add 2 cups sugar snap peas, cover and cook for 2 minutes. Drain; add 2 tablespoons chopped fresh mint or dill and 2 teaspoons butter. Season with salt and freshly ground pepper.

Potato Galette

Preheat oven to 450°F. Very thinly slice 1 pound small Yukon Gold potatoes. Toss with 1 tablespoon extra-virgin olive oil, and salt and freshly ground pepper to taste. Lightly oil a baking sheet and arrange the potato slices in an overlapping 10-inch circle on it, forming a layered potato cake. Bake until tender and golden brown, 25 to 30 minutes.

Quesadillas

Grate 4 ounces Monterey Jack or Cheddar cheese. Spread 1 ounce on a corn tortilla. Top with another tortilla and place in a nonstick skillet over high heat. Cook until the bottom is lightly toasted, about 1 1/2 minutes. Turn over and cook until the cheese is melted and the second side is lightly toasted. Transfer to a plate and keep warm. Repeat with 6 more tortillas and the remaining cheese to make 4 quesadillas altogether. Cut each into quarters and serve with salsa.

Wilted Greens & Pasta Salad

Cook 1 cup small pasta, such as bow ties. Drain and toss with 4 cups baby arugula, 1 shredded carrot, 1/2 cup chopped red bell pepper, 2 tablespoons reduced-fat mayonnaise, 2 tablespoons white-wine vinegar, and salt and freshly ground pepper to taste.

VEGETABLE SIDES

Asparagus with Fresh Tomato Garnish

Steam 1 pound asparagus. Combine 2 chopped tomatoes, 1 minced shallot, 1 tablespoon each extra-virgin olive oil and balsamic vinegar, and salt and freshly ground pepper to taste. Serve the asparagus topped with the tomato garnish.

Balsamic-Roasted Onions

Preheat oven to 450°F. Peel 4 large red onions and cut through the root end into 8 wedges. Place in a 9-by-13-inch baking dish and toss with 1 tablespoon extra-virgin olive oil. Pour 1/3 cup balsamic vinegar over and sprinkle with 1/2 teaspoon salt. Cover with foil; bake until almost tender, about 45 minutes. Uncover and cook until soft and caramelized, 5 to 10 minutes more.

Grilled Red Onions

Preheat grill. Peel 4 red onions and cut through the root end into quarters. Toss with 4 teaspoons olive oil. Grill, cut-side down, until well-browned and tender, about 5 minutes on each side. Season with salt and freshly ground pepper.

Roasted Green Beans & Red Peppers

Preheat oven to 500°F. Trim 12 ounces green beans. Cut 1 large red bell pepper into strips. Toss the vegetables with 1 tablespoon extra-virgin olive oil, and salt and freshly ground pepper to taste. Spread in an even layer on a rimmed baking sheet. Roast, turning once halfway through cooking, until browned and tender, about 10 minutes.

Sautéed Cherry Tomatoes with Chives

Sauté 2 pints cherry tomatoes in 2 teaspoons extra-virgin olive oil over medium-high heat until the skins start to split, 3 to 4 minutes. Remove from heat; toss with 2 tablespoons chopped fresh chives and season with salt and freshly ground pepper.

Sesame Green Beans

Preheat oven to 500°F. Trim 1 pound green beans. Toss with 2 teaspoons extra-virgin olive oil. Spread in an even layer on a rimmed baking sheet. Roast, turning once halfway through cooking, until tender and beginning to brown, about 10 minutes. Toss with 2 teaspoons toasted sesame seeds, 1 teaspoon sesame oil, and salt and freshly ground pepper to taste.

Vegetable Stir-Fry

Stir-fry a 16-ounce package of frozen stir-fry vegetables with 1 teaspoon peanut oil or canola oil. Toss with 2 tablespoons oyster sauce or hoisin sauce and 1 tablespoon rice vinegar.

Wilted Spinach with Garlic

Remove tough stems from 1 pound spinach. Heat 1 tablespoon extra-virgin olive oil in a large skillet over medium-high heat. Add 1 finely chopped garlic clove and cook, stirring, until fragrant, about 30 seconds. Add spinach and cook, stirring, until just wilted, 2 to 4 minutes. Season with salt and freshly ground pepper.

Zucchini & Mushroom Sauté

Cut 2 small zucchini into julienne strips. Heat 2 teaspoons extra-virgin olive oil in a large nonstick skillet over high heat. Sauté the zucchini for 2 minutes. Add 1 1/2 cups sliced mushrooms and 2 teaspoons chopped fresh basil and sauté until softened, about 1 minute. Season with salt and freshly ground pepper.

Zucchini Noodles

Run a vegetable peeler down the length of 4 small zucchini, creating long strips ("noodles"). Steam or microwave for 2 minutes; toss with pasta sauce or creamy low-fat salad dressing.

How to Quick-Cook 20 Vegetables

Start with 1 pound untrimmed raw vegetables.

1. Artichokes, Baby

Look for: Tight, small heads without browning or bruising.

Prep: Snip off tough outer leaves; cut off top quarter and trim off woody stem.

Braise: Heat 2 teaspoons extra-virgin olive oil in a large skillet; add baby artichokes and cook for 1 minute, stirring constantly. Add 1 cup each white wine (or dry vermouth) and water and 1 teaspoon dried thyme (or rosemary or tarragon). Bring to a simmer; cover, reduce heat and cook until tender, about 15 minutes.

Grill: Halve artichokes, scoop out the choke if necessary, then toss with 1 tablespoon extra-virgin olive oil and 1/2 teaspoon kosher salt. Preheat grill. Place the artichokes over direct, medium-high heat and cook, turning once or twice, until tender, about 8 minutes.

Microwave: Place artichokes in a large glass pie pan or baking dish, add 1/2 cup white wine (or dry vermouth), 1/2 teaspoon salt and 1 teaspoon dried thyme. Cover tightly and microwave on High until tender, about 8 minutes.

Steam: Place artichokes in a steamer basket over 2 inches of water in a large pot set over high heat. Cover and steam until tender, about 15 minutes.

2. Asparagus

Look for: Sturdy spears with tight heads; the cut ends should not look desiccated or woody. Fresh asparagus should snap when bent.

Prep: Trim off stem ends; shave down any woody bits with a vegetable peeler.

Braise: Place a large skillet over high heat. Add asparagus, 1/2 cup water and a slice of lemon. Cover, bring to a simmer, and cook until tender, about 5 minutes.

Grill: Preheat grill; lightly oil rack. Place asparagus over direct, medium heat; cook until browned, turning occasionally, about 6 minutes.

Microwave: Place asparagus on a glass platter or pie pan; add 1/4 cup water, drizzle with 1 teaspoon extra-virgin olive oil, and cover tightly. Microwave on High until tender, about 3 minutes.

Roast: Preheat oven to 500°F. Spread asparagus on a baking sheet or in a pan large enough to hold it in a single layer. Coat with 2 teaspoons extra-virgin olive oil. Roast, turning once halfway through cooking, until wilted and browned, about 10 minutes.

3. Beets

Look for: Small beets with firm, dark ruby or bright orange skins.

Prep: Peel.

Microwave: Cut beets into 1/4-inch-thick rings; place in a large glass baking dish or pie pan. Add 1/4 cup water, cover tightly and microwave on High for 10 minutes. Let stand, covered, for 5 minutes before serving.

Roast: Preheat oven to 500°F. Cut beets into 1 1/2-inch chunks. Spread on a baking sheet or in a pan large enough to hold them in a single layer. Coat with 2 teaspoons extra-virgin olive oil. Roast, turning once halfway through cooking, until tender, about 30 minutes.

Sauté: Heat 1 tablespoon extra-virgin olive oil in a large skillet over medium heat. Grate beets into the pan using the large-hole side of a box grater. Add 1 minced garlic clove. Cook, stirring constantly, for 1 minute. Add 1/3 cup water and bring to a simmer. Cover, reduce heat to low and cook until tender, about 8 minutes.

Steam: Cut beets into quarters. Place in a steamer basket over 2 inches of water in a large pot set over high heat. Cover and steam until tender, about 15 minutes.

4. Broccoli

Look for: Sturdy, dark-green spears with tight buds, no yellowing and a high floret-to-stem ratio.

Prep: Cut off florets; cut stalks in half lengthwise and then into 1-inch-thick half-moons.

Microwave: Place stems and florets in a large glass baking dish. Cover tightly and microwave on High until tender, about 4 minutes.

Roast: Preheat oven to 500°F. Spread on a baking sheet or in a pan large enough to hold them in a single layer. Coat with 1 tablespoon extra-virgin olive oil. Roast, turning once halfway through cooking, until tender and browned in places, about 10 minutes.

Steam: Place stems in a steamer basket over 2 inches of water (with 1 tablespoon lemon juice added to it) in a large pot set over high heat. Cover and steam for 2 minutes. Add florets; cover and continue steaming until tender, about 5 minutes more.

5. Brussels Sprouts

Look for: Tight, firm, small deep-green heads without yellowed leaves or insect holes. The sprouts should preferably still be on the stalk.

Prep: Peel off outer leaves; trim stem.

Braise: Place sprouts and 1 cup dry white wine in a large skillet over medium-high heat. Cover and braise until tender, about 7 minutes. Remove sprouts with a slotted spoon; increase heat to high, add 1 teaspoon butter and reduce liquid to a glaze. Pour over sprouts.

Microwave: Place sprouts in a large glass baking dish. Add 1/4 cup broth (or water), cover tightly and microwave on High until tender, about 6 minutes.

Roast: Preheat oven to 500°F. Cut sprouts in half. Spread on a baking sheet or in a pan large enough to hold them in a single layer. Coat with 1 tablespoon extra-virgin olive oil. Roast, turning once halfway through cooking, until browned and tender, about 20 minutes.

Steam: Place sprouts in a steamer basket over 2 inches of water in a large pot set over high heat. Cover and steam until tender, 6 to 8 minutes.

6. Carrots

Look for: Orange, firm spears without any gray, white or desiccated residue on the skin. The greens should preferably still be attached.

Prep: Peel; cut off greens.

Microwave: Cut carrots into 1/8-inch-thick rounds. Place in a large glass baking dish or pie pan. Add 1/4 cup broth (or white wine). Cover tightly and microwave on High until tender, about 3 minutes.

Roast: Preheat oven to 500°F. Cut carrots in half lengthwise then slice into 1 1/2-inch-long pieces. Spread on a baking sheet or in a pan large enough to hold them in a single layer. Coat with 2 teaspoons extra-virgin olive oil. Roast, turning once halfway through cooking, until beginning to brown, about 15 minutes.

Sauté: Cut carrots into 1/8-inch-thick rounds. Melt 1 tablespoon butter in a large skillet over medium-low heat. Add carrots; stir and cook until tender, about 4 minutes. Add 1 teaspoon sugar; stir until glazed.

Steam: Cut carrots into 1/8-inch thick rounds. Place in a steamer basket over 1 inch of water in a large pot set over high heat. Cover and steam for 4 minutes.

7. Cauliflower

Look for: Tight white or purple heads without brown or yellow spots; the green leaves at the stem should still be attached firmly to the head, not limp or withered.

Prep: Cut into 1-inch-wide florets; discard core and thick stems.

Braise: Place florets in a large skillet with 1/2 cup dry white wine and 1/2 teaspoon caraway seeds. Bring to a simmer, reduce heat, cover and cook until tender, about 4 minutes.

Microwave: Place florets in a large glass baking dish. Add 1/4 cup dry white wine (or dry vermouth). Cover tightly and microwave on High until tender, about 4 minutes.

Roast: Preheat oven to 500°F. Spread florets on a baking sheet or in a pan large enough to hold them in a

single layer. Coat with 1 tablespoon extra-virgin olive oil. Roast, turning once halfway through cooking, until tender and beginning to brown, about 15 minutes.
Steam: Place florets in a steamer basket over 2 inches of water in a large pot set over high heat. Cover and steam for 5 minutes.

8. Corn

Look for: Pale to dark green husks with moist silks; each ear should feel heavy to the hand, the cob filling the husk well.
Grill: Pull back the husks without removing them; pull out the silks. Replace the husks; soak the ears in water for 20 minutes. Preheat grill. Place corn (in husks) over high heat and grill, turning occasionally, until lightly browned, about 5 minutes. Remove husks before serving.
Microwave: Husk corn and cut ears in thirds; place in a large glass baking dish or microwave-safe container. Cover tightly and microwave on High until tender, about 4 minutes.
Sauté: Remove kernels from cobs. Melt 2 teaspoons butter in a large skillet over medium heat. Add corn kernels; cook, stirring constantly, until tender, about 3 minutes. Stir in 1/2 teaspoon white-wine vinegar before serving.
Steam: Husk corn, then break or cut ears in half to fit in a steamer basket. Set over 2 inches of water in a large pot over high heat. Cover and steam until tender, about 4 minutes.

9. Eggplant

Look for: Smooth, glossy skins without wrinkles or spongy spots; each eggplant should feel heavy for its size.
Prep: Slice into 1/2-inch-thick rounds (peeling is optional).
Braise: Cut eggplant slices into cubes. Mix with an 8-ounce jar of salsa. Pour into a pan and place over medium heat. Cover and cook, stirring often, until thick, about 15 minutes.
Grill: Preheat grill. Brush eggplant slices lightly with extra-virgin olive oil. Place over medium-high heat and grill, turning once, until browned, about 8 minutes.
Roast: Preheat oven to 500°F. Brush both sides of eggplant slices with 2 teaspoons extra-virgin olive oil and arrange on a baking sheet or pan large enough to hold them in a single layer. Roast, turning once halfway through cooking, until tender, about 15 minutes.
Sauté: Cut eggplant slices into cubes; mix with 2 teaspoons salt. Let stand for 5 minutes, then blot dry with paper towels. Heat 2 teaspoons extra-virgin olive oil in a large skillet over medium heat. Add the eggplant; cook until tender, stirring often, about 4 minutes.

10. Fennel

Look for: Small, white, unbruised bulbs with brilliant green stalks and feathery fronds.
Prep: Cut off the stalks and fronds where they meet the bulb, remove any damaged outer layers, cut 1/4 inch off the bottom and remove the core.
Braise: Slice bulb into 1-inch pieces. Heat 1 tablespoon extra-virgin olive oil in a large skillet over medium heat. Add fennel and 2 teaspoons dried rosemary, crushed. Cook 1 minute, stirring constantly. Add 1/2 cup dry white wine (or dry vermouth). Cover, reduce heat and cook until tender, about 15 minutes.
Roast: Preheat oven to 500°F. Slice bulb into 1/4-inch pieces. Spread on a baking sheet or in a pan large enough to hold them in a single layer. Coat with 2 teaspoons extra-virgin olive oil. Roast, turning once halfway through cooking, until tender and beginning to brown, 18 to 20 minutes.
Steam: Slice bulb into 1-inch pieces. Place in a steamer basket over 2 inches of water (with 1 teaspoon mustard seeds and bay leaves added to it) in a large pot set over high heat. Cover and steam until tender, about 15 minutes.

11. Green Beans

Look for: Small, thin, firm beans.

Prep: Snip off stem ends.

Microwave: Place beans in a large glass baking dish. Add 1/4 cup broth (or water). Cover and microwave on High for 4 minutes.

Roast: Preheat oven to 500°F. Spread beans on a baking sheet or in a pan large enough to hold them in a single layer. Coat with 1 tablespoon extra-virgin olive oil. Roast, turning once halfway through cooking, until tender and beginning to brown, about 10 minutes.

Sauté: Heat 2 teaspoons walnut oil in a large skillet. Add beans; cook, stirring constantly, for 2 minutes.

Steam: Place beans in a steamer basket over 1 inch of water in a large pot set over high heat. Cover and steam for 5 minutes.

12. Leeks

Look for: Long, thin stalks that do not bend and are not bruised; the outer layers should not be wrinkly or dried out.

Prep: Trim off the thick green leaves, leaving only the pale green and white parts; pull off damaged outer layers, leaving the root end intact. Split in half lengthwise. Under cold running water, fan out inner layers to rinse out grit and sand.

Braise: Place leeks in a large skillet with 1/2 cup vegetable (or chicken broth), 1 sprig fresh rosemary (or 6 juniper berries and 6 black peppercorns). Bring to a simmer over high heat. Cover, reduce heat and cook until tender, about 12 minutes. Serve warm or cold with a vinaigrette dressing.

Grill: Preheat grill. Brush leeks with 1 tablespoon extra-virgin olive oil. Place over direct, medium heat and grill, turning occasionally, until lightly browned, about 8 minutes.

Roast: Preheat oven to 500°F. Trim off root ends of leeks, slice in half crosswise and then into 1/4-inch-thick slices lengthwise. Spread on a baking sheet or pan large enough to hold them in a single layer. Coat with 2 teaspoons extra-virgin olive oil. Roast, stirring once halfway through cooking, until browned and tender, 10 to 15 minutes.

Sauté: Thinly slice leeks into half-moons. Heat 1 tablespoon butter in a large skillet over medium heat. Add leeks; cook, stirring often, until softened and very aromatic, about 5 minutes.

13. Peas

Look for: If fresh, look for firm, vibrant green pods without blotches and with the stem end still attached.

Prep: If fresh, zip open the hull, using the stem end as a tab. If frozen, do not defrost before using.

Microwave: Place peas in a glass baking dish or microwave-safe bowl; add 2 tablespoons broth (or unsweetened apple juice). Cover tightly and microwave on High for 2 minutes.

Sauté: Heat 2 teaspoons butter in a large skillet over medium heat. Add peas; cook, stirring often, until bright green, about 3 minutes.

Steam: Place peas in a steamer basket over 1 inch of water in a large pot set over high heat. Cover and steam for 2 minutes.

14. Potatoes, red-skinned or yellow-fleshed

Look for: Small potatoes with firm skins that are not loose, papery or bruised.

Prep: Scrub off any dirt (peeling is optional; the skin is fiber-rich and the nutrients are clustered about 1/2 inch below the skin).

Braise: Cut potatoes into 1/2-inch pieces. Place in a large skillet with 1/2 cup each vegetable broth and nonfat milk and 1 teaspoon butter. Bring to a simmer, cover, reduce heat and cook until tender and most of the liquid has been absorbed, about 20 minutes.

Roast: Preheat oven to 500°F. Halve potatoes then cut into 1/2-inch wedges. Spread on a baking sheet or in a pan large enough to hold them in a single layer. Coat with 2 teaspoons extra-virgin olive oil. Roast, stirring once halfway through cooking, until crispy and browned on the outside and tender on the inside, 20 to 25 minutes.

Sauté: Peel potatoes (if desired), then shred using the large-hole side of a box grater. Heat 1 tablespoon canola oil in a large skillet over medium heat. Add potatoes; reduce heat. Cook, pressing down with the back of a wooden spoon, for 6 minutes. Flip the cake over and continue cooking until browned, about 5 minutes more.

Steam: Place potatoes in a steamer basket over 2 inches of water in a large pot set over high heat. Cover and steam until tender when pierced with a fork, about 10 minutes.

15. Spinach & Swiss Chard

Look for: Supple, deeply colored leaves without mushy spots.

Prep: Rinse thoroughly to remove sand; remove thick stems and shred leaves into 2-inch chunks. Rinse leaves again but do not dry.

Braise: Heat 2 teaspoons walnut oil (or canola oil) in a large skillet over medium heat. Add spinach or chard and toss until wilted. Add 1/2 cup dry white wine or dry vermouth. Cover, reduce heat and cook until wilted, about 5 minutes. Uncover and cook until liquid is reduced to a glaze. Sprinkle 2 teaspoons balsamic vinegar (or rice vinegar) over the greens.

16. Squash, Acorn

Look for: Green, orange or white varietals with firm, smooth skins and no spongy spots.

Prep: Cut in quarters and scoop out the seeds.

Braise: Place squash in a pot with 2 cups unsweetened apple juice. Set over medium-high heat and bring to a simmer. Cover, reduce heat and cook until tender when pierced with a fork, about 20 minutes.

Microwave: Place squash in a large glass baking dish; add 1/2 cup water. Cover and microwave on High for 15 minutes; let stand, covered, for 10 minutes.

17. Squash, Delicata

Look for: Small, firm squash with bright yellow or orange skins that have green veins branching like lightning through them.

Microwave: Place squash in a large glass baking dish or microwave-safe bowl with 1/4 cup broth (or water). Cover tightly and microwave on High for 10 minutes.

Prep: Cut squash in half lengthwise, scoop out the seeds and slice into thin half-moons (peeling is optional).

Sauté: Melt 2 teaspoons butter in a large skillet over medium heat. Add squash slices; cook, stirring frequently, until tender, about 10 minutes. Stir in a pinch of grated nutmeg before serving.

Steam: Place squash slices in a steamer basket over 1 inch of water in a large pot set over high heat. Cover and cook until tender, about 6 minutes.

18. Squash, Summer & Zucchini

Look for: No breaks, gashes or soft spots; smaller squash (under 8 inches) are sweeter and have fewer seeds; do not peel, but scrub off any dirt.

Prep: Cut off stem ends.

Grill: Cut squash lengthwise into 1/4-inch strips. Preheat grill; brush strips lightly with 1 tablespoon extra-virgin olive oil. Place over direct, medium heat; grill, turning once, until marked and lightly browned, 3 to 4 minutes.

Roast: Preheat oven to 500°F. Cut squash lengthwise into 1/4-inch-thick slices. Spread on a baking sheet or in a pan large enough to hold them in a single layer. Coat with 2 teaspoons extra-virgin olive oil. Roast, turning once halfway through cooking, until tender, about 10 minutes.

Sauté: Cut squash into 1/4-inch-thick rings. Heat 1 tablespoon extra-virgin olive oil in a large skillet over medium heat. Add 1 minced garlic clove and squash; cook, stirring frequently, until tender, about 7 minutes.

Steam: Cut squash into 1/2-inch-thick rings. Place in a steamer basket with a small onion, thinly sliced. Place over 1 inch of water in a large pot set over high heat. Cook until tender, about 5 minutes.

19. Sweet Potatoes

Look for: Taut if papery skins with tapered ends.

Prep: Scrub.

Braise: Peel sweet potatoes and cut into 1-inch pieces. Place in a large skillet with 1 cup vegetable broth, 1 teaspoon honey and 1/2 teaspoon dried thyme. Bring to a simmer over high heat; reduce heat, cover and cook until almost tender, about 15 minutes. Uncover, increase heat and cook until the liquid is reduced to a glaze, about 2 minutes.

Microwaving: Place 2 to 3 medium sweet potatoes in a large glass baking dish; pierce with a knife. Microwave on High until soft, 8 to 12 minutes. Let stand for 5 minutes.

Roast: Preheat oven to 500°F. Halve sweet potatoes, then slice into 1/2-inch wedges. Spread on a baking sheet or in a pan large enough to hold them in a single layer. Coat with 2 teaspoons extra-virgin olive oil. Roast, turning once halfway through cooking, until browned and tender, 20 to 25 minutes.

Steam: Peel sweet potatoes and cut into 1-inch pieces. Place in a steamer basket over 2 inches of water in a pot set over high heat. Cover and steam until tender, about 20 minutes.

20. Turnips

Look for: Smaller turnips with firm, white skins; they should feel heavy to the hand. The greens should preferably still be attached.

Prep: Cut off the root end and the greens; peel, then cut into thin slices.

Grill: Steam turnip slices (*see below*) for 5 minutes; meanwhile, preheat grill. Place slices over direct, medium-high heat and grill, turning once, until lightly browned and tender, about 8 minutes.

Roast: Preheat oven to 500°F. Spread turnip slices on a baking sheet or in a pan large enough to hold them in a single layer. Coat with 2 teaspoons extra-virgin olive oil. Roast, turning once halfway through cooking, until tender, about 15 minutes.

Sauté: Cut turnip slices into matchsticks. Heat 1 teaspoon each butter and extra-virgin olive oil in a large skillet over medium heat; add slices and cook, stirring frequently, until tender, about 12 minutes.

Steam: Place turnip slices in a steamer basket over 2 inches of water in a large pot set over high heat. Cover and cook until tender when pierced with a fork, about 12 minutes.

Grain-Cooking Guide

Directions are for 1 cup of uncooked grain.

Grain	Liquid (*water/broth*)	Directions	Yield	Per 1/2-Cup Serving
Barley				
Quick-cooking	1 3/4 cups	Bring liquid to a boil; add barley. Reduce heat to low and simmer, covered, 10-12 minutes.	2 cups	86 calories; 1 g fat (0 g sat, 0 g mono); 0 mg cholesterol; 19 g carbohydrate; 3 g protein; 3 g fiber; 2 mg sodium.
Pearl	2 1/2 cups	Bring barley and liquid to a boil. Reduce heat to low and simmer, covered, 35-50 minutes.	3-3 1/2 cups	117 calories; 0 g fat; 0 mg cholesterol; 26 g carbohydrate; 3 g protein; 5 g fiber; 6 mg sodium.
Bulgur	1 1/2 cups	Bring bulgur and liquid to a boil. Reduce heat to low and simmer, covered, until tender and most of the liquid has been absorbed, 10-15 minutes.	2 1/2-3 cups	96 calories; 0 g fat; 0 mg cholesterol; 21 g carbohydrate; 3 g protein; 5 g fiber; 7 mg sodium.
Couscous				
Whole-wheat	1 3/4 cups	Bring liquid to a boil; stir in couscous. Remove from heat and let stand, covered, 5 minutes. Fluff with a fork.	3-3 1/2 cups	140 calories; 1 g fat (0 g sat, 0 g mono); 0 mg cholesterol; 30 g carbohydrate; 5 g protein; 5 g fiber; 1 mg sodium.
Quinoa	2 cups	Rinse in several changes of cold water. Bring quinoa and liquid to a boil. Reduce heat to low and simmer, covered, until tender and most of the liquid has been absorbed, 15-20 minutes. Fluff with a fork.	3 cups	106 calories; 2 g fat (0 g sat, 0 g mono); 0 mg cholesterol; 20 g carbohydrate; 4 g protein; 2 g fiber; 8 mg sodium.
Rice				
Brown	2 1/2 cups	Bring rice and liquid to a boil. Reduce heat to low and simmer, covered, until tender and most of the liquid has been absorbed, 40-50 minutes. Let stand 5 minutes, then fluff with a fork.	3 cups	98 calories; 1 g fat (0 g sat, 0 g mono); 0 mg cholesterol; 20 g carbohydrate; 2 g protein; 1 g fiber; 3 mg sodium.
Wild	At least 4 cups	Cook rice in a large saucepan of lightly salted boiling water until tender, 45-55 minutes. Drain.	2-2 1/2 cups	82 calories; 0 g fat; 0 mg cholesterol; 17 g carbohydrate; 3 g protein; 1 g fiber; 4 mg sodium.

Desserts in a Hurry

Aromatic Rice Pudding

Stir 2 tablespoons each pine nuts and golden raisins and 1 teaspoon freshly grated lemon zest into 2 cups prepared rice pudding, found in the supermarket dairy case.

Banana-Cinnamon Frozen Yogurt

Soften 1 pint nonfat vanilla frozen yogurt. Mash together 2 small bananas, 1 teaspoon lemon juice and 1/2 teaspoon ground cinnamon. Add the frozen yogurt and mix well with a whisk. Scoop into 4 dessert dishes, cover and freeze until firm, about 30 minutes.

Black-Fruit Compote

Combine 2 tablespoons each honey, tawny port and orange juice in a small saucepan over low heat until blended. Let cool 5 minutes. Toss the honey mixture with 1 cup each blackberries, blueberries and cherries in a medium bowl.

Broiled Pineapple

Brush 8 pineapple slices with canola oil. Sprinkle with freshly ground pepper and broil until lightly browned, about 7 minutes. Flip the pineapple, brush with oil, sprinkle with freshly ground pepper and broil 5 to 7 minutes. Sprinkle with brown sugar. Cut into wedges and serve with lime wedges.

Chocolate & Nut Butter Bites

Top eight 1/4-ounce squares of bittersweet chocolate with 1/2 teaspoon nut butter of your choice (almond, cashew, pistachio).

Cinnamon Oranges

With a sharp knife, remove rind and white pith from 4 navel oranges. Cut each into 5 or 6 slices and arrange on 4 plates. Whisk together 2 tablespoons each orange juice and lemon juice, 1 tablespoon sugar and 1/4 teaspoon ground cinnamon. Spoon over orange slices.

"Cocoa-Nut" Bananas

Slice 2 small bananas on the bias, roll each slice in cocoa, shake off the excess, then dip in toasted unsweetened coconut.

Aromatic Rice Pudding

Strawberries Dipped in Chocolate

Iced Lychees

Chocolate & Nut Butter Bites

Tea-Scented Mandarins

Coffee-Cognac Coupe

Bring 1/3 cup sugar, 1/4 cup water and 2 teaspoons instant coffee powder to a boil; boil until slightly thickened, 2 to 3 minutes. Remove from heat; stir in 2 tablespoons cognac or brandy. Let cool. Layer in parfait glasses with nonfat vanilla frozen yogurt.

Frosted Grapes

Wash and pat dry 2 cups seedless grapes. Freeze 45 minutes. Let stand for 2 minutes at room temperature before serving.

Gingered Peach Gratin

Halve and pit 4 peaches. Place the peaches cut-side up in a shallow 1-quart baking dish. Simmer 1/3 cup sugar, 1/4 cup lemon juice, 2 tablespoons water and 1/2 teaspoon ground ginger. Pour over the peaches and sprinkle with 4 crushed gingersnaps. Bake 15 to 20 minutes, or until the peaches are tender and the syrup is thickened.

Iced Lychees

Drain 1 can lychees (found in the Asian section of supermarkets) and freeze on a sheet pan for at least 2 hours before serving.

Pineapple with Mango Coulis

Dice 1 small mango. Puree the mango with 1 1/2 tablespoons each dark rum and lime juice and 1 teaspoon lime zest in a food processor or blender. Add sugar to taste. Serve over fresh pineapple spears or chunks.

Raspberries & Mangoes

Toss 1 cup each raspberries and diced mango with 1 teaspoon sugar. Sprinkle with sliced almonds before serving.

Raspberry Sorbet with Sliced Kiwis

Thinly slice two kiwis. Top four 1/2-cup scoops of raspberry sorbet with the kiwi slices and 2 tablespoons toasted coconut.

Roasted Plums

Halve and pit 1 1/2 pounds plums. Place skin-side down in a 9-by-13-inch baking dish. Sprinkle with 1/3 cup sugar and 2 tablespoons lemon juice; bake for 30 to 40 minutes, or until juices are thickened and plums are tender, shaking pan occasionally to distribute juices. Stir in 1 tablespoon brandy and 1 teaspoon grated lemon zest.

Stewed Rhubarb with Orange

Bring 4 cups diced rhubarb, 1/2 cup orange marmalade, 1/4 cup sugar, 2 tablespoons water and a pinch each cinnamon and nutmeg to a simmer over medium heat. Reduce to low, cover and cook until rhubarb is tender, 6 to 8 minutes.

Strawberries Dipped in Chocolate

Melt 2 ounces high-quality dark chocolate over barely simmering water or in the microwave. Dip 12 strawberries in the chocolate.

Strawberries with Ginger & Pine Nuts

Hull and quarter 1 1/2 pints strawberries. Coarsely chop and toast 1 tablespoon pine nuts. Let cool slightly and toss with the strawberries, 2 tablespoons orange juice, 1 tablespoon chopped crystallized ginger and 2 teaspoons sugar. Let stand 10 minutes.

Strawberries with Minted Yogurt

Whisk together 1/2 cup each nonfat plain yogurt and buttermilk, 1 tablespoon sugar, 1 1/2 teaspoons chopped mint and 1/8 teaspoon vanilla extract until smooth. Spoon over 3 cups sliced strawberries.

Strawberry Shortcakes

Line a sieve with cheesecloth and set over a bowl. Spoon in 1 cup low-fat vanilla yogurt and let drain in the refrigerator 30 to 60 minutes. Hull and slice 1 pint strawberries and toss with 3 tablespoons sugar. Let stand 30 minutes, stirring occasionally. Top 4 slices of fat-free pound cake with strawberries and drained yogurt.

Summer Blackberries

Stir together 3 tablespoons orange juice, 1 tablespoon lemon juice, 1 tablespoon sugar and 1 teaspoon lime zest until sugar dissolves. Toss with 3 cups fresh blackberries.

Tea-Scented Mandarins

Pour 1/2 cup hot black tea over 2 cups mandarin oranges or clementines; drizzle with 2 tablespoons honey and sprinkle with ground cardamom.

Tropical Fruits with Pistachios & Coconut

Drizzle 4 teaspoons "lite" coconut milk over 16 slices ripe mango, pineapple and/or papaya slices; sprinkle with 2 tablespoons chopped pistachios.

Tropical Fruits with Pistachios & Coconut

"Cocoa-Nut" Bananas

COOKING TIPS

To make fresh **breadcrumbs**: Trim crusts from firm sandwich bread. Tear bread into pieces and process in a food processor until a coarse crumb forms. One slice of bread makes about 1/3 cup crumbs.

To make **croutons**: Toss 1 cup whole-grain bread cubes with 1 tablespoon extra-virgin olive oil, a pinch each of salt, pepper and garlic powder. Spread out on a baking sheet and toast at 350°F until crispy, turning occasionally, 15 to 20 minutes.

To oil a **grill rack**: Oil a folded paper towel, hold it with tongs and rub it over the rack. (Do not use cooking spray on a hot grill.)

To **grill with wooden skewers**: Wrap the exposed parts with foil to keep them from burning. (Contrary to conventional wisdom, soaking skewers in water doesn't protect them.)

To cook **lentils**: Place in a saucepan, cover with water and bring to a boil. Reduce heat to a simmer and cook until just tender, about 20 minutes for green lentils and 30 minutes for brown. Drain and rinse under cold water.

To cut a **mango**: 1. Slice both ends off the mango, revealing the long, slender seed inside. Set the fruit upright on a work surface and remove the skin with a sharp knife. 2. With the seed perpendicular to you, slice the fruit from both sides of the seed, yielding two large pieces. 3. Turn the seed parallel to you and slice the two smaller pieces of fruit from each side. 4. Cut the fruit into the desired shape.

To **peel peaches**: Bring a medium saucepan of water to a boil. Immerse peaches in boiling water for 1 minute. Remove with a slotted spoon and plunge into a bowl of ice water to cool slightly. Transfer to a cutting board. Remove the skins with a paring knife.

To remove **portobello mushroom gills**: The dark gills found on the underside of the cap are edible, but will turn soups and sauces an unappealing gray/black color. Remove the gills with a spoon, if desired.

To **segment a citrus fruit**: Using a sharp knife, cut off the peel and white pith from the fruit. To make attractive segments, hold the fruit over a bowl (to catch the juice) and slice between each segment and its surrounding membranes.

To defrost **frozen shrimp**: Place in a colander under cold running water until thawed.

To **skin a salmon fillet**: Place it on a clean cutting board, skin-side down. Starting at the tail end, slip the blade of a long, sharp knife between the fish flesh and the skin, holding the skin down firmly with your other hand. Gently push the blade along at a 30° angle, separating the fillet from the skin without cutting through either. Or have your fishmonger do it for you.

To **toast chopped nuts or seeds**: Cook in a small dry skillet over medium-low heat, stirring constantly, until fragrant and lightly browned, 2 to 4 minutes.

To **toast whole nuts**: Spread on a baking sheet and bake at 350°F, stirring occasionally, until fragrant and lightly browned, 7 to 9 minutes.

INGREDIENT NOTES

Arugula: Also called "rocket," this aromatic green lends a peppery mustard flavor to salads. Sold in supermarkets or farmers' markets. Watercress is a good substitute.

Beans, canned: When you use canned beans in a recipe, be sure to rinse them first in a colander under cold running water, as their canning liquid often contains a fair amount of sodium.

Black bean-garlic sauce: This savory, salty sauce used in Chinese cooking is made from fermented black beans, garlic and rice wine. Found in the Asian-food section of large supermarkets or at Asian markets. Use it in stir-fries and marinades for beef, chicken or tofu.

Broccolini: A cross between broccoli and Chinese kale, broccolini is sweet and tender—both the florets and stalks are edible.

Broccoli rabe: Also known as broccoli raab and rapini, this is a pleasantly pungent and mildly bitter member of the cabbage family, commonly used in Mediterranean cooking.

Bulgur: Fiber-rich, made from whole-wheat kernels that are precooked, dried and cracked. Found in natural-foods stores and large markets.

Chicken, rotisserie: Store-bought rotisserie chicken is convenient and practical—but much higher in sodium than a home-roasted bird (4 ounces home-roasted chicken: less than 100 mg sodium; 4 ounces rotisserie chicken: 350-450 mg sodium). Even the unseasoned varieties have been marinated or seasoned with salty flavorings. People with hypertension should think twice before choosing store-bought.

Chicken tenders: The virtually fat-free strips of rib meat typically found attached to the underside of the chicken breasts can also be purchased separately. Four 1-ounce tenders will yield a 3-ounce cooked portion. Tenders are perfect for quick stir-fries, chicken satay or kid-friendly breaded "chicken fingers."

Chile-garlic sauce: A blend of ground chiles, garlic and vinegar, it's commonly used to add heat and flavor to Asian soups, sauces and stir-fries. It can be found in the Asian section of large supermarkets (sometimes labeled as chili-garlic sauce or paste) and keeps up to 1 year in the refrigerator.

Chinkiang vinegar: A dark, slightly sweet rice vinegar with a smoky flavor. Available in many Asian specialty markets. Balsamic vinegar is an acceptable substitute.

Chipotle peppers in adobo sauce: Canned smoked jalapeños, which add heat and smokiness to dishes; the adobo sauce alone adds a spicy zest without extra heat. Look for small cans with other Mexican foods in large supermarkets. Once opened, chipotles will keep for up to 2 weeks in the refrigerator or 6 months in the freezer.

Couscous: Resembling a grain, these granules of semolina meal are actually a type of pasta. A staple throughout North Africa, it is traditionally steamed over broth but is now available in a precooked form that only requires 5 minutes of soaking in hot broth or water. Whole-wheat couscous can be found in natural-foods stores and large supermarkets.

Cremini mushrooms: A strain of button mushrooms (also called baby bella) prized for their dark hue, firm texture and rich flavor.

Curry powder, Madras: Named for a city in southern India; hotter than standard curry powder. Found in specialty stores and large supermarkets.

Dried egg whites: Powdered brands like Just Whites are in the baking aisle or natural-foods section; fresh pasteurized whites are in the dairy case of most supermarkets.

Fish sauce: A pungent Southeast Asian sauce made from salted, fermented fish. Found in the Asian section of large supermarkets and in Asian specialty markets.

Hoisin sauce: This dark brown, thick, spicy-sweet sauce is made with soybeans and a complex mix of spices. Look for it in the Chinese section of supermarkets and in Asian markets.

Marsala: A fortified wine that is a flavorful and wonderfully economical addition to many sauces. An opened bottle can be stored in a cool, dry place for months—unlike wine, which starts to decline within hours of its being uncorked.

Mirin: A low-alcohol rice wine essential to Japanese cooking. Look for it in the Asian or gourmet-ingredients section of your supermarket. An equal portion of sherry or white wine with a pinch of sugar may be substituted for mirin.

Miso: Fermented bean paste made from barley, rice or soybeans used in Japanese cooking to add flavor to dishes such as soups, sauces and salad dressings. A little goes a long way because of its concentrated, salty taste. Miso is available in different colors, depending on the type of grain or bean and how long it's been fermented. In general, the lighter the color, the more mild the flavor. It will keep, in the refrigerator, for more than a year.

Olive oil, extra-virgin: This flavorful, heart-healthy oil is unrefined and thus high in antioxidants and polyphenols that are a tonic to cardiovascular health. Less expensive but so-called "pure" olive oil (not extra-virgin) is refined and more tolerant to heat but also less nutrient-dense. Don't bother with "light" olive oil; it has virtually no character and even fewer polyphenols. Use extra-virgin in moderate-heat cooking, baking and dressings.

Portobello: A mature cremini, this is a large, dark brown mushroom with a wide, flaring, flat cap. While the stems are usually too woody to eat, the caps have an especially rich and meaty texture.

Prosciutto: A spiced and salt-cured Italian ham that is air-dried then pressed, resulting in a firm, dense texture. Usually sold very thinly sliced, it can be found in specialty-foods stores, Italian markets and deli counters.

Quinoa: This delicately flavored grain was a staple in the ancient Incas' diet. It is available in most natural-foods stores and the natural-foods sections of many supermarkets. Toasting the grain before cooking enhances its flavor, and rinsing removes any residue of saponin, quinoa's natural, bitter protective covering.

Rice or rice-wine vinegar: A mild vinegar made from glutinous rice; bottlings range from clear to aged (extremely dark). Substitute cider vinegar for clear rice vinegar in a pinch. (*See also Chinkiang.*)

Saffron: Literally the stigma from *Crocus sativus*, saffron is the world's most expensive spice. Each crocus produces only 3 stigmas, requiring over 75,000 flowers for each pound of saffron. Fortunately, a little goes a long way. It's used sparingly to add golden yellow color and flavor to a wide variety of Middle Eastern, African and European-inspired foods. Find it in the specialty-herb section of large supermarkets, gourmet-food shops and www.tienda.com. Wrapped in foil and placed in a container with a tight-fitting lid, it will keep in a cool, dry place for several years.

Sake: A dry rice wine generally available where wines are sold. Junmai, a special designation for sake, denotes sake brewed from rice that has been milled less than other special-designation sakes. More pure than other sakes, junmai has no distilled alcohol added. It is characterized by a well-rounded, rich flavor and body and more acidity than most sakes.

(Continued on page 246)

SOME SUBSTITUTIONS

Although substitutions can be tricky business, we've all faced that moment when we're ready to cook supper and we've still managed to forget some little ingredient that throws the whole affair off. Here are some acceptable substitutions that will keep things on track.

Balsamic Vinegar: 1 tablespoon = 2 1/2 teaspoons white wine vinegar + 1/4 teaspoon molasses + 1/4 teaspoon Worcestershire sauce

Butter: 1 tablespoon = 2 1/4 teaspoons non-trans-fatty-acid solid shortening

Buttermilk: 1 cup = 1 cup plain yogurt = 1 tablespoon lemon juice *or* cider vinegar + 1 cup milk (let stand for 10 minutes at room temperature)

Chocolate, semisweet: 1 ounce = 1/2 ounce unsweetened chocolate + 1 1/4 tablespoons sugar

Chocolate, unsweetened: 3 tablespoons unsweetened cocoa + 1 tablespoon non-trans-fatty-acid solid vegetable shortening, melted and cooled

Eggs: 1 large egg = 3 tablespoons pasteurized egg substitute

Milk: 1 cup nonfat milk = 1/2 cup nonfat evaporated milk + 1/2 cup water

SOME EQUIVALENCIES

Food is sold by a variety of measures: weight, volume, bunch and even handful (at some farmers' markets). It's not always easy to tell what's what; here's a simple list of measurements that can help.

Almonds, shelled: 1 lb. = about 3 1/2 cups whole almonds, about 4 cups slivered almonds
Anchovies: 2-oz. can = about 12 fillets; 1 fillet = 1/2 teaspoon anchovy paste
Apples: 1 lb. = about 3 cups chopped
Apricots: 1 lb. = about 2 1/2 cups sliced
Asparagus: 1 lb. = about 15 spears
Bacon: 1 lb. = about 20 thin slices
Bananas: 1 lb. = about 2 cups sliced or 1 1/2 cups mashed
Barley, quick-cooking: 1 cup raw = about 2 cups cooked
Beans, canned: 15-oz. can = about 1 1/2 cups; 19-oz. can = about 2 cups
Beans, dried: 1 lb. (2 cups) unsoaked raw = 5-6 cups cooked
Beets: 1 lb. = about 2 cups chopped
Bell Peppers: 1 lb. = about 2 1/2 cups chopped; 1 medium bell pepper = about 1 cup chopped
Blueberries, fresh: 1 pint = 2 cups
Blueberries, frozen: 10-oz. package = about 1 1/3 cups
Breadcrumbs, dried: 1 slice toast, crust removed = about 1/4 cup dried breadcrumbs
Breadcrumbs, fresh: 1 slice bread, crust removed = about 1/3 cup fresh breadcrumbs
Broccoli, fresh: 1 lb. = about 2 1/4 cups chopped
Broccoli, frozen: 10-oz. package = about 1 1/2 cups chopped
Cabbage: 1 lb. (cored) = 4 cups shredded (raw) = 1 3/4 cups shredded (cooked)
Cantaloupe: 1 medium = about 3 cups peeled, seeded and chopped
Carrots, fresh: 1 lb. = about 3 cups (chopped) = about 2 1/2 cups (shredded)
Cauliflower, fresh: 1 lb. = about 3 cups florets
Celery: 1 stalk = about 1/4 cup chopped
Cherries, fresh: 1 lb. unpitted = about 2 cups pitted
Cherries, frozen: 10-oz. bag pitted = about 1 1/4 cups
Chicken: 1 lb. raw with bones = about 1 cup cooked, boned meat
Chocolate: 6 ounces chocolate chips = about 1 cup
Coconut: 7-oz. bag shredded, sweetened or unsweetened = about 2 3/4 cups
Cottage or Ricotta Cheese: 16 ounces = 2 cups
Cranberries: 12-oz. bag = 3 cups whole berries or 2 1/2 cups chopped berries
Cream Cheese: 8 ounces = 1 cup
Cucumbers: 1 medium = about 1 1/3 cups seeded and chopped
Dates, pitted: 8-oz. package = about 1 cup chopped
Dates, unpitted: 1 lb. = about 2 cups pitted and chopped
Eggplant: 1 lb. = about 3 cups peeled and chopped
Fennel: 2 small bulbs = about 1 lb. = about 1 3/4 cups trimmed and sliced
Garlic: 1 medium clove minced = about 1teaspoon
Ginger: 2-inch piece = about 1 1/2 tablespoons peeled and minced
Grapefruit: 1 lb. = about 1 1/4 cups segments = about 1 cup juice
Grapes: 1 lb. seedless = about 3 cups; 1 lb. with seeds = about 2 cups seeded
Green Beans: 1 lb. = about 2 3/4 cups trimmed
Greens (spinach, kale, chard, etc.): 1 lb. raw = about 1 2/3 cups stemmed and cooked
Hazelnuts, shelled: 1 lb. skinned = about 3 cups whole = about 2 cups chopped
Herbs: 1 tablespoon fresh = 1 teaspoon dry
Horseradish: 1 tablespoon jarred = 2 teaspoons freshly grated
Jicama: 1 lb. = about 3 cups peeled and chopped
Leeks: 1 lb. = about 1 1/2 cups trimmed and chopped
Lemons: 1 medium lemon = about 3 tablespoons juice and 2 teaspoons grated zest
Mangoes: 1 medium mango = about 3/4 cup peeled, pitted and chopped
Milk, Dry: 1/3 cup = 1 cup reconstituted; 1 1/3 cups = 1 quart reconstituted
Mushrooms, dried: 1 oz. reconstituted = about 1/3 lb. fresh
Mushrooms, fresh: 1 lb. = 6 cups sliced
Okra: 1 lb. raw = about 2 cups chopped
Onions, fresh: 1 lb. = about 4 cups chopped; 1 large = about 1 1/2 cups chopped; 1 medium = about 1 cup chopped; 1 small = about 1/2 cup chopped
Onions, frozen, chopped: 12-oz. bag = about 3 cups
Oranges and Tangerines: 1 medium = about 1/2 cup juice and 1 1/2 tablespoons grated zest
Parsnips: 1 lb. = about 2 cups peeled and chopped
Peaches and Nectarines: 1 lb. = about 2 1/2 cups peeled and sliced
Peanuts: 1 lb. in the shells = about 2 1/2 cups shelled
Pears: 1 lb. = 2 cups cored and chopped
Peas: 1 lb. in the shells = about 1 cup shelled
Pineapple: 1 lb. = about 3 cups peeled, cored and chopped
Pistachios: 1 lb. in the shells = about 2 cups shelled
Potatoes: 1 lb. = about 3 baking potatoes or 6 round potatoes or about 12 small "new" potatoes
Radishes: 1 lb. = about 3 cups sliced
Raspberries, fresh: 1 pint = about 2 1/3 cups
Raspberries, frozen: 10-oz. bag = about 1 1/2 cups
Rice, brown: 1 cup raw = about 3 cups cooked
Rice, white: 1 cup raw = about 3 cups cooked
Rice, wild: 1 cup raw = 2-2 1/2 cups cooked
Scallions (or green onions): 1 medium = about 1/3 cup sliced
Shallots: 1 medium (both bulbs) = about 1/2 cup chopped
Squash, Summer or Zucchini: 1 lb. = about 3 cups raw, chopped
Strawberries, fresh: 1 quart = about 3 1/2 cups sliced
Strawberries, frozen: 10-oz. bag = about 1 1/3 cups
Tofu: 1 lb. = about 2 1/2 cups cubed or 1 2/3 cup pureed
Tomatoes, canned: 14-oz. can = 1 3/4 cups (tomatoes and juice)
Tomatoes, fresh: 1 lb. = about 2 cups chopped
Tomato paste: 1 oz. = scant 1 tablespoon
Turnips: 1 lb. = 2 1/3 cups peeled and chopped
Walnuts: 1 lb. in the shells = 2 cups walnut halves; 1 lb. shelled walnuts = 3 1/2 cups walnut pieces
Wine: 750-ml bottle = generous 3 cups

Scallops: Be sure to request "dry" sea scallops, which have not been treated with sodium tripolyphosphate (STP). They are more flavorful and will brown the best.

Sherry: Don't use the "cooking sherry" sold in many supermarkets—it can be surprisingly high in sodium. Instead, purchase dry sherry that's sold with other fortified wines in your wine or liquor store.

Shrimp: Raw, frozen and cooked shrimp are all sold by the number needed to make one pound—for example, "21-25 count" or "31-40 count"—and by more generic size names, such as "large" or "extra large." Size names don't always correspond to the actual "count size." To be sure you're getting the size you want, order by the count (or number) per pound.

Soba: These thin buckwheat noodles from Japan are traditionally served cold with a soy-based dipping sauce or hot in a broth. They should be cooked in simmering, not boiling, water and then rinsed well under cold water. Look for soba in natural-foods stores, Asian markets or the specialty-food section of the supermarket.

Sole: The term "sole" is widely used for many types of flatfish from both the Atlantic and Pacific. Flounder and Atlantic halibut are included in the group that is often identified as sole or grey sole. The best choices are Pacific, Dover or English sole. Other sole and flounder are overfished.

Tahini: This smooth, thick paste made from ground sesame seeds is commonly used in Middle Eastern foods. Look for it in the Middle Eastern section or near other nut butters in large supermarkets.

Tofu: "Soybean curd" is made by heating soymilk and a curdling agent in a process similar to dairy cheesemaking. Allowed to stand and thicken, the curds form silken tofu. When stirred and separated from the whey, the pressed curds, with their spongier texture, are known as "regular" tofu. The longer the pressing, the firmer and denser the tofu—soft, firm or extra-firm. The secret to great-tasting tofu with appealing texture is to start with water-packed tofu from the refrigerated section of the supermarket and crumble it into uneven pieces, creating more surface area for improved texture.

Vegetable broth: Commercial vegetable broth is readily available in natural-foods stores and many supermarkets. We especially like the Imagine and Pacific brands, sold in convenient aseptic packages that allow you to use small amounts and keep the rest refrigerated.

Tuna: Canned white tuna comes from the large albacore and can be high in mercury content. Chunk light, on the other hand, which comes from smaller fish, skipjack or yellowfin, is best for health-conscious eaters. According to a recent study, canned white tuna samples averaged about 315 percent more mercury than chunk light samples.

Turkey tenderloin: An all-white piece that comes from the rib side of the breast. Tenderloins typically weigh between 7 and 14 ounces each and can be found with other turkey products in the meat section of most supermarkets.

Whole-wheat pasta: A good source of dietary fiber and a smart choice for a healthy diet: it hasn't been stripped of the grain's important trace nutrients and phytochemicals.

Special Index: Healthy Weight

An index of all the recipes marked with the **Healthy**)(**Weight** icon: CALORIES ≤ 350, CARBS ≤ 33g, TOTAL FAT ≤ 20g, SAT FAT ≤ 10g

Vegetarian

Chicken, Duck & Turkey

Fish & Seafood

Beef, Pork & Lamb

Special Index:
30 Minutes or Less

*Recipes marked with * are ready in 20 minutes or less.*

Special Index:
Family-Friendly

Comprehensive Recipe Index

Page numbers in italics indicate photographs.

T

Contributors

Our thanks to the fine cooks whose work has appeared in EatingWell *Magazine.*

Baggett, Nancy: Spiced Pork Chops & Peaches, 206; Easy Pork Chop Sauté with Cranberries, 213

Brennan, Georgeanne: Cod with Grapefruit, 154

Farrell-Kingsley, Kathy: Tomato-&-Olive-Stuffed Portobello Caps, 95; Asian-Style Grilled Tofu with Greens, 99; Tandoori Chicken with Tomato-Cucumber Raita, 136; Chile-Crusted Scallops with Cucumber Salad, 172; Grilled Shrimp Rémoulade, 179; Korean-Style Steak & Lettuce Wraps, 190; Tomato-Cucumber Raita, 227

Fritschner, Sarah: Florentine Ravioli, 79; Stir-Fried Spicy Chicken Tenders, 128

Hendley, Joyce: Jerk Chicken Breasts, 121; Jerk Seasoning Blend, 226

Iyer, Raghavan: Shrimp with Mango & Basil, 182; Indian Spiced Shrimp, 183

Kalen, Wendy: Chicken & Spiced Apples, 116

Niall, Mani: Honey-Mustard Chicken, 129

Riccardi, Victoria Abbott: Warm Shrimp & Arugula Salad, 35; Wok-Seared Chicken Tenders with Asparagus & Pistachios, 111; Chicken Stuffed with Golden Onions & Fontina, 114; Japanese Chicken-Scallion Rice Bowl, 118; Turkey with Cherries & Port, 148; Cajun Pecan-Crusted Catfish, 151; Midori Salmon, 158; Veal Scaloppine with Lemon, Capers & Leeks, 204

Romagnoli, G. Franco: Fettuccine & Bells, 80; Rigatoni with Turkey Sausage, Cheese & Pepper, 144; Spaghetti with Caramelized Onions & Anchovies, 166; Fusilli with Walnuts & Prosciutto, 220

Simmons, Marie: Crispy Potatoes with Green Beans & Eggs, 89

Weinstein, Bruce & Mark Scarbrough: Seafood Salad with Citrus Vinaigrette, 26; Light Salade aux Lardons, 42; Greek Diner Salad, 51; Asparagus Soup, 70; Wasabi Salmon Burgers, 160; Pacific Sole with Oranges & Pecans, 162; Inside-Out Cheeseburgers, 201; Boneless Pork Chops with Mushrooms & Thyme, 212, Basic Basil Pesto, 226; Mint Pesto, 227

Young, Grace: Sichuan-Style Tofu with Mushrooms, 101; Sichuan-Style Shrimp, 177; Sichuan Sauce, 227